Greater
Mekong Subregion

The **Institute of Southeast Asian Studies (ISEAS)** was established as an autonomous organization in 1968. It is a regional centre dedicated to the study of socio-political, security and economic trends and developments in Southeast Asia and its wider geostrategic and economic environment. The Institute's research programmes are the Regional Economic Studies (RES, including ASEAN and APEC), Regional Strategic and Political Studies (RSPS), and Regional Social and Cultural Studies (RSCS).

ISEAS Publishing, an established academic press, has issued more than 2,000 books and journals. It is the largest scholarly publisher of research about Southeast Asia from within the region. ISEAS Publishing works with many other academic and trade publishers and distributors to disseminate important research and analyses from and about Southeast Asia to the rest of the world.

Greater Mekong Subregion

From Geographical to Socio-economic Integration

edited by
Omkar L. Shrestha
Aekapol Chongvilaivan

LSEAS
Institute of Southeast Asian Studies
Singapore

First published in Singapore in 2013 by
ISEAS Publishing
Institute of Southeast Asian Studies
30 Heng Mui Keng Terrace
Pasir Panjang
Singapore 119614

E-mail: publish@iseas.edu.sg
Website: <http://bookshop.iseas.edu.sg>

The responsibility for facts and opinions in this publication rests exclusively with the authors and their interpretations do not necessarily reflect the views or the policy of the publisher or its supporters.

ISEAS Library Cataloguing-in-Publication Data

Greater Mekong subregion : from geographical to socio-economic integration / edited by Omkar L. Shresta and Aekapol Chongvilaivan.
    Papers originally presented at a Regional Conference on Greater Mekong Sub-Region: from Geographical Corridor to Socio-Economic Corridor, organised by Institute of Southeast Asian Studies on 18–19 October 2010.
    1. Mekong River Region—Economic integration—Congresses.
    2. Mekong River Region—Economic conditions—Congresses.
    3. Mekong River Region—Social conditions—Congresses.
    4. Southeast Asia—Economic integration—Congresses.
    5. Southeast Asia—Economic conditions—Congresses.
    6. Southeast Asia—Social conditions—Congresses.
    I. Shresta, Omkar L.
    II. Aekapol Chongvilaivan.
    III. Institute of Southeast Asian Studies.
    IV. Regional Conference on Greater Mekong Sub-Region : from Geographical Corridor to Socio-Economic Corridor (2010 : Singapore)
HC441 G782   2013

ISBN 978-981-4379-68-7 (soft cover)
ISBN 978-981-4379-69-4 (e-book, PDF)

Cover Photo: Construction of the Bai Chay Bridge over the Cua Luc Straits, Vietnam © Nikolay Chervonenko/Dreamstime.com.

Typeset by Superskill Graphics Pte Ltd
Printed in Singapore by Oxford Graphic Printers Pte Ltd

CONTENTS

Preface   vii

List of Abbreviations   xi

Contributors   xv

1   Greater Mekong Subregion: From Geographical
    Corridors to Socio-economic Corridors   1
    Omkar L. Shrestha and Aekapol Chongvilaivan

2   Cambodia, Its Development, and Integration into
    the GMS: A Work in Progress   18
    Larry Strange

3   Subregional Connectivity in the Lao PDR: From Land-locked
    Disadvantage to Land-linked Advantage   31
    Oudet Souvannavong

4   The Economic Development of Myanmar and the Relevance
    of the Greater Mekong Subregion   47
    Michael von Hauff

5   GMS Challenges for Thailand   74
    Narongchai Akrasanee

6   Deepening GMS Cooperation in a More Integrated ASEAN
    and East Asia   84
    Vo Tri Thanh

7   China (Yunnan)–GMS Economic Cooperation:
    New Development and New Problems   103
    Guangsheng Lu

8   Trade and Investment in the Greater Mekong Subregion:
    Remaining Challenges and the Unfinished Policy Agenda   119
    Jayant Menon and Anna Cassandra Melendez

9   Enhancing Financial Cooperation among the GMS Countries   162
    Ulrich Volz

10 The Challenges of GMS Regional Integration:
    Case Study of Governance of the Logistics Industry in Thailand 172
    Narong Pomlaktong, Chaiyasit Anuchitworawong,
    Rattana Jongwilaiwan, and Prakai Theerawattanakul

11 Energy Sector Integration for Low-carbon Development in
    the GMS: Towards a Model of South-South Cooperation   216
    Yongping Zhai and Anthony J. Jude

12 Linking the Social to the Economic: Broadened Ambitions
    and Multiple Mitigations in New Mekong Corridors   233
    Chris Lyttleton

Index   253

PREFACE

It has been nearly two decades since the Greater Mekong Subregion (GMS) regional economic strategy was initiated in 1992, aimed at promoting and integrating the economies of Cambodia, the Lao PDR, Myanmar, Thailand, Vietnam, and Yunnan Province and Guangxi autonomous region of China. Together, they encompass a huge population of over 316 million people (bigger than the United States) and a vast land area of around 2.6 million square kilometres (roughly the size of Europe), enjoying a rich agricultural base, considerable mineral and energy resources (renewable and non-renewable), and a strategic location at the heart of Asia between the burgeoning economies of China and India.

Several regional infrastructure projects in the transport and energy sectors have facilitated the process of integration of the GMS economies. For instance, the 1,320-kilometre-long East-West Economic Corridor cross-border project, triggered by the landmark trade accord signed in 1999, stretches from Danang in Vietnam, through the Lao PDR and Thailand to Myanmar, forming a land bridge connecting the South China Sea at Danang Port to the Andaman Sea at Mawlamyine Port in Myanmar. There is a growing recognition that these cross-border infrastructure projects have helped raise the GMS economies' degree of connectivity and competitiveness, achieve accelerated shared prosperity, and expand intraregional trade and investment activities. Indeed there is a widely held perception that Asia's success story is not only about rise in income and decline in poverty, but is also the story of increased integration among the regional countries through various regional and subregional infrastructure projects.

Enhanced regional integration and cooperation also help build resilient economies through well-coordinated and timely responses to global crises. Hence, notwithstanding the recent international financial crisis, several GMS countries have made remarkable achievement in terms of their sustained economic growth (6 to 10 per cent per year) for the past decade. The intraregional trade among the GMS countries is now estimated at 30–50 per cent of their total trade. Foreign direct investment flows to the GMS countries have increased considerably and so have tourist arrivals.

Despite the above positive developments, several of the GMS economies remain the weakest link in the ASEAN chain. The economic divide that exists between these economies and other ASEAN nations remains a major concern for the ASEAN quest to achieve the ASEAN Economic Community vision by the year 2015. Some of their basic fundamentals remain very fragile, particularly in terms of their high poverty incidence, low life expectancy, weak human capital development, basic physical and financial infrastructure, and institutional capability, among other things.

Accordingly, many more cross-border projects are either under implementation or in the pipeline with clear timelines. For instance, the North-South Economic Corridor multimodal transport, when completed, will link China with Thailand and Vietnam, thus serving as China's gateway with ASEAN. The Southern Economic Corridor strategically connects Bangkok, Phnom Penh, and Ho Chi Minh City. While these cross-border transport projects are desirable, there is an emerging concern that the cross-border transport corridors, which are supposed to act as the backbone of the economic corridors, have not provided the economic impact on the GMS economies at the expected level. These "two faces" of regional integration therefore require careful analysis, attention, and action so as to mitigate the potential socio-economic and environmental "costs" of regional cooperation and integration. It will also be essential to build and expand regional knowledge to ensure that the benefits of regional integration can be more equitably shared among the economies in the GMS region, thereby minimizing the development divide.

It is against the above background that the conference on the "Greater Mekong Subregion: From Geographical Corridor to Socio-economic Corridor", was organized by the Institute of Southeast Asian Studies (ISEAS) in 2010 with a thorough debate on the GMS economies, followed by discussions on several thematic issues that are common to all of them. The aim was to come up with a series of pragmatic policy options and suggestions for addressing those issues and helping to build economic corridors from the ongoing cross-border transport corridors projects.

In convening this conference, we are grateful to Konrad-Adeneuer Stiftung for generous funding support. Thanks are also due to Karthi Nair for her excellent assistance, and to the ISEAS Publications Unit, in particular, Triena Ong.

Finally, we would like to thank Ambassador Kesavapany, former Director of ISEAS, for his encouragement of and support for the GMS Regional Conference.

ABBREVIATIONS

AEC	ASEAN Economic Community
AFTA	ASEAN Free Trade Agreement
AMRO	ASEAN+3 Macroeconomic Research Office
ASEAN	Association of Southeast Asian Nations
ASP	ASEAN Surveillance Process
BAU	business as usual
BIMSTEC	Bay of Bengal Initiative for Multi-Sectoral Technical and Economic
BOOT	build-own-operate-transfer
BOT	build-operate-transfer
BRTA	bilateral road transport agreement
CADP	Comprehensive Asia Development Plan
CAFTA	China-ASEAN Free Trade Area
CBM	Central Bank of Burma
CBTA	cross-border transport agreement
CCA	common control area
CDM	clean development mechanism
CEPT	common effective preferential tariff
CF	clean fuels
CLM	Cambodia, Laos, Myanmar
CLMV	Cambodia, Laos, Myanmar, Vietnam
CMIM	Chiang Mai Initiative Multilateralization
CNPC	China National Petroleum Corp
COP	community of practice
CPP	Cambodian People's Party

CSR	corporate social responsibility
CTS	customs and transit systems
DLT	Department of Land Transport (Thailand)
DSM	demand-side management
EC	energy conservation
ECF	Economic Corridors Forum
EE	energy efficiency
ERIA	Economic Research Institute for ASEAN
ESCAP	United Nations Economic and Social Commission for Asia and the Pacific
EWEC	East-West Economic Corridor
FDI	foreign direct investment
FIMC	Foreign Investment Management Committee (Laos)
FTA	free trade agreement
GFC	global financial crisis
GMS	Greater Mekong Subregion
GNI	gross national income
GoL	Government of Laos
HDI	Human Development Index
IAI	Initiatives of ASEAN Integration
IEAI	Initiative for East Asian Integration
IGA	Inter-Governmental Agreement on Regional Power Trade
IRM	Integrated Resource Management
IRR	Impoverishment Risks and Reconstruction Model
LDC	least-developed country
LECS	Lao Expenditures and Consumption Survey
LPI	Logistics Performance Index
MDGs	Millennium Development Goals
MESSAGE	Model of Energy Supply Systems Alternatives and their General Environmental Impacts
MFN	most favoured nation
MFSO	Macroeconomic and Finance Surveillance Office
MICE	meetings, incentives, conferences, and exhibitions
MMR	maternal mortality ratio
MoP	margin of preference
NBC	National Bank of Cambodia
NSEC	North-South Economic Corridor
NSEDP	National Social and Economic Development Plan (Laos)
NSW	National Single Window
NTFC	National Transport Facilitation Committee (Thailand)

ODA	official development assistance
PGB	Pan Beibu Gulf
POLIS	Police Information System (Thailand)
PPA	power purchase agreement
PPP	public-private partnership
PRC	People's Republic of China
PTA	preferential trade agreement
RE	renewable energy
RETA	Regional Technical Assistance
RoO	rules of origin
RPTCC	Regional Power Trade Coordinating Committee
SAP	strategies and action plans
SEA	strategic environmental assessment
SEC	Southern Economic Corridor
SEE	state economic enterprise
SEZ	special economic zone
SLORC	State Law and Order Restoration Council (Myanmar)
SME	small and medium enterprises
SOE	state-owned enterprise
SSI	Single-Stop Inspection
SWI	Single Window Inspection
TEU	twenty-foot equivalent unit
UNFCC	United Nations Framework Convention for Climate Change
UNFPA	United Nations Fund for Population Activities
UNTAC	United Nations Transition Administration in Cambodia
WGI	Worldwide Governance Indicators
WTO	World Trade Organization

CONTRIBUTORS

Narongchai Akrasanee is Chairman of Steering Committees, Mekong Institute, and a former Minister of Commerce and Senator of Thailand.

Chaiyasit Anuchitworawong is Research Fellow, Sectoral Economics Program, Thailand Development Research Institute (TDRI), Thailand.

Aekapol Chongvilaivan is Fellow of the Regional Economic Studies Programme, Institute of Southeast Asian Studies (ISEAS), Singapore.

Rattana Jongwilaiwan is former Researcher at the Thailand Development Research Institute (TDRI), Thailand.

Anthony J. Jude is Director, Energy and Water Division, Southeast Asia Department, Asian Development Bank (ADB).

Chris Lyttleton is Associate Professor, Department of Anthropology, Macquarie University, Australia.

Guangsheng Lu is Professor and Director, Southeast Asian Institute, Yunnan University, China.

Jayant Menon is Lead Economist (Trade and Regional Cooperation), Office of Regional Economic Integration, Asian Development Bank (ADB).

Anna Cassandra Melendez is Research Assistant at the Asian Development Bank (ADB).

Narong Pomlaktong is Research Director for Transport and Logistics, Human Resources and Social Development Program, Thailand Development Research Institute (TDRI), Thailand.

Omkar L. Shrestha is Visiting Senior Research Fellow, Institute of Southeast Asian Studies (ISEAS), Singapore.

Oudet Souvannavong is Secretary General, GMS Business Forum (GMS-BF), Vientiane.

Larry Strange is Executive Director, Cambodia Development Resource Institute (CDRI), Cambodia.

Vo Tri Thanh is Vice-President, Central Institute for Economic Management (CIEM), Vietnam.

Prakai Theerawattanakul is Former Senior Researcher at the Thailand Development Research Institute (TDRI), Thailand.

Ulrich Volz is Senior Researcher at the German Development Institute/ Deutsches Institut für Entwicklungspolitik (DIE), Germany.

Michael von Hauff is Professor of Economics, University of Kaiserslautern, Germany.

Yongping Zhai is Principal Energy Specialist at the Asian Development Bank (ADB).

1

GREATER MEKONG SUBREGION
From Geographical Corridors to Socio-economic Corridors

Omkar L. Shrestha and Aekapol Chongvilaivan

The Greater Mekong Subregion (GMS) embraces the nations and territories located in the Mekong river basin, including Cambodia, China (Yunnan Province and Guangxi Zhuang Autonomous Region), the Lao PDR, Myanmar, Thailand, and Vietnam.[1] This diverse, dynamic subregion encompasses a huge market of more than 240 million people and a vast land area of 2.3 million square kilometres. The gross domestic product of the subregion was projected to reach US$863 billion in 2010 — more than triple the 1996 level — with Cambodia, the Lao PDR, Myanmar, Vietnam, and Yunnan Province, PRC, experiencing startling output growth rates of 6–10 per cent, despite the current global economic hardships. This is attributed fundamentally to their abundant resources, including a large motivated, cheap workforce, a rich agricultural base, extensive timber and fisheries resources, considerable mineral potentials, and vast energy resources in the form of hydropower and large coal and petroleum resources. The GMS is increasingly being recognized as a new frontier of the Southeast Asian economic strength.

The GMS enjoys a strategic location at the heart of East Asia and between the burgeoning economies of China and India. Closer economic

1

ties to external markets offer the GMS opportunities to tap benefits from boosts in trade, tourism, and investment, which have been a crucial driving force of impressive economic growth in the subregion. The last two decades since its inception in 1992 witnessed strong growth in intra-GMS trade and investment. Cross-border trade is now estimated to account for 30–50 per cent of the GMS economies' total trade, and has increased sharply at a compound average annual rate of nearly 10 per cent, while intra-GMS net foreign direct investment nearly doubled during the period of 2000–2002.

This chapter aims to assess the recent economic, social, and political developments in the GMS, and identify emerging opportunities and challenges facing the region's successful transition towards a market-driven economy. The GMS countries are at a critical juncture where subregional efforts and cooperation must be made to address fully the rapidly evolving issues which are vital to appropriate policy formation, yet remain widely debatable. The deliberation in this chapter sheds light on what the development stages of GMS countries are, and gives an overview of the contributions of the ensuing chapters.

The remainder of this chapter is organized as follows. The next section examines the recent economic developments in the GMS, with emphasis on the impact of the global financial crisis. The following section provides the state of social and political developments in the GMS subregion and identifies emerging issues and concerns. After this comes a synopsis of the book, followed by the conclusion.

RECENT ECONOMIC DEVELOPMENT: OPPORTUNITIES AND CHALLENGES

Since the inception of the GMS programme in 1992, the GMS countries have achieved several milestones of closer economic ties in the subregion and leveraged the seamless transitions from centrally planned to market economies (except for Thailand, which was already a market-driven economy). The GMS demonstrated strong economic performance, achieving an average GDP growth rate of 7.6 per cent from 1992 to 2009 — with 10.5 per cent for China (Yunnan Province), 9.1 per cent for Myanmar, 7.8 per cent for Cambodia, 7.5 per cent for Vietnam, 6.6 per cent for the Lao PDR, and 4.1 per cent for Thailand (Figure 1.1). Against the backdrop of the global financial crisis, the GMS countries (except for Cambodia and Thailand) remained resilient, as output continued to grow strongly — 9.1 per cent for China (Yunnan Province), 6.4 per cent for the Lao PDR, 5.3 per cent for Vietnam, and 4.4 per cent for Myanmar.

FIGURE 1.1
Real GDP Growth in GMS Countries, 1994–2009

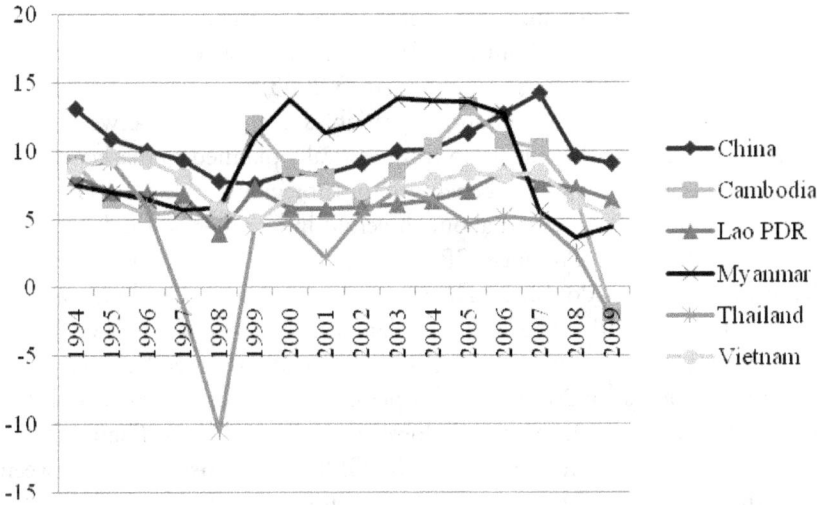

Source: *World Development Indicators*, World Bank, various years.

At least three main reasons explain why the GMS stands to gain from its economic synergies and optimize its economic potentials. First, ever-increasing regional economic integration in Asia and the Pacific has resulted in a considerable increase in intraregional trade. A closer trade nexus within and outside the Asian region allowed the GMS to thrive on export-led growth strategies, whereby diversification of export markets and specialization of production offered respectable economic growth through rapid industrialization and urbanization, in addition to strengthening comparative advantage. GMS initiatives that have helped tighten economic integration with regional countries and the rest of the world include facilitating trade and investment, improving procedures and transparency for custom clearance, and enhancing technical skills to improve the application of various regulatory systems. Second, a decision by the Association of Southeast Asian Nations (ASEAN) to establish the ASEAN Economic Community (AEC) by 2015 set the stage for the burgeoning GMS because success in transforming the subregion into an economic and transportation corridor is a crucial stepping stone towards the AEC. Last, but not least, the aftermath of the global financial crisis witnessed the rise of China and India as new global economic powerhouses. The unwinding global imbalances also implied a shift of global demand towards Asia. The strategic location of the GMS as a "landbridge" from Southeast Asia to China, therefore, offers abundant opportunities for the subregion as well as the Southeast Asian region as a whole to reap benefits from large emerging markets in China (ADB 2005).

A comparison of various economic variables in the GMS between 1993 and 2009 reveals that the transition from centrally planned to market-driven economies has offered immense benefits to the subregion (Table 1.1). The gross national income (GNI) soared about threefold in Cambodia, the Lao PDR, Vietnam, and Yunnan Province, PRC, while the GNI of the market-driven Thai economy nearly doubled.[2] The subregion's economic development was also raised significantly. The GNI per capita of Cambodia, the Lao PDR, Vietnam, and Yunnan Province, PRC, exponentially increased between 1993 and 2009. In fact, as of 2009, the GNI per capita in Yunnan Province, PRC, amounted to US$3,650, marginally lower than US$3,760 in Thailand.

The share of international trade in GDP rose considerably between 1993 and 2009 in Vietnam, Thailand, Cambodia, the Lao PDR, and Yunnan Province, PRC (Table 1.1). Myanmar is the only exception, as its share of international trade in GDP declined from 3.4 per cent in 1993 to 0.6 per cent in 2009. It should be highlighted that the removal of non-tariff barriers, including the improvement of customs clearance procedures, trade facilitation, and transparency and enhancement in institutional and physical infrastructure, will serve as key catalysts in escalating trade openness in the subregion. Nevertheless, the most favoured nation (MFN) tariff rates were higher than 10 per cent in most GMS countries as of 2009 and, in some countries such as the Lao PDR and Vietnam, jumped between 1993 and 2009, thanks to the subregion's undue emphasis on bilateral trade liberalization and stalled multilateral trade talks under the World Trade Organization (WTO). Foreign direct investment (FDI) had also been a source of economic growth in the subregion, especially in the Lao PDR, Thailand, and Vietnam, where the proportion of FDI in GDP rose between 1993 and 2009.

Within the GMS, Thailand is an important trade partner with Cambodia, the Lao PDR, and Myanmar (CLM countries). Ishida (2005) showed that as of 2003, the share of imports from Thailand in total imports amounted to 27.0 per cent in Cambodia, 59.4 per cent in the Lao PDR, and 14.3 per cent in Myanmar. Thailand is the largest import partner of both Cambodia and the Lao PDR, and the third-largest partner for Myanmar, following China (29.5 per cent) and Singapore (21.1 per cent). The share of exports to Thailand in total exports from the Lao PDR and Myanmar was also significant — 30.7 per cent for Myanmar and 21.4 per cent for the Lao PDR (but only

TABLE 1.1
Selected Economic Variables in the GMS

Variables	Cambodia 1993	Cambodia 2009	Lao PDR 1993	Lao PDR 2009	Myanmar 1993	Myanmar 2009	Thailand 1993	Thailand 2009	Vietnam 1993	Vietnam 2009	Yunnan 1993	Yunnan 2009
Gross National Income (billion US$)	3.18	9.4	1.76	5.8	—	—	165.3	252.0	20.5	85.2	716.2[a]	5,028.8[a]
Gross National Income per capita (US$)	310.0[b]	610.0	280.0	880.0	—	—	2,100.0	3,760.0	170.0	930.0	410.0	3,650.0
Unemployment (%)	2.5[c]	4.6[d]	2.6[c]	1.4[d]	6.0[c]	—	2.0[c]	1.6[d]	2.3[c]	2.3[d]	2.8[c]	4.0[d]
Vulnerable Employment (% of total employment)	84.5[c]	85.1[d]	90.1[c]	—	—	—	62.6[c]	54.6[d]	80.5[c]	76.6[d]	42.0[a]	49.1[a]
International trade (% of GDP)	48.7	122.3	52.6	74.5[d]	3.4	0.6	80.2	135.0	66.2	142.1	42.0[a]	49.1[a]
MFN Tariff Rates (%)	—	15.5[d]	9.5[c]	9.7[d]	—	5.6[d]	31.2[c]	13.8[d]	15.3[c]	16.7[d]	16.1[a,c]	11.0[a,d]
Foreign Direct Investment Inflows (% of GDP)	6.0[c]	5.3	2.3	5.4	—	—	1.4	1.9	7.0	8.4	6.2[a]	1.6[a]
Gross Capital Formation (% of GDP)	11.9	21.3	28.3[c]	37.1	13.1[c]	11.2[d]	40.0	21.8	24.2	38.1	44.5[a]	47.7[a]
Agriculture Value Added (% of GDP)	46.5	35.3	57.5	34.7	63.0	52.6[d]	10.3[c]	10.5[d]	29.9	20.9	19.7	10.3
Manufacturing Value Added (% of GDP)	8.9	15.0	13.1	14.3[d]	6.8	9.6[d]	29.6	34.1	15.2	20.1	33.9	33.9
Services Value Added (% of GDP)	40.5	42.0	24.7	37.1	28.1	33.8[d]	50.9	45.1	41.2	38.8	33.7	43.4

Notes: a The figures refer to the PRC.
  b The figure refers to the year 1997.
  c The figures refer to the average during the period 1990–2000.
  d The figures refer to the average during the period 2001–9.

Source: *World Development Indicators*, World Bank, various years.

0.6 per cent for Cambodia). Bilateral trade flows with Vietnam are vital only to Cambodia and the Lao PDR, but not Myanmar. The share of exports to Vietnam in the Lao PDR's total export reached 17.3 per cent (but only 1.5 per cent for Cambodia). Imports from Vietnam to the Lao PDR and Cambodia accounted for 10.4 and 4.7 per cent respectively of Vietnam's total imports. Yunnan Province, PRC, has close trade linkages with Myanmar, Vietnam, the Lao PDR, and Thailand. Of the total exports from Yunnan Province, PRC, Myanmar, Vietnam, the Lao PDR, and Thailand took up 48.9, 17.8, 9.2, and 5.8 per cent respectively. Imports from Myanmar, Vietnam, the Lao PDR, and Thailand to Yunnan Province, PRC, amounted to 29.7, 6.4, 1.9, and 1.4 per cent respectively of its total imports. Intra-GMS FDI has also increased rapidly. Outward FDI flows from Thailand in the GMS were the largest among other GMS riparian countries; the Lao PDR was the largest host country of outward FDI from Thailand, followed by Myanmar and Vietnam (Thanh 1997). China, has also emerged as an active investor in Myanmar, Cambodia, and the Lao PDR. Most FDI flows within the subregion went to tourism and natural resources extraction, with the exception of FDI in Thailand, which was concentrated on the manufacturing sector.

A structural shift away from the traditional agricultural sectors towards manufacturing and service sectors has also been observed in the GMS. Except in Thailand, where the agricultural sector has been relatively small, the share of the agricultural sector in GDP contracted substantially between 1993 and 2009 in the subregion; in some GMS countries such as Cambodia, the Lao PDR, and Yunnan Province, PRC, the share of the agricultural sector nearly halved during the same period. At the same time, the proportion of manufacturing sectors in GDP expanded in all GMS countries and, as of 2009, reached 34.1 per cent in Thailand, 33.9 per cent in Yunnan, PRC, 20.1 per cent in Vietnam, 15.0 per cent in Cambodia, and 14.3 per cent in the Lao PDR. The proliferation of the service sector was also remarkable in most GMS countries, except in Thailand and Vietnam, where the share of the service sector in GDP slightly declined.

Rapid economic development has spawned vulnerabilities in the labour markets in the GMS. Despite ongoing industrialization and urbanization, vulnerable employment, for example, unpaid family workers and own-account workers, remains uncomfortably high. The figures in Table 1.1 indicate that vulnerable employment constituted the major part of total employment in the GMS countries — approximately 90 per cent for the Lao PDR, 85 per cent in Cambodia, 80 per cent in Vietnam, and 55 per cent in Thailand. The global financial crisis further aggravated the problem of expanding vulnerable employment as a shutdown of manufacturing plants in the aftermath of the global economic meltdown forced a shift towards vulnerable employment in the agricultural sector. Therefore, inadequate social security and growing informal sectors constituted a major challenge to sustainable economic development in the GMS.

A number of regional GMS infrastructure projects have made significant progress in shoring up the development of North-South, East-West, and Southern Economic Corridors, including road and rail networks and air transport (Table 1.2). The average volume of freight air transport in 2001–9 increased substantially for the period 1990–2000 in all GMS countries, particularly Thailand, Vietnam, and Yunnan Province, PRC. Rail lines likewise were markedly augmented in Yunnan Province, PRC, while roads were more than doubled in Thailand and Yunnan Province, PRC. Nevertheless, little has been done in terms of communication development. For example, the number of telephone lines was remarkably insufficient in Cambodia, the Lao PDR, and Myanmar, while exponential increases in telephone lines were observed in Thailand, Vietnam, and Yunnan Province, PRC. Expenditure on information and telecommunication technology (ICT) constituted merely 6–7 per cent of GDP in Thailand, Vietnam, and Yunnan Province, PRC. Expenditure on research and development (R&D) showed no progress as it accounted for less than one per cent of GDP in the subregion. The underinvestment in productivity-enhancing infrastructure projects ultimately constrains the growth prospect of the GMS. A recent study conducted by the ADB estimated that Vietnam, for instance, will require an investment of US$12.5 billion a year in power generation alone in order to sustain an average growth rate of 7–9 per cent (ADB 2004). Large infrastructure projects such as highways, railways, and energy networks, more importantly, are infeasible for most individual countries in the subregion due to several capacity constraints, including their lack of capital and human resources, regulatory and institutional limitations, and small markets.

RECENT SOCIAL AND POLITICAL DEVELOPMENT: OPPORTUNITIES AND CHALLENGES

Economic potentials emerging from the fast pace towards the economic corridors in the GMS bring about numerous socio-economic gains in terms of upgrading standards of living and accelerating poverty reduction. Along with rising income per capita (Table 1.1), the average poverty gap of US$2 per day declined substantially in all GMS countries. In the period 1990–2000, millions in Cambodia, the Lao PDR, Vietnam, and Yunnan Province, PRC, lived with an income of less than US$2 a day (Table 1.3). From 2001–9,

TABLE 1.2
Infrastructure Development in the GMS

Variables	Cambodia		Lao PDR		Myanmar		Thailand		Vietnam		Yunnan	
	1990–2000	2001–9	1990–2000	2001–9	1990–2000	2001–9	1990–2000	2001–9	1990–2000	2001–9	1990–2000	2001–9
Freight Air Transport (million tonnes/km)	n.a.	2.2	1.1	2.2	2.6	2.3	1,267	1,997	99.9	208.6	1,941[a]	7,470[a]
Rail Lines (kilometres)	600.0	618.7	n.a.	n.a.	3,335.9	n.a.	3,967.8	4,121.0	2,859.9	2,844.1	55,499[a]	61,266[a]
Roads (thousand kilometres)	35.8	38.2	17.2	31.8	26.9	27.0	61.6	180.1	110.2	191.1	1,175[a]	2,504[a]
Telephone Lines (per 100 people)	0.1	0.3	0.4	1.4	0.4	1.0	5.7	10.3	1.3	18.3	4.3	23.0
ICT Expenditure (% of GDP)	n.a.	n.a.	n.a.	n.a.	n.a.	n.a.	n.a.	6.2	n.a.	6.2	n.a.	7.0
R&D Expenditure (% of GDP)	n.a.	0.05	n.a.	0.04	0.06	0.12	0.18	0.25	n.a.	0.19	0.71	1.23

Note: a The figures refers to the PRC.
Source: *World Development Indicators*, The World Bank, various years.

Selected Social Development Variables in the GMS

Variables	Cambodia 1990–2000	Cambodia 2001–9	Lao PDR 1990–2000	Lao PDR 2001–9	Myanmar 1990–2000	Myanmar 2001–9	Thailand 1990–2000	Thailand 2001–9	Vietnam 1990–2000	Vietnam 2001–9	Yunnan 1990–2000	Yunnan 2001–9
Poverty and Economic Inequality:												
Poverty Gap at $2 a day (%)	33.3	24.1	36.0	31.0	—	—	4.2	2.4	38.9	20.7	32.3	16.4
Food Production Index (1999–2000 = 100)	78.0	127.5	69.4	119.3	78.5	130.4	90.2	110	76.6	117.6	78.7	114.6
GINI Index	38.3	43.0	32.7	32.6	—	—	43.5	42.2	35.6	38.1	—	41.5
Income Share held by highest 10%	32.7	35.9	27.4	27.0	—	—	34.3	33.5	29.2	30.6	—	31.4
Education:												
Education Expenditure (% of GNI)	1.1	1.7[a]	1.7	1.2[a]	0.9	0.8[a]	3.5	4.8[a]	2.6	2.8[a]	1.9	1.8[a]
Literacy Rate[b]	67.3	75.6	64.9	70.7	89.9	91.9	92.6	93.5	90.2	92.5	84.6	93.7
Secondary School Enrolment (%)	19.6	29.3	26.2	42.3	27.5	45.5	42.1	68.6	44.8	66.9	50.4	69.4
Tertiary School Enrolment (%)	1.2	3.9	2.0	7.4	5.4	10.9	24.7	43.4	4.5	9.7	4.5	17.6
Health:												
Health Expenditure (% of GDP)	—	6.3[c]	—	4.3[c]	—	2.1[c]	—	3.6[c]	—	6.1[c]	—	4.5[c]
Life Expectancy at birth (years)	55.8	59.0	57.9	63.3	59.4	60.6	68.5	68.4	69.1	73.5	69.7	72.4
Prevalence of Undernourishment (% of population)	39.0	25.5	30.0	24.5	41.0	22.5	22.0	17.0	26.5	14.0	15.0	10.0
Environment:												
Energy Depletion (% of GNI)	—	—	0.0	0.0	—	—	0.74	3.16	4.57	9.66	3.28	3.83
Mineral depletion (% of GNI)	—	—	—	—	—	—	0.02	0.01	0.03	0.05	0.21	0.63
Forest Depletion (% of GNI)	1.31	0.28	—	—	—	—	0.20	0.25	2.11	0.37	0.15	0.01
Arable Land (% of land areas)	21.0	21.1	3.6	4.4	14.7	15.4	32.6	29.9	17.3	20.8	13.5	14.4
Forest Area (% of land areas)	69.4	60.4	73.3	70.3	56.4	50.0	30.1	28.5	32.5	40.9	17.9	20.7

Notes: a The figures show the average during the period 2001–8.

b The literacy rate is represented as the percentage of people ages 15 and above.

c The figures show the average during the period 2003–7.

Source: World Development Indicators, World Bank, various years.

however, the proportion of the poor was trimmed down to merely 16.4 per cent in Yunnan Province, PRC, 20.7 per cent in Vietnam, 24.1 per cent in Cambodia, and 31 per cent in the Lao PDR. Food shortage was also alleviated significantly in the same period as the index of food production increased persistently across all GMS countries. Despite the progress made in poverty reduction in the subregion, the achievement of the Millennium Development Goals (MDGs), such as those relating to health and drinking water, etc., remains at risk.

The progress on social development has been slow and patchy, owing to the absence of sound economic, social, and political fundamentals. A rapid momentum towards a market-driven economy inflicted widening income inequality in the various societies, thereby complicating social development policy in the subregion. Table 1.3 underlines the incidence of the worsening income gap emerging in the GMS. For instance, a significant rise in the GINI index during the period 1990–2009 is observed in various GMS countries, especially Cambodia and Vietnam. This evidence is also confirmed by the soaring income share held by the highest 10 per cent — from 32.7 per cent in 1990–2000 to 35.9 per cent in 2001–9 for Cambodia, and from 29.2 per cent in 1990–2000, to 30.6 per cent in 2001–9 for Vietnam.

The Kunming Declaration at the Second GMS Summit in July 2005 saw this income inequality as a crucial threat to peace and prosperity in the subregion. It called for a new phase of social development policy that is well targeted at the poor. In particular, the GMS leaders agreed to "(i) accelerate connectivity and associated software elements and expand cooperation in air, rail, and water transport; (ii) enhance competitiveness by facilitating trade and investment, and promoting knowledge and technology; and (iii) promote environmental sustainability through the core environment program, which will address the impacts of rapid growth and development in the sub-region" (ADB 2005).

These three key thrusts of the Kunming Declaration are interrelated. Enhancing connectivity, both hardware and software, essentially helps put forward competitiveness through burgeoning trade and investment, in addition to transfers of knowledge and technology. As the GMS countries are moving towards a seamlessly integrated region, several pre-emptive measures are equally important to tackle the negative impacts of rapid economic and social development, such as environmental degradation, communicable diseases (e.g., HIV/AIDS and malaria) and inaccessible health care, and inadequate human capital, among others. These rising challenges necessitate a wide range of social protection programmes that put emphasis on empowering vulnerable groups, and ensuring equitable gains from strengthening connectivity and escalating competitiveness in the subregion.

While the transition towards a market-driven economy has produced favourable economic performance, several social and environmental concerns have however arisen, which may impose serious constraints to the future growth of the subregion. First and foremost, although several indicators point to improvements in education levels from 1990 to 2009, such as the literacy rate and (secondary and tertiary) school enrolment, the proportion of education expenditure in GNI has remained stunningly low — less than two per cent in all GMS countries except Thailand. In some GMS countries such as the Lao PDR and Myanmar, the share of education expenditure in GNI actually showed a decline (Table 1.3). Ishida (2005) pointed out that the major problem of educational development in the GMS rests with the differences between urban and rural accessibility to schools. The derisory investment in human capital underscores the fact that rising competitiveness and accumulated gains from the economic corridors will soon reach their limit as the shortage of skilled labour sources will impede the domestic industries from moving up the value chain, making the countries unattractive as hosts of FDI.

Second, access to health care services is also a serious concern. Although the past decade witnessed some encouraging signs, such as prolonged life expectancy at birth and waning prevalence of undernourishment, health expenditure as a proportion of GDP was particularly low from 2003 to 2007 — merely 2.1 per cent in Myanmar, 3.6 per cent in Thailand, 4.3 per cent in the Lao PDR, 4.5 per cent in Yunnan Province, PRC, and 6.3 per cent in Cambodia (Table 1.3). Public health protection schemes and insurance are typically absent in most GMS countries, forcing the poor to relinquish appropriate health care and resort to ineffective alternatives. The lack of access to health care, which aggravates morbidity and mortality, ultimately further propels millions into poverty. The United Nations Economic and Social Commission for Asia and the Pacific (ESCAP) articulated that "only the serious commitment on behalf of the Governments can break this vicious cycle of poverty and morbidity".[3] However, individual GMS countries severely lack sufficient and sustainable resources for health and accurate, reliable data on the quantum and effectiveness of health expenditures, making a successful health protection programme very difficult in the subregion.

The recent rapid economic growth in the subregion was achieved with environmental costs. The proliferation of manufacturing plants and agricultural industries has resulted in the persistent deterioration of natural resources, such as energy and mineral sources and forests. Specifically, energy sources were depleted in Thailand, Vietnam, and Yunnan Province, PRC; mineral sources have been excessively exploited in Vietnam and Yunnan Province, PRC; and forests have been devastated in Thailand. Compared with the period 1990–2000, the average forest areas as a share of total land areas plunged significantly from 2001 to 2009 in Cambodia, the Lao PDR, Myanmar, and Thailand (Table 1.3). The stern degradation of energy sources, forests, and habitats accelerates environmental damages at an unprecedented pace. Linde et al. (2009) estimated that if concrete environmental protection measures are not seriously carried out, the GMS will lose 50 per cent of its remaining forests and natural resources over the next century with one-third of it expected to be devastated over the next few decades.

Political stability is a necessary condition for successful subregional coordination. Only if domestic and cross-border political conflicts are resolved could meaningful reforms and solid development momentum be put in place. Smooth steps forward, nevertheless, have been critically hampered by political developments in the GMS. Political stampedes in Myanmar are perhaps the most definitive obstacles for future progress and development of this cooperation. For the time being, the political situation in Myanmar does not indicate where the country is moving, even though the country was an active participant in the initial stages of the GMS projects in the early 1990s. "Without genuine democratization and political reforms in Myanmar, it is unlikely that Myanmar will be or could be accepted as a bona fide good or trusting member in the GMS, let alone in ASEAN or in the international community" (Krongkaew 2004, p. 995). As Myanmar is left behind politically, the country is on the verge of losing development opportunities that stem from foreign assistance from, and trade relations with, the world. Likewise, the Cambodian Government, despite its successful foundation of a democratic government, has been plagued by domestic chaos and disorganization. More recently, the long-drawn out political deadlock at the Cambodia-Thailand border virtually froze the next rounds of regional economic and social cooperation and necessary reforms at the GMS subregional platform, as well as at the wider regional ties such as ASEAN.

OVERVIEW OF THE BOOK

This book is structured in two parts. The first part pertains to country-specific chapters (Chapters 2–7) that discuss recent developments and emerging issues facing each GMS country. The other part is concerned with thematic chapters (Chapters 8–12), highlighting the issues that are commonly relevant to all countries in the GMS. Each chapter examines a key subject surrounding the progress of a transition from a geographic corridor to a socio-economic corridor, including trade and investment; regional financial cooperation; governance enhancement; energy development; and transportation infrastructure development.

Larry Strange (Chapter 2) paints a balanced picture of Cambodia's recent development even though its constitutional, political, and military crisis in the early 1990s severely set back the social, political, and economic progress of this small, yet strategically important country. Cambodia in the run-up to the global financial crisis in 2008 had achieved several milestones leading to its economic integration in the GMS, such as its accession to ASEAN and the WTO, and strengthening physical and institutional infrastructure, among many others. The buoyant scenario for Cambodia in the next decade envisages that the country "is no longer aid-dependent, has graduated from LDC-status, and has made significant progress in achieving sustainable socio-economic development, poverty reduction, and a more equitable distribution of national wealth".

Oudet Souvannavong (Chapter 3) provides a comprehensive, realistic assessment of the Lao PDR's economic situation in the aftermath of the global economic meltdown in 2008. Although several problems and constraints have, by and large, perturbed its smooth economic development, particularly the lack of basic infrastructure, scarce skilled human resources, a weak private sector, limited financial development, and prevalent corruption, the Lao PDR stands in good stead to "turn its 'land-locked' disadvantage into a 'land-link' advantage" and to embrace the full potentials of economic integration in the GMS. To realize this, it is imperative for the Lao PDR to insert itself into the regional value chain whereby enhanced transport connectivity offers abundant business opportunities and economic gains through growing flows of goods and services.

Michael von Hauff (Chapter 4) illuminates Myanmar's economic development trends and identifies challenges that confront its transition from a centrally planned economy to a market-oriented economy. Since the inception of reforms and liberalization policies initiated after 1988, no significant steps forward have been made, and various figures point to economic stagnation, if not regression, due mainly to the weak commitment of the military regime to a free and open economy, and partly to economic sanctions by the Western countries, and the impact of cyclone Nargis in 2008. As its economic isolation has left Myanmar behind, comprehensive economic and social reforms, such as free trade and investment, financial market development, investment in human capital, and labour market and industry development, hold a key towards meaningful connectivity in the GMS.

Narongchai Akrasanee (Chapter 5) provides perspectives on the GMS through Thailand's lens. While Thailand has long been tied to the GMS economically, socially, and historically, its most important gains from the GMS as a subregional grouping is secured access to natural resources, particularly natural gas from Myanmar and hydropower from the Lao PDR.

Although connectivity in the GMS has improved physically through a number of infrastructure projects supported by the ADB, various cross-border problems of rules and regulations have not been resolved. They could hamper the cross-border flows of goods and services, at the Thailand-Myanmar and Thailand-Cambodia borders and other border points. The subregion also suffers from uneven development. To address these challenges, Thailand, as a relatively advanced member, must play a critical role in the provision of development assistance, negotiation of trade and investment facilitation, entrepreneurship development, and business promotion.

Vo Tri Thanh (Chapter 6) examines GMS socio-economic development and cooperation in the wider context of ASEAN and East Asia with an emphasis on perspectives from Vietnam. While increases in intraregional trade and investment have brought about substantial benefits to the GMS countries in terms of rapid output growth, narrowing income gaps, and rapid human development, the subregion differs critically in the development levels of labour and industrial structures. The differences in constraints and socio-economic conditions facing the GMS members have complicated integration and development processes. The new phase of subregional cooperation requires the GMS Strategic Framework to address various emerging issues, including inclusive and green growth, rethinking the East Asian growth paradigm, and attempts in going beyond trade and investment liberalization to include facilitation and connectivity.

Guangsheng Lu (Chapter 7) envisages that Yunnan Province, PRC, is now embracing a big opportunity to strengthen its economic cooperation with the GMS. Since mid-2009, it has been drawing up a grand development plan, namely the Bridgehead Strategy, which gives the Yunnan Province an exceptional chance for economic cooperation with the GMS. Nevertheless, there are some problems to be addressed, such as the unbalanced trade between Yunnan Province and the GMS, insufficient complementarities, environmental concerns, and corporate social responsibility, among others.

Jayant Menon and Anna C. Melendez (Chapter 8) articulate that the strong rates of economic growth in the GMS since the early 1990s have been fuelled by increased trade and FDI, attributable to unilateral policy reforms and greater economic cooperation through the GMS Programme and, more recently, its membership of the WTO and participation in the ASEAN Free Trade Agreement (AFTA). Despite these achievements, the trade reform agenda remains incomplete. It is important for the GMS members of AFTA to multilateralize their preferences to avoid trade diversion and deflection, and remain open globally. Intrasectoral diversification of both export commodities and markets is equally important to reduce vulnerability to external shocks. It is unlikely, however, that any rebalancing of growth from foreign to domestic sources will be required in the GMS countries to enhance their resilience to external shocks.

Ulrich Volz (Chapter 9) explores the extent to which subregional cooperation on financial market development, financial regulation, and the advancement of cross-border financial integration helps the GMS countries put forward a well-functioning financial market. While the need for deepening financial cooperation and development in the subregion is apparent, he emphasizes that the GMS countries have to meet certain necessary conditions through domestic reforms, including macroeconomic stability, property rights, and law enforcement. To achieve this, the GMS countries potentially bank on existing initiatives and institutions such as the Macroeconomic and Finance Surveillance Office (MFSO) at the ASEAN Secretariat, the ASEAN+3 Macroeconomic Research Office (AMRO), and the Chiang Mai Initiative Multilateralization (CMIM).

Narong Pomlaktong et al. (Chapter 10) discuss the governance issues in the GMS countries using case studies from Thailand's logistic industry. As the GMS countries stand in good stead to tap a well-connected subregion, effective national road infrastructure and coherent coordination of transport policies in the subregion would require improved governance of institutional and regulatory frameworks, on top of pricing and law enforcement. They highlight several policy recommendations that shed light on strengthening governance in the GMS, such as the inclusion of stakeholders and provision of the right incentives; appropriate institution arrangements; sharing costs of infrastructure investment; capacity building; enhancing a public-private partnership (PPP); and the facilitation of customs clearance formalities.

Yongping Zhai and Anthony J. Jude (Chapter 11) contemplate a model of South-South cooperation based on energy sector integration and low-carbon development in the GMS. While the subregion is characterized by its uneven energy resource endowment, different levels of economic development, diverse cultures, and distinct government systems, the common challenge to all GMS countries is how to sustain their economic growth and, at the same time, limit adverse environmental impacts. In light of this, the GMS countries have embarked on implementing a road map of power interconnection and expanded energy sector cooperation. The experience of GMS cooperation offers a unique example of regional collaboration to address the challenges of climate change.

Chris Lyttleton (Chapter 12) focuses specifically on interpersonal social interactions in local communities, rather than economic dimensions accompanying infrastructure development in the GMS. In place of quantitative tables, descriptions and vignettes are used to highlight certain elements of social change incurred by rapid development. The aim of this chapter is to examine how the impact of new corridors extends in multiple ways to local populations as entrepreneurial opportunities allow income diversification and livelihood improvement. Insofar as expanding neoliberal structures underpin economic growth, so too they affect how people make choices and what resources they use to do this. Thus, this chapter suggests that social impact assessment is a crucial part of understanding the transition from geographic linkages to socio-economic growth.

CONCLUSION

The transition to a market-driven economy in the GMS through ever-increasing connectivity has borne some fruit. The GMS Programme that kicked off in 1992 and, not least, the strong commitment of the various governments to leverage on economic, social, and political complementarities have made the GMS one of the most dynamic subregions on earth. GMS countries have enjoyed substantial economic benefits in terms of robust economic growth, growing employment, macroeconomic stability, and swift industry and labour market development as a result of a persistent upward shift in intraregional trade and investment. These have been translated into escalating standards of living, accelerating poverty reduction, narrowing economic and social inequality, rapid human resource development, and improved social security.

Yet various challenges to the subregion remain: GMS countries are significantly diverse in terms of developmental pace and level, ranging from leading countries such as Thailand and Yunnan Province, PRC, with GDP per capita of over US$3,000, to the relatively less-developed ones such as Cambodia, the Lao PDR, and Myanmar (CLM), with GDP per capita of under US$500. The ways GMS countries can fully tap benefits from the cooperation lies with bridging the development gap. Failure to do so would result in these countries being left behind, making the GMS a stumbling block to regionalism and multilateralism. The economic corridor development must therefore target equipping CLM with capabilities to catch up with their neighbouring countries, including having access to health care services and quality food, technology development, and affordable education.

The ensuing chapters in this book address a wide range of key socio-economic and political issues related particularly to the economy, the environment, governance, and human security, among others. It sheds light on how to narrow the gap between potentials and what the GMS countries are realizing. They illuminate the way to (i) harness the rich resources for regional development, (ii) mitigate the development gap, and (iii) explore sustainable ways to enhance connectivity and capacity.

Notes

1. Guangxi Zhuang Autonomous Region joined the GMS at the 13th GMS Ministerial Conference in Vientiane, Lao PDR, in December 2004. Because of the very recent accession to the subregion, this book's analyses do not touch on it, but only on Yunnan Province.
2. Myanmar's GNI is not available in the dataset.
3. See <http://www.unescap.org/esid/hds/projects/UC/index.asp>.

References

Asian Development Bank. "The Greater Mekong Subregion: Beyond Borders". Regional Cooperation Strategy and Program Update 2006–2008. 2005 <http://www.adb.org/Documents/Reports/Beyond-Borders/default.asp>.

————. "The GMS beyond Borders". Regional Cooperation Strategy and Program Update 2004–2008 <http://www.adb.org/Documents/CSPs/GMS/2004/GMS-RCSP.pdf>.

Ishida, M. "Effectiveness and Challenges of Three Economic Corridors of the Greater Mekong Sub-region". Institute of Developing Economies Discussion Papers, No. 35, 2005.

Krongkaew, M. "The Development of the Greater Mekong Subregion (GMS): Real Promise or False Hope?" *Journal of Asian Economics* 15, no. 5 (2004): 977–98.

Linde, L., I. Watson, and T. Tekelenburg. "Environmental Performance Assessment in the Greater Mekong Subregion". RAP Publication, no. 3, 2009, pp. 405–17.

Than, M. "Economic Co-operation in the Greater Mekong Subregion". *Asia-Pacific Economic Literature* 11, no. 2 (1997): 40–57.

2

CAMBODIA, ITS DEVELOPMENT, AND INTEGRATION INTO THE GMS
A Work in Progress

Larry Strange

CAMBODIA AND THE GMS IN CONTEXT

In international development literature Cambodia is often defined as a post-conflict, aid-dependent, least-developed country, all terms with potentially negative implications. This chapter will present a more balanced overview of Cambodia's recent development and its historical, geopolitical, and economic contexts, highlighting its achievement — until the setback of the global financial crisis and economic downturn — of high levels of economic growth, significant socio-economic development, slow but steady poverty reduction, and significant but uneven progress in state institution-building and reforms. It will also present a positive future scenario for Cambodia and the strengths and weaknesses that will determine whether this scenario can be achieved. A major factor will be Cambodia's further integration into subregional and regional economies, institutions, and strategic relationships, in the Greater Mekong Subregion, as a member of the Association of South East Asian Nations (ASEAN), and the emerging East Asian configuration of ASEAN+3, that is ASEAN, China, South Korea, and Japan or other emerging East Asia regional architecture.

BUILDING BACK FROM YEAR ZERO

On 17 April 1975, soldiers of the Khmer Rouge entered the Cambodian capital, Phnom Penh. They were greeted by the local people with a mixture of relief and trepidation — relief that they might bring some prospect of an end to the civil war, and trepidation as to what this new military and ideological force might bring for Cambodia. Over the next three days the city was emptied of people. Long columns of people headed out of the city, the rationale provided to them that it was to protect the citizens of Phnom Penh from the inevitable American bombing that would follow the Khmer Rouge victory. Year Zero had begun. While the Khmer Rouge was in power, from April 1975 to January 1979, their programmes of forced labour, repression, torture, and executions, as well as disease, saw the loss of almost two million Cambodian lives, including the purging of Khmer Rouge members themselves and their leaders. Most of a generation of educated Cambodians was lost.

On 7 January 1979, the Vietnamese army, along with many Cambodians and former Khmer Rouge members who had earlier fled the Democratic Kampuchea regime, including the current Prime Minister of Cambodia, Hun Sen, invaded Cambodia, defeating the Khmer Rouge regime. To this day the public holiday in Cambodia on 7 January celebrating this event remains sensitive and contested. Was it an invasion or a liberation? Or both? This depends on where one sat in the complex Cold War geopolitical situation at the time, and whose interests were at stake. Objectively, it might best be described as a "self-interested liberation", Vietnam moving both to secure its borders and defeat the Khmer Rouge, and to install a sympathetic regime in Phnom Penh.

The reality that was encountered by the Vietnamese army and the Cambodian returnees, and the first international humanitarian workers who arrived over the next twelve months, was at first difficult to comprehend — the wholesale destruction of infrastructure, of productive agricultural activity, and the massive dislocation of people throughout the country — but most of all, the gradual unearthing of what became known as "the killing fields", the many mass graves of the millions of Cambodians who had either been executed, tortured to death, or had died through forced labour and disease. A complex set of geopolitical developments that then befell Cambodia — a victim of not only the Khmer Rouge, but also of the broader Cold War — including the international embargo of the Vietnamese-backed regime in Phnom Penh through the decade of the 1980s, brought further suffering and hardship, poverty, and hunger to the Cambodian people. The efforts of the Vietnam-backed regime during the 1980s, and humanitarian efforts by some international NGOs and Soviet bloc and Scandinavian nations, saw a stabilizing of the country and some rehabilitation and reconstruction of infrastructure and basic agricultural activity. It also saw continued conflict with the Khmer Rouge in many areas, with the Khmer Rouge leadership retaining its seat at the United Nations with the support of China, the United States and its ASEAN allies, and most western nations, and the creation of a Khmer diaspora of refugees in Europe, North America, and Australia.

A PEACE SETTLEMENT, UNTAC, ELECTIONS, DEVELOPMENT ASSISTANCE

In the early 1990s, with the end of the Cold War and the Paris Peace Settlement, Cambodia experienced another quite different invasion — the United Nations Transition Administration in Cambodia, or UNTAC, which saw an international peacekeeping force help build peace and security; the drafting of a new constitution, the first national elections under this constitution in 1993, and the beginning of large-scale international development assistance. During the 1990s the rudiments of a market economy were established with the reintroduction of private property, privatization of state-owned companies, and the decollectivization of agriculture. However, the political conflict between Hun Sen's Cambodian People's Party (CPP) and Prince Norodom Ranariddh's FUNCIPEC Party continued until 1997–98, deteriorating into armed military conflict and, finally, the consolidation of power by Prime Minister Hun Sen and the CPP.

The decades of conflict in Cambodia did not end until 1998, just over a decade ago, when the final armed conflict between political opponents in Cambodia was concluded, and the last remnants of the Khmer Rouge and its leadership were neutralized and disarmed, with successful policies for the integration of former Khmer Rouge zones, the dismantling of their political and military organization, and land distribution to former Khmer Rouge soldiers. This is important to any understanding of the dimensions of Cambodia's recent record of peace, stability, and socio-economic development.

1999–2008: A DECADE OF RECONSTRUCTION, GROWTH, DEVELOPMENT, AND CONFIDENCE

Following the setback of the 1998 constitutional, political, and military crisis, and the subsequent achievement of an uneasy political stability, international recognition of the Cambodian Government was re-established and, in 1999, Cambodia became a member of ASEAN. New constitutional democratic institutions were built, ambitious subnational governance reforms, "decentralization and deconcentration", were implemented, with the first successful local commune council elections held in 2002, and national elections held in 2003, which resulted in a strong ruling party, with a smaller but vocal opposition. Over the same period a series of reforms focusing on macroeconomic management, public financial management, and the governance of the financial sector were implemented, along with significant progress in the rehabilitation and reconstruction of physical infrastructure, especially national road networks.

The following period, 2004–8, saw high levels of growth for the Cambodian economy, an average of 10.3 per cent, with an average for the decade of 7 per cent, but concentrated within a narrow band of economic activity — garment manufacturing, tourism, and construction. In 2004, consistent with the constitutional and political commitment to an open market economy, Cambodia became the first least-developed country (LDC) to accede to the World Trade Organization (WTO). This period saw the implementation of a second generation of reforms under the first phase of a Public Financial Management Programme. Major infrastructure development also progressed — roads, bridges, dams, energy generation, and telecommunications, with continued investment in provincial and rural roads. Socio-economic development outcomes also improved, particularly in poverty reduction, which fell from 45 per cent to 30 per cent over the decade, but unevenly distributed, with a persistent concentration of the poor and very poor in the Tonle Sap (Great Lake) region in central Cambodia.

CAMBODIA AND THE "DEVELOPMENT PARADIGM": BENEFITS AND LIABILITIES

The provision of high levels of official development assistance (ODA) loans and grants from multilateral and bilateral government agencies and from international NGOs, has been a major factor in Cambodia's development over the past decade, with significant assistance for critical areas of development such as infrastructure, public financial management, health, and education. However, many questions have been raised about the effectiveness of the model of development assistance delivery to Cambodia. Despite the uncontested value of much of this assistance to the achievement of Cambodia's development, critics point to the need to address the waste, duplication, competition, and "supply-driven" policies and practices of the international development community, and, until recently, the lack of a coordinated government response to this, so that development assistance might be more "demand-driven", that is, reflecting the real priorities of the Cambodian Government and people, and genuinely addressing Cambodia's needs rather than the needs, agendas, and ideological orientations of "donors" themselves.

In 2010 Cambodia received ODA commitments of more than US$1 billion, with strong statements of donor confidence, even with specific concerns expressed on governance and corruption issues. Despite the impact of the global financial crisis and economic downturn, Cambodia can anticipate high levels of assistance for the foreseeable future, allowing for predictability and the alignment of ODA with the priorities of the government's National Strategic Development Plan 2009–13, especially on macro-economic and public financial management, infrastructure, agriculture and rural development, health, and education. China is now Cambodia's largest provider of both ODA and foreign direct investment, with Japan still a major provider of ODA, both bilaterally, and through the Asian Development Bank, and the U.S. Government providing ODA direct to the Cambodian Government rather than through civil society organizations as was its practice in the past. The provision of ODA and associated economic and development cooperation is taking on an increasingly subregional and regional character, with deepening relationships with other nations in the Greater Mekong Subregion, ASEAN, and ASEAN+3 (ASEAN plus China, Japan, and South Korea).

However, despite the commitment of Cambodia and its development partners to the Paris Declaration on Aid Effectiveness, there is still very uneven progress in donor harmonization and coordination, and the elimination of competition, duplication, and waste, although there has been some progress in the achievement of "sector wide approaches" to ODA delivery, but less discernible change in ODA delivery practice. ODA to Cambodia is still too much "supply driven" rather than "demand driven", and not reflective enough of local initiative and ownership. "Short termism" in ODA commitments and delivery, and associated country programme design, remain a constraining factor in aid effectiveness, with, too often, a failure or incapacity to invest in the long-term strengthening of local institutions, and examples of ideological and institutional "favouritism" in the choice of Cambodian institutions where major investment is to be made. There is also an overreliance on expensive international consultants and technical advisers, often short-term, rather than long-term investment in building local capacity and ownership, a practice which constitutes capacity substitution rather than capacity development, and entrenches dependency.

THE 2008–9 CRISIS: IMPACT AND RESPONSES

From 1998 to 2008 Cambodia experienced a decade of peace and stability, strong political leadership and sound macroeconomic management, sustained economic growth, and significant achievement in socio-economic development and poverty reduction. In 2008–9 the global financial crisis and associated regional economic downturn had a significant negative impact on Cambodia. It was particularly felt in the key pillars of the Cambodia economy — the garment industry, tourism, and construction, with only agriculture continuing to perform strongly. Prior to the crisis, Cambodia was among the ten fastest-growing economies in the world. In the first quarter of 2009, garment exports fell by 18.7 per cent, compared with the same period in 2008; there was a severe drop in high-end tourism income; construction contracted; FDI flows halved. In 2008–9 Cambodia's growth saw one of the steepest contractions in developing East Asia, with negative GDP growth of –2.5 per cent in 2009. The crisis also had a significant impact on the poor and vulnerable, with a decline in real incomes and consumption, and increased vulnerability; and the unemployment and displacement of young female workers in the garment industry, with associated economic and social impact on remittances and family livelihoods, and in some cases "reverse remittances", with rural families subsidizing the livelihoods of urban-based workers.

The Cambodian Government responded quickly to the crisis through both fiscal and monetary policy, running a high budget deficit in 2009 and 2010. To support the garment industry, hard hit by the dramatic fall in demand in the U.S. market, the government suspended the monthly turnover tax of one per cent on garment factory expenditures, and extended the profit-tax holiday for garment factories established prior to 2006. A special fund was set up to provide rice mills with more space to buy and process paddy for export. The National Bank of Cambodia's (NBC) decrease of the reserve requirements of commercial banks from 16 per cent to 12 per cent (after raising it from 8 per cent to curb the spiking inflation in the first half of 2008), and its lifting of the 15 per cent cap on their real estate lending as a condition, opened up some room for monetary easing. These interventions prevented the Cambodian economy from contracting too seriously in 2009 and helped it to recover well in 2010.

Three main lessons were learnt from the crisis for sustaining growth and development in Cambodia. Firstly, the economic growth of the prior decade was unlikely to be sustainable in its current form. Secondly, with a focused growth strategy to increase competitiveness and diversify the economy, Cambodia can achieve sustainable growth. Thirdly, Cambodia is well positioned to benefit from three important opportunities — harnessing the benefits of regional integration; managing natural resources in a sustainable way; and investing in its future through agriculture, infrastructure, education, and higher savings. The crisis, and responses to it, also helped identify or confirm some fundamental priorities for Cambodia's future economic health and socio-economic development:

(i)   A stable, well-managed macroeconomic environment that enables and promotes economic diversification, competitiveness and productivity, and domestic consumption;

(ii) The strengthening of key export-oriented sectors such as agriculture and rural development, tourism, construction, energy and infrastructure, along with trade facilitation and investment;

(iii) Effective implementation of government policies in the National Strategic Development Plan 2009–13 to achieve high, sustainable paddy growth, and the 2010 Policy on Rice Production and Export Promotion and its key success factors — rural infrastructure, paddy productivity, crop diversification, access to credit, extension services, vocational education and training;

(iv) The strategic integration of Cambodia's economy and its key trade and investment relationships in the Greater Mekong Subregion (GMS), ASEAN, the broader ASEAN-China, Korea, and Japan region, and targeted international markets.

Following the crisis and downturn, and the remedial action that was taken, a broadening export-led recovery was under way in 2010–11, with garment exports and tourism growing strongly (14.5 and 9 per cent respectively), agriculture (13.3 per cent), and, particularly, rice production, milling, and export also growing, but construction growth remaining flat. Cambodia's trade with China and South Korea increased dramatically in 2010 (42 per cent and 30 per cent respectively) following the implementation of the China-ASEAN and South Korea–ASEAN Free Trade Areas and associated tariff reductions.

A GDP growth of 5.5 per cent was achieved in 2010, with a GDP growth of 6 per cent for 2011 projected by Cambodia's Ministry of Economy and Finance, the World Bank, and ADB, and 6.8 per cent by the IMF. Inflation was running at 6–7 per cent. Official reserves rose modestly. Credit growth has recovered from 6.5 per cent at the end of 2009, to more than 20 per cent in late 2010.

However, while GDP growth is relatively high and there has been progress in poverty reduction, poverty incidence remains high and inequality has increased. As a result of the setback of the crisis and downturn, the poverty rate remains at approximately 27 per cent, but is higher in some regions of Cambodia. Progress towards the achievement of the Cambodia Millennium Development Goals (MDGs) is uneven, with poverty reduction goals only partially on track; reduction in child mortality and HIV/AIDS, malaria, dengue, and tuberculosis achieved; strong performance on ODA and ICT goals; primary education, literacy rates, and gender equality lagging behind; and weak performances on maternal mortality, natural resource protection, and land management. Further success in achieving poverty reduction and socio-economic development objectives will depend on the maintenance of high levels of more sustainable and equitable growth.

REGIONAL AND SUBREGIONAL INTEGRATION: HARD AND SOFT INFRASTRUCTURE FOR "CONNECTIVITY" IN THE GMS, ASEAN, ASEAN+3: IMPERATIVES FOR CAMBODIA

Cambodia is involved in a complex set of initiatives and processes to promote "connectivity", achieve socio-economic development, reduce poverty, and bridge the development gap in the GMS and ASEAN — infrastructure, transport, logistics and trade facilitation, special economic zones and corridors, environmental and natural resource management, and human resource development; but its "soft" infrastructure, the legal and regulatory framework and associated institutional capacity to support cross-border movement of goods and people and promote regional economic integration, is lagging well behind the "hard" infrastructure. A major issue — the complexity of ASEAN-GMS institutional arrangements — has implications for the pace and effectiveness of regional integration and on the "absorptive capacity" in CLMV GMS countries where institutional capacity is still being built; this constitutes another "spaghetti or noodle bowl" effect just like in the case of the proliferation of free trade agreements.

An imperative for Cambodia is the strategic coordination of ASEAN-GMS integration initiatives, more realistic time frames for the implementation of complex reforms, and associated investment in long-term institutional capacity building, for example, the GMS Cross-Border Transport Agreement and the synchronicity of the Master Plan on ASEAN Connectivity with GMS connectivity initiatives and processes, and a greater awareness of and engagement in ASEAN Economic Community mechanisms and opportunities.

"BRIDGING THE DEVELOPMENT GAP" IN THE GMS AND ASEAN: PRIORITIES FOR THE GMS LDCS IN GMS, ASEAN AND EAST ASIAN REGIONAL COOPERATION AND INTEGRATION

ASEAN LDCs such as Cambodia need GMS, ASEAN and ASEAN+3 partnerships to deliver on the ASEAN Charter commitment "to alleviate poverty and narrow the development gap within ASEAN through mutual assistance and cooperation". Cambodia needs to exploit the real and potential benefits of the ASEAN–China/Korea/Japan FTAs better, especially provisions such as the Early Harvest Programme in the ASEAN-China FTA, as an agricultural producer and potential food processor, and to promote awareness and engagement of the Cambodian private sector in the ASEAN Economic Community and GMS opportunities and processes.

Ultimately it would be in Cambodia's long-term interest, while remaining an open economy with an international market perspective, to be part of an East Asian free trade and economic cooperation area or community, linked to or including specific strategies for East Asian development cooperation and integration strategies to "narrow or bridge the development gap" in East Asia. Related to this will be the importance of ensuring the coordination and synchronization of GMS–ASEAN–East Asian development cooperation and regional integration processes to include a focus on sustained growth and "bridging the development gap", with the associated regional investment in long-term institutional capacity development in the LDCs — Cambodia, the Lao PDR, and Myanmar.

A POSITIVE FUTURE SCENARIO FOR CAMBODIA AND HOW TO GET THERE

What then would a positive and achievable scenario look like for Cambodia ten years from now, and what major factors will determine whether or not that scenario can be achieved? Building on the positive indicators in 2010–11, and lessons learned from the crisis and downturn, we see a positive and achievable scenario for a future peaceful, stable, and prosperous Cambodia as *a Cambodia that is no longer aid-dependent, has graduated from its LDC-status, and has made significant progress in achieving sustainable socio-economic development, poverty reduction, and a more equitable distribution of national wealth.*

This could be achieved through:

• High levels of growth based on economic diversification, increased competitiveness and productivity, the strengthening of key export-oriented sectors such as agriculture and rural development, private sector development, tourism, construction, energy and infrastructure, intraregional trade and investment, the flow of benefits from the exploitation of offshore oil and gas resources, and the strategic integration of Cambodia's economy into the GMS, ASEAN, and the broader ASEAN, China, Korea and Japan (East Asian) region;

- Cambodia and the GMS: The prospect of an integrated Greater Mekong Subregional production network and market, extending from southern China, through the GMS countries to the rest of Southeast Asia, provides opportunities for Cambodia in terms of infrastructure, the movement of people, private sector development and trade and investment flows, and a more integrated production and marketing network, with significant benefits for Cambodian growth, prosperity, private sector development, and poverty reduction;
- Significant poverty reduction, agricultural and rural development, with improvements in agricultural productivity, especially in the quality and quantity of rice production for both domestic consumption and export, crop diversification, extension services, access to credit and markets, and improved infrastructure for affordable energy and transport;
- The strengthening of democratic development, public institutions, and national and subnational governance, with progress in key areas of public sector reform, including service delivery, civil service salaries, capacity building of civil servants, judicial reform, the rule of law and anti-corruption measures;
- Improved management and governance of natural resources — land, water, forest, and fishery — and environmental management, adaptivity in response to climate change, particularly for the agricultural sector, and more transparent and equitable access to natural resources for rural livelihoods and poverty reduction, and a more effective land management policy for the productive use of economic and social land concessions;
- Greater commitment to and resources for social development in key areas of health care, particularly for women and children, access to affordable quality primary, secondary, vocational, and tertiary education, in response to market needs and changing demography, opportunities for youth, and broader human security and social protection.

Cambodia has some real strengths and opportunities to utilize in reaching this positive future scenario. It has a strong, stable political leadership and a system with a track record, although uneven, in macroeconomic management and development planning and results. It has abundant land, water, and other natural resources — minerals, gas and oil, forest, and fisheries — as great national assets if well managed. It has an open market economy responsive to global and regional opportunities, a dynamic entrepreneurial private sector, both large enterprises and SMEs, and continued high levels of ODA, particularly for critical areas of infrastructure, agriculture, and rural development, health, and education. Importantly, it has a young population hungry for education and employment opportunities; with an expanding "talent pool" of young professionals with international experience, but who are Cambodia-committed and family-oriented. It has a strong national and cultural identity; a high-value tangible and intangible cultural heritage, and an increasingly vibrant, contemporary cultural life. But, perhaps most importantly, it has a very advantageous geopolitical and economic "location", at the heart of the GMS, ASEAN, and East Asia, with great potential to be a beneficiary of China's development and the "competition" for regional economic and strategic opportunities between China, the United States, and Japan. Cambodia's genuine commitment to the GMS, ASEAN, and broader East Asian cooperation and integration will serve it well in securing a positive future.

However, Cambodia also faces some serious challenges and weaknesses that will need to be addressed if the positive future scenario is to be achieved. It still has relatively weak public institutions, low civil service salaries, poor but improving taxation collection, and an overly complex decentralization model for subnational governance. Its economy remains too narrowly based, with unexploited potential for agriculture, agribusiness and food processing, and other light industry, and poor private sector awareness of and engagement in the opportunities presented by regional integration. It has comparatively poor-quality tertiary and vocational education that does not meet the aspirations of a very young population or the labour market needs of a growing private sector. It remains aid-dependent with all the challenges of the international development paradigm, the "donor treadmill", and a more complex donor landscape. It has a weak and uneven commitment to the rule of law and "transparency" in government, business, and societal relations and carries the historical burden of the legacy of damaged "trust" from decades of conflict and genocide. Despite recent government initiatives, corruption remains corrosive, with elite land and natural resource grabbing, associated deforestation, and poor land policy and management, particularly in the opportunistic administration of economic and social land concessions. The major gap between hard and soft infrastructure development in Cambodia and the GMS, and the underutilization of Cambodia's Special Economic Zones, constrain investment and the physical and people-to-people "connectivity" imperative for the smooth cross-border movement of people and goods, and for deeper subregional and regional integration.

CONCLUSION: CAMBODIA, THE GMS, AND ITS ASIAN FUTURE

Despite its tragic history and the associated economic, social, political, and psychological legacy of this relatively recent history — still scarcely one generation ago — modern Cambodia has many positive assets: its physical character, its stability, its human and natural resources, its economic potential, and, most of all, its geopolitical situation. Cambodia is a small, strategically important country at the heart of the Greater Mekong Subregion, a member of ASEAN, and the ASEAN+3 configuration with China, South Korea, and Japan, and a part of the processes of subregional and regional integration in which it is both a committed player and a beneficiary.

Cambodia, a member of ASEAN since 1999, has ratified the ASEAN Charter and has been an active supporter of the ASEAN role in the ASEAN+3 processes. Cambodia also acceded to the WTO in 2004, with its complex compliance programme still in train. Cambodia currently stands to gain significantly from the ASEAN–China Free Trade Agreement and others of its kind, particularly the provisions of the ASEAN-China FTA's Early Harvest Programme, which could bring significant potential benefits for Cambodia as an agricultural producer. It can also reap potential benefits from other ASEAN+1 FTAs with Japan, Korea, Australia, and New Zealand, and ultimately an East Asia–wide FTA or economic cooperation agreement. It is significant that in 2010 as a result of implementation of provisions of the ASEAN–China and ASEAN–South Korea Free Trade Agreements, trade between Cambodia and these two economic giants to the north has dramatically increased.

The ASEAN Charter includes as one of ASEAN's purposes, "to alleviate poverty and narrow the development gap within ASEAN through mutual assistance and cooperation", with associated policy commitments to "narrowing of the development gap" as "an important task which will ensure that the benefits of ASEAN's integration efforts are fully realised". There is also the commitment that efforts to narrow and eventually bridge the development gap, such as the Initiatives for ASEAN Integration (IAI), should be better resourced and better aligned with the broader objectives of ASEAN's integration efforts and the GMS subregional development programme.

An integrated Greater Mekong Subregion, extending from southern China through the GMS countries to the rest of Southeast Asia and beyond, provides great opportunities for Cambodia for infrastructure development, the movement of people and goods, private sector development and trade and investment flows, and an integrated production and marketing network, with significant benefits for Cambodian business, growth, prosperity, poverty reduction, and the future well-being of the Cambodian people. It may also prove to be "transformational" for the least-developed countries of the GMS — Cambodia, the Lao PDR, and Myanmar.

3

SUBREGIONAL CONNECTIVITY IN THE LAO PDR
From Landlocked Disadvantage to Land-linked Advantage

Oudet Souvannavong

The Lao People's Democratic Republic (Lao PDR) is a landlocked country in Southeast Asia surrounded by the People's Republic of China and Myanmar to the north, Thailand to the west, Vietnam to the east, and Cambodia to the south. The country has a large area of 236,800 square kilometres, a population of 6.6 million inhabitants, and a very low population density of twenty-five persons per square kilometre.

The country is mountainous in the north and the east, and has in the west a number of plains along the Mekong River. The Mekong River and its tributaries are the main water sources that provide abundant natural resources with high socio-economic development potential for agriculture, forestry, fisheries, hydropower, and mining. In addition to those resources, the country has large ethnic diversity and an ancient Lao cultural heritage.

Despite its natural and cultural resources, the Lao PDR has a number of constraints that hamper economic development, such as large mountainous terrain, remote settlements, low population density, and widespread poverty. The country is one of the least-developed countries (LDC) because of its underdeveloped physical infrastructure and human resources, its largely non-monetized economy, and undeveloped public administration and governance frameworks, which have resulted in institutional and regulatory deficiencies that are posing problems and challenges to development.

In the late 1980s the Government of the Lao PDR (GoL) introduced New Economic Mechanisms that aim at reforming public governance from a centrally planned economy to a market oriented economy. Trade liberalization is one pillar of economic reform and this has been accelerated when the Lao PDR joined the Association of South East Asian Nations (ASEAN) in 1987 and agreed to the ASEAN Free Trade Area (AFTA) in 1997. The desire of the government is to develop the country's unfavourable landlocked situation into an effective land-linked position by leveraging the growing market of the neighbouring countries forming the Mekong River subregion of ASEAN and East Asia.

In 1992 the Lao PDR joined a programme of economic cooperation that aims to promote development through closer economic linkages in the Greater Mekong Subregion[1] (the GMS Programme). The GMS Programme, with support from the Asian Development Bank (ADB) and other donors, supported the implementation of high-priority subregional projects in transport, energy, telecommunications, the environment, human resource development, tourism, trade, private sector investment, and agriculture. One of the main components of the GMS Programme is the development of Economic Corridors that would entail integrating infrastructure development with other economic opportunities. These include trade and investment and efforts to address social and other impacts arising from increased connectivity. This chapter highlights the Lao PDR's economic situation right after the global financial crisis and economic downturn of 2009 and the country's potential and challenges for regional economic integration, especially within the GMS and East Asia.

ECONOMIC AND SOCIAL CONDITIONS

The Lao PDR remains one of the least-developed countries (LDCs) in the world, with life expectancy at birth of 53.1 years, an adult literacy rate of 47.3 per cent, and a human development index of 0.476 in 2005. The ultimate goal of the government is to eradicate poverty and move the country from the list of LDCs by 2020. Since 1992, the GoL has embarked on large poverty reduction programmes that have resulted in the reduction of its poverty incidence from 45 per cent in 1992, to 26.8 per cent in 2008. According to the Lao Expenditures and Consumption Survey (LECS) (Figure 3.1), the poverty ratio decreased from 11 (LECS 1992/93) to 8 (LECS 2002/03).

FIGURE 3.1

Poverty Incidence in the Lao PDR

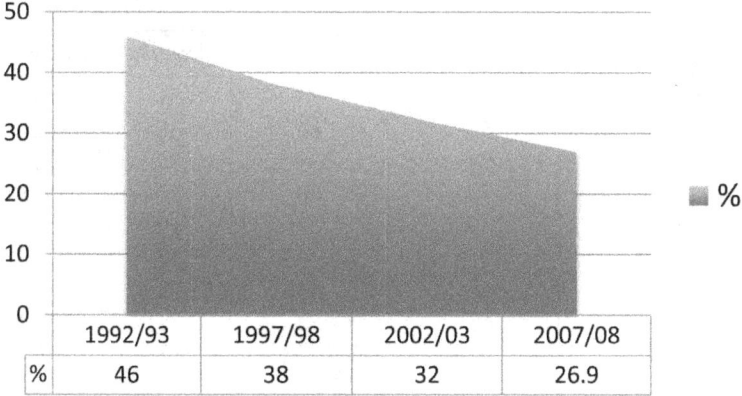

	1992/93	1997/98	2002/03	2007/08
%	46	38	32	26.9

Source: Laos Expenditures and Consumption Survey, various years.

The proportion of its population below the food poverty line reduced from 32.5 per cent (LECS 1997/98) to 19.8 per cent (LECS 2002/03).

The LECS further indicates that the dietary patterns are different in rural and urban areas. This shows that there are large development disparities between urban and rural areas. In rural areas rice is the main component of household meals. Consumption of meat and fish is high, as well as the consumption of non-timber forest products (NTFP), which is the main source of food in the rural areas. In urban areas there is an increase in transport and communication household expenditures.

In terms of access to clean water supply and sanitation (Table 3.1), the proportion of the population having access to improved drinking water sources increased from 38 per cent (1990) to 66 per cent (2008), and the proportion of the population using improved sanitation facilities increased from 8 per cent (1990) to 53 per cent (2008). The infant mortality rate (IMR) decreased from 104 (1995) to 70 (2005). The maternal mortality ratio (MMR) decreased from 650 (1995) to 38 (2005). The contraceptive prevalence rate increased from 20 (1994) to 38 (2005).

Education is a priority of the GoL and access to education is high at the primary level. However, the access to secondary, vocational, and higher education remains low. School attendance is also low, especially in remote,

TABLE 3.1
Social Development Indicators in the Lao PDR

Access to	Whole Country	Urban Area	Rural Area	
			Accessible	non-accessible
Improved drinking	57	72	51	23
Improved sanitation	53	84	38	24
Vaccination	98	97	99	95
Malaria treatment	76	80	75	68
Medical drugs	30	60	19	3
Birth assistance	51	39	57	50
Health volunteers	56	43	60	72
Medical services	45	82	31	12

TABLE 3.2
School Development in the Lao PDR

	Whole Country	Urban Area	Rural Area	
			Accessible	non-accessible
School attendance				
6–10-year-old girls	78	94	76	69
6–10-year-old boys	80	93	80	67
11–15-year-old girls	90	98	90	77
11–15-year-old boys	95	99	95	91
Illiteracy rate				
Women	14	9	15	16
Men	13	7	15	16

non-accessible rural areas (Table 3.2). The illiteracy rate is still high, particularly for females living in rural areas.

Access to basic infrastructure such as roads and electricity has improved substantively. The actual electricity network coverage is up to 99 per cent in urban areas, but is only at 26 per cent in rural areas. All-weather road access in rural areas is low (17 per cent).

ECONOMIC PERFORMANCE

Since the introduction of the New Economic Mechanism, the economy grew by an average of 6.2 per cent from 1990 to 1999; 5.5 per cent from 2000 to 2005; and 7 per cent from 2006 to 2009. GNP per capita increased to US$986 in 2008 from US$114 in 1985 (Figure 3.2).

In the seventh National Social and Economic Development Plan (NSEDP 2006–11) the GoL forecasted a significant, increased GDP growth in the natural resource and manufacturing sectors. The GDP per capita reached US$986 in 2008. In comparison to the other countries in Southeast Asia, the GDP value is the lowest. Real GDP growth is estimated at 7 per cent in 2009, and is expected to increase to 7 per cent in 2010, with 3.3 per cent from the power sector (hydropower), 0.9 per cent from agriculture, 0.4 per cent from mining and construction, 0.8 per cent from manufacturing, 1.7 per cent from the service sector, which comprises tourism, trade, transport, finance, banking, and telecommunications. There is a slight growth in the service sector that is the result of a recent sharp increase in bank lending and transport and telecommunication services. According to the World Bank, the real GNI is expected to slow down to 6 per cent in 2010, compared with 9.5 per cent in 2009. This is due to significant outflows of income from profit repatriation and interest payment from the mining and hydropower sectors.

FIGURE 3.2
GDP per capita in the GMS, 2008

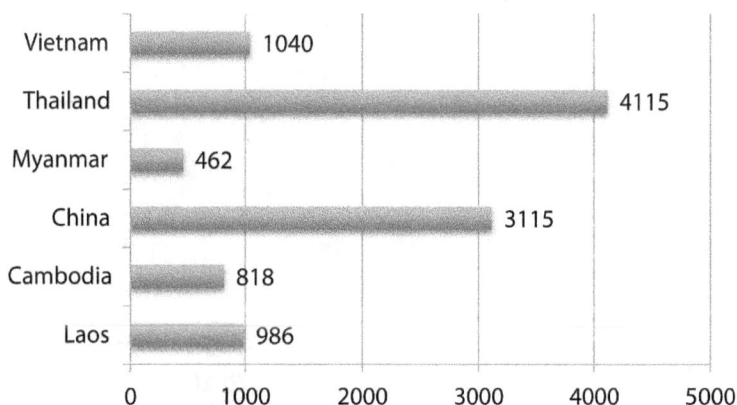

Source: National Social and Economic Development Plan (NSEDP), 2008.

If the global economy recovers from the crisis, the real GDP is projected to grow on average by 7.7 per cent per annum in the next five years (2011–15). The real GNI will also grow by 7.3 per cent.

Headline inflation rose in 2010 largely due to the recent recovery of fuel and food prices (Figures 3.3 and 3.4). Year-on-year inflation increased from 1.5 per cent at the end of 2009 to 4.8 per cent in the second quarter of 2010. The inflation is 2 per cent from energy costs, 1.6 per cent from food, and 1.2 per cent from core prices. Inflation is expected to reach 7.1 per cent in 2011.

TRADE DEVELOPMENT

Since the announcement of its open door policy, the Lao economy has been gradually integrated into regional and global economies. The economic integration of the Lao PDR is derived from the growth of foreign direct investment (FDI), foreign trade, including border trade, and regional cooperation, which have produced valuable contributions to the development of the country, especially in the form of job creation and income generation. The GoL has recognized the importance of trade for poverty reduction, hence, the trade sector in the Lao PDR has gradually been developed and is integrated into the regional economy under the ASEAN Free Trade Area

FIGURE 3.3
Inflation Rates in the GMS

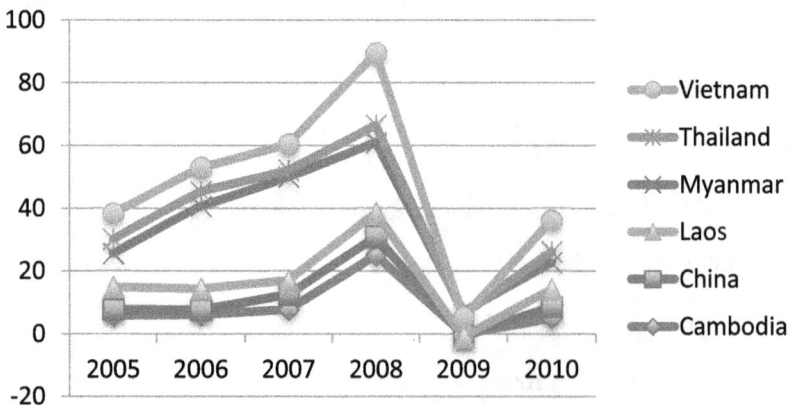

FIGURE 3.4
Consumer Price Inflation in the Lao PDR

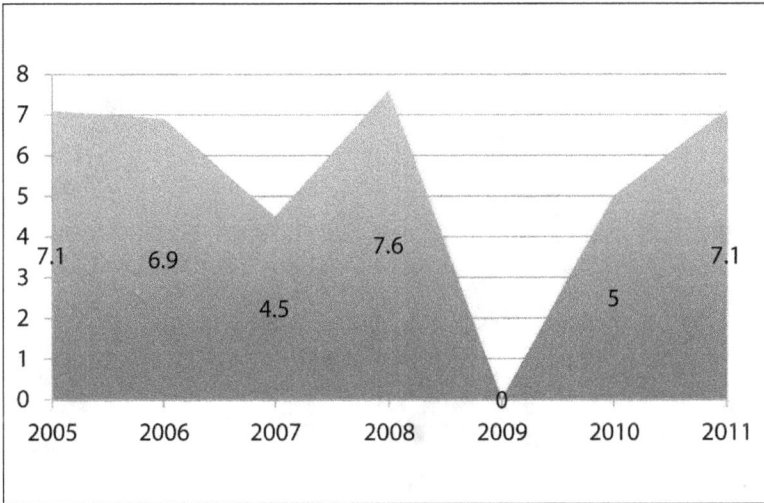

(AFTA), the trade programme under GMS cooperation, and border trade development with neighbouring countries.

Export and import growth, which has been on the increase since 2005, plunged in 2009 due to the global crisis (Figure 3.5). Driven by electricity and minerals, exports were expected to increase by more than 30 per cent in 2010. The new hydropower plant, Nam Theun 2, is expected to generate US$115 million in 2010, and US$240 million per year from 2011. Mineral exports are expected to increase by 32 per cent. Exports of agriculture, garments, and wood products are projected to increase by 33 per cent. Garment export is expected to rebound to over US$200 million (Figure 3.6).

Imports are also expected to rise by over 15 per cent due to increased demand and prices from the implication of export growth and the increased demand for capital goods and the infrastructure construction of large hydropower and industrial plants. The Lao PDR currently has a deficit trade balance. The current account balance is expected to improve, driven by a trade surplus in the natural resource sector that is related to the export of gold, copper, and electricity.

The Lao PDR share of exports with Southeast Asian countries and, especially with its neighbours in the GMS, is high. A share of 54.9 per cent

FIGURE 3.5
Export and Import Growth in the Lao PDR

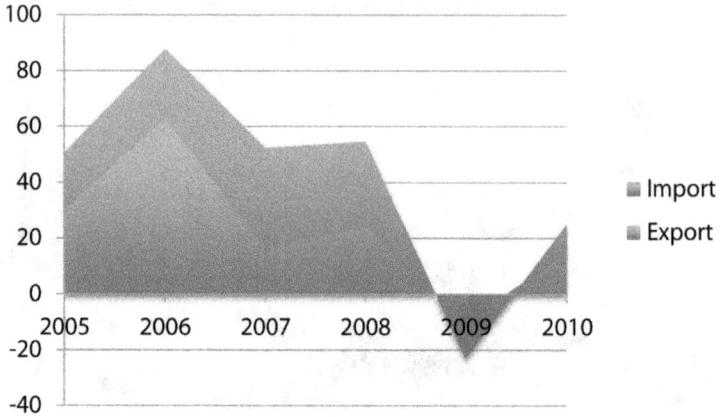

FIGURE 3.6
Direct Export (% of total exports) in the Lao PDR

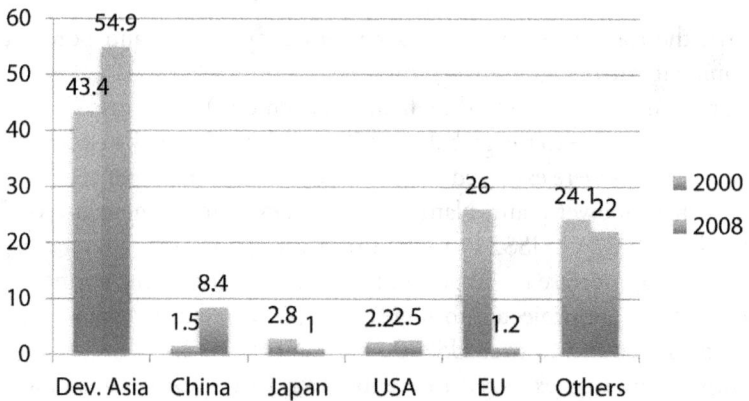

of its exports is within the GMS and Asia. The Lao PDR and Myanmar are mostly exporting in the GMS, compared with other countries in the GMS.

INVESTMENT

The Lao PDR public investment depends a lot on official development assistance (ODA). Domestic capital investment (DCI) represents only 3 per cent of the total public investment. The structure of investment is led by FDI at 65 per cent and ODA at 18 per cent. Domestic investment represents 14 per cent, and public investment, 3 per cent of the investments (Figure 3.7).

FDI declined by almost 23 per cent in 2009 due to the impact of the global financial crisis. It is expected to recover in 2010 by 5.7 per cent. FDI in the natural resource sector (mining and energy) is expected to grow. The non-resource sector will also grow in processing industries, construction, and services, especially trade and tourism.

There is also a large discrepancy between FDI approved and implemented projects (Figure 3.8). That has made the GoL review investment concessions, especially in the natural resource sector (mining).

BUSINESS ENVIRONMENT

The implementation of new economic reforms brought changes in the roles of various economic sectors. Price liberalization, land, agricultural, fiscal, trade, exchange rates, the banking and financial sector, foreign investments, and public enterprise reforms have enabled the private sector to increase its contribution to the economy by creating more income and employment.

Since the early 1990s there has been a consistent and high rate of annual employment growth in private sector growth of 10 to 15 per cent per annum. The increase in manufacturing value added produced by the private sector, including private FDI, has reached more than four times the manufacturing value added produced by state enterprises at the beginning of the century, and

FIGURE 3.7
Investment in the Lao PDR, 2005–9

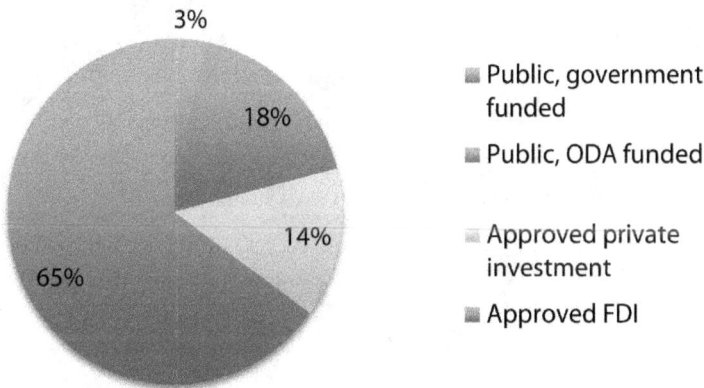

FIGURE 3.8
FDI Projects in the Lao PDR

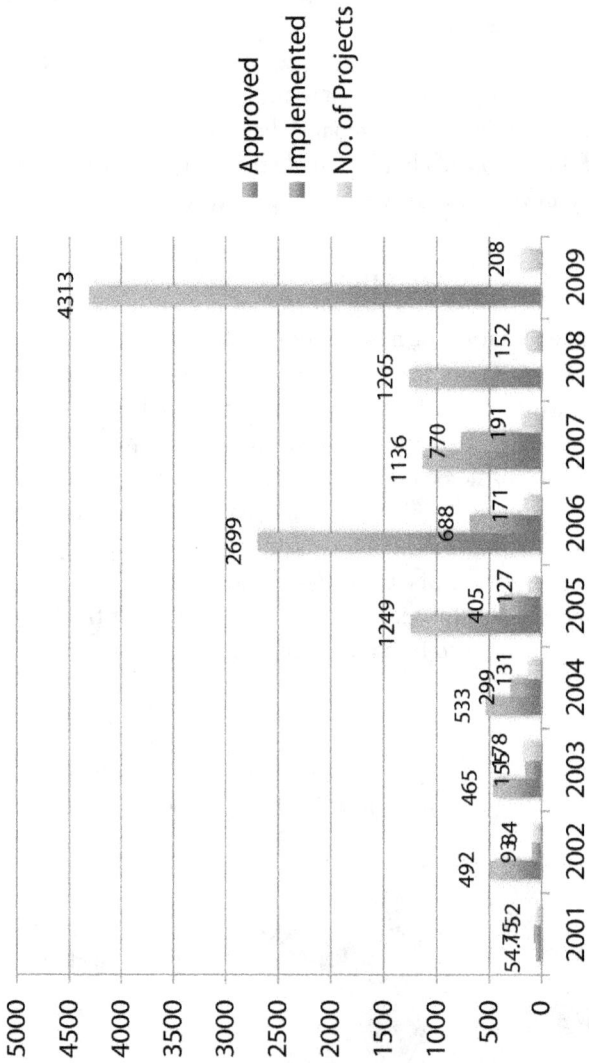

about one third of the private manufacturing value added has been created by local private investors.

In the service sector, private entrepreneurship rapidly evolved to occupy the major share in the economy and in employment. However, the number of private businesses in the Lao PDR is small and most of the businesses are classified as small and medium enterprises (SMEs).

Private enterprises are important to the economy and are considered the engine of growth by the government. Nonetheless, they are facing many problems in realizing their full potential despite ongoing reforms. The World Bank's "Doing Business Ranking" places the Lao PDR at 167 out of 183 — the lowest ranking compared with other countries in the GMS and Southeast Asia (Figure 3.9). The business environment in the Lao PDR is considered not favourable by the private sector. The country's tax rate is considered one of the biggest constraints in doing business. Corruption and access to finance are the issues that concern local enterprises most (Figure 3.10).

TRADE AND INVESTMENT OPPORTUNITIES IN LAOS

Despite the above problems and constraints, the Lao PDR has large potential for development. The country lies in the middle of vibrant larger economies in the GMS with a combined population of over 360 million. Their abundant natural resources, such as forests, water, and minerals, are actually the prime sources for wood, hydropower, and mining industries. The country's natural and cultural diversity have large potential for tourism development. Its young population and labour force provide potential for the development of manufacturing and service industries. Its political stability and open market policies and reforms have made an impact through the enhancement of capital and FDI flows into the country.

Southeast Asia and the GMS represent a large natural resource–based market for the Lao PDR. With a large potential in hydropower energy generation of over 23,000 MW, the Lao PDR is viewed as the future energy source for the GMS and for Southeast Asia. Mineral resources are yet untapped and comprise a number of commercial products such as tin, lead, zinc, iron, copper, gold, gypsum, lignite, precious stones, etc.

The increasing population in Southeast Asia and the GMS represents a large food and agriculture based market for the Lao PDR. There are agri-business projects in forestry plantation and industrial wood, agro-industry products (sugar cane, maize, rice, and fruits and vegetables) to be developed for those markets.

FIGURE 3.9
Doing Business Ranking in the Lao PDR, 2009–10

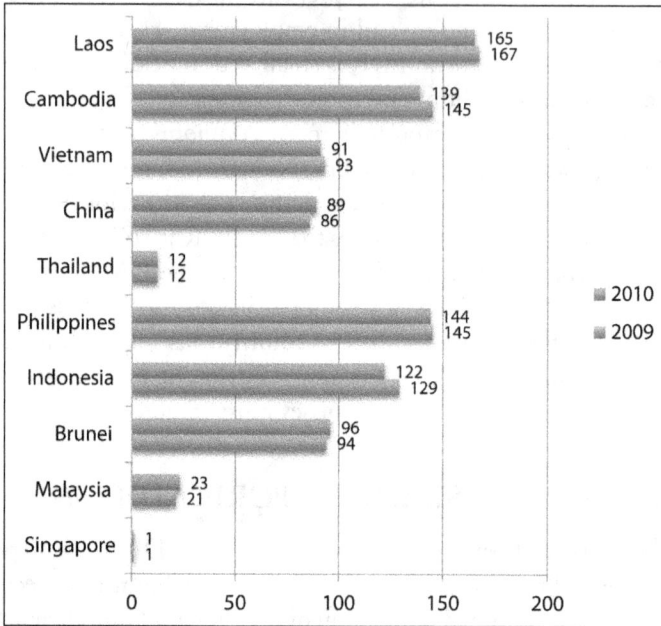

Source: Doing Business Ranking, World Bank.

With regard to its young population, the development of labour-intensive industries is a must for the GoL — to encourage young people to work in the country and limit labour migration to Thailand and other countries. The potential labour-intensive industries are in garments, electrical and auto parts, construction materials, and components using raw materials from the primary resource industry (copper).

The Lao PDR has a large potential for tourism. The country's water and forestry resources and its ancient history and ethnic and cultural diversity have recently been an attraction for large numbers of tourists. Luangprabang, the ancient royal capital, and Vat Phou Champasak (Khmer Temple) that are registered as world heritage sites by UNESCO as well as a number of ecotourism sites are to be further developed to increase tourism arrivals. In 2009 the number of inbound tourists reached two million, of whom more than one million came from Thailand, Vietnam, and China.

FIGURE 3.10
Business Environment in the Lao PDR

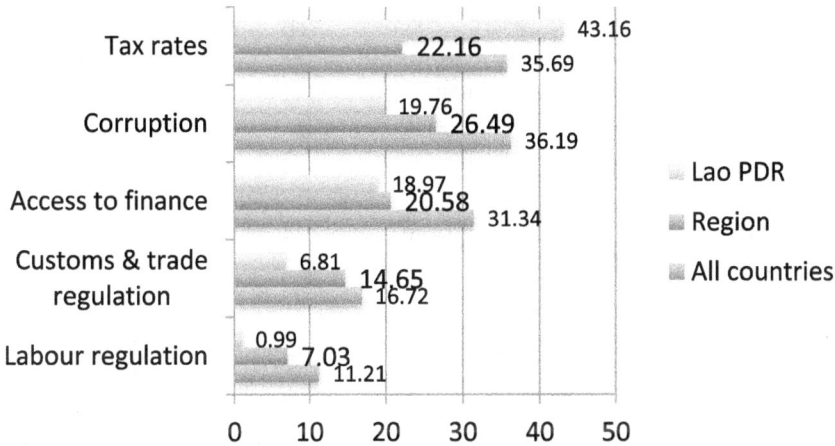

CONSTRAINTS FOR REGIONAL ECONOMIC
INTEGRATION

There are a number of constraints that slow down development in the Lao PDR. The most important one is the lack of basic infrastructure, such as access roads, electricity, and water supplies that would support rural and industrial development of the country. Despite its young population structure, other constraints are the low population density and the low level of knowledge and education among the population and labour force. There are large urban and rural disparities and the movement of young workers to the cities and neighbouring countries decreases the availability of a labour force for the agriculture sector, and increases social tension.

Weak public governance capacity, the slowdown in the application of necessary structural changes in the market economy, and the application of the rule of law in the country have substantial impact on the business environment and private sector investment. The Lao private sector is weak and there is a large, non-formal sector that is benefiting from non-transparent public procurement concessions, particularly in construction and natural resource exploitation. The corruption level is on the increase because of an incomplete legal system and the weak application of the rule of law.

The large economic disparity between the Lao PDR and the rest of the GMS and Southeast Asian countries is a big constraint for regional integration. If the Lao PDR is not part of the regional value chain, the economic benefits from enhanced regional transport connectivity may not be equally profitable for the Lao PDR, and regional road networks developed through the GMS Corridors Programme could pass through the Lao PDR without bringing any meaningful economic benefit to its people. In fact, increased traffic may become a burden on the economy because of the incurred cost of maintenance. At the same time, 95 per cent of Lao businesses are SMEs. There are concerns that SMEs in the Lao PDR may be marginalized by the more integrated larger businesses in larger economies in the GMS.

SOME THOUGHTS FOR THE DEVELOPMENT OF REGIONAL INTEGRATION

The GoL made efforts through subregional cooperation to turn its "landlocked" disadvantage into a "land-linked" advantage by taking the opportunity from the flow of goods derived from the new industrial value chain within the region. The GMS development strategy to develop transport corridors into economic corridors has been taken seriously to enable the development of the "East–West Corridor" and "North–South Corridors".

Leveraging the gap between the Lao PDR and other economies in the GMS, and the rest of the world, is necessary for boosting trade and investment and developing the country. This needs to be done through ambitious development programmes, which need large investments and great contributions from the private sector under public and private partnership (PPP) programmes.

There is the need to make existing GMS economic corridors more competitive and interesting for international and local transport and logistics operators. Actually, the flow of commodities along the GMS's economic corridors are not proceeding smoothly due to inefficient customs and transit systems (CTS) and the lack of road and transport and logistics infrastructure, especially in the Lao PDR.

Therefore, the development of infrastructure projects that aim to increase the traffic volume in the GMS economic corridors is most important for the Lao PDR. This comprises upgrading existing infrastructure, such as reinforcing Road No. 9 and completing planned infrastructure on the East-West Economic Corridor (EWEC). There is also the need to develop more "feeder roads" to connect the existing economic corridors to industrial agglomeration centres and new potential markets in East Asia. On this issue, the GMS Business

Forum[2] recommended a change of the EWEC's focus to linking Bangkok to Hanoi, and further north to China.

Regional economic integration will depend highly on the integration of the Lao PDR's domestic industries into the regional value chains, especially to existing high-tech production chains that are linking the industries in China, Vietnam, and Thailand. The promotion of "industrial clusters" that are linked to the existing industrial agglomerations in the GMS should be a priority. For example, the development of Special Economic Zones (SEZs) in nodal cities that are primary industrial agglomeration centres of the Lao PDR, such as the Savan-Seno Economic Zone located along the EWEC, must be given more attention and more incentives need to be provided to industries located in the SEZs. The SEZs in the Lao PDR are lagging behind, with incomplete industrial infrastructure, and cannot compete with existing or newly planned industrial zones in other GMS countries. The SEZs in the Lao PDR should comprise logistic parks or inland container depots (ICD) with bonded facilities and environmentally sound urban infrastructure.

Domestic energy supply is also a problem for local industries as the current policy is focused on the export of electricity. The development of efficient energy supply system for the industry agglomeration and nodal cities in the GMS will be required to make the SEZ and other developments more attractive to investors. The Lao PDR still has 23,000 MW of hydropower potential for generating electricity and it is important that major power generation is used to increase domestic industries.

The effective exploitation of the abundant mineral resources would require the development of railways to transport raw materials and equipment. The construction of the railways linking Bangkok to Vientiane and China, and linking Thakhek and Vung Aung Port, are important investment projects.

With 80 per cent of the population working in the agriculture sector, this is an important sector that should not be neglected. Agribusiness and modern "smart" agriculture need to be promoted to develop and link rural agriculture production with retail food and agriculture markets and industries in Vietnam, Thailand, and other countries.

Little income is actually generated from tourism along the portion of the corridors in the Lao PDR. Tourism attractions and related hospitality and MICE (meetings, incentives, conferences, exhibitions) industries need to be promoted along the corridors.

SMEs represents 95 per cent of the enterprises in the Lao PDR, so enhancing the capacity of local SMEs and supporting industries is important. This should be made throughout the promotion of FDI and local SMEs for them to penetrate regional and global markets. It is also important to enhance

SME financing in the course of a "two-step loan" for the establishment of a regional SME Development Fund.

Notes

1. The Greater Mekong Subregion (GMS) is made up of Cambodia, the People's Republic of China (PRC, specifically Yunnan Province and Guangxi Zhuang Autonomous Region), the Lao People's Democratic Republic (Lao PDR), Myanmar, Thailand, and Vietnam. The GMS is a natural economic area bound together by the Mekong River. It covers 2.6 million square kilometres and has a combined population of around 326 million.
2. Established in 2000, the Greater Mekong Subregion Business Forum (GMS-BF) is a multi-country, independent, non-government organization, and a joint initiative of the chambers of commerce of the six GMS countries. It plays a key role in promoting and facilitating cross-border trade and investment in the region.

4

THE ECONOMIC DEVELOPMENT OF MYANMAR AND THE RELEVANCE OF THE GREATER MEKONG SUBREGION

Michael von Hauff

In 1992 the six GMS countries, with the support of the Asian Development Bank (ADB), introduced a programme of subregional economic cooperation (GMS Programme) to enhance their economic relations. Building on their shared histories and cultures, the programme covers nine priority sectors: agriculture, energy, environment, human resource development, investment, telecommunications, tourism, transport infrastructure, and transport and trade facilitation. The programme basically offers member nations positive impulses for diverse development opportunities. Member countries have yet another mutual interest: they all want to use the Mekong River to further their national interests and goals which are not always free of conflict (Schmeier 2010, p. 28). This is where the union can offer opportunities to foster positive cooperation among the states.

In terms of cooperation, the member states of the Greater Mekong Subregion (GMS) reflect a range of very different political situations and economic development levels (Ishida 2005, p. 1). Specifically, issues arise in Cambodia, the Lao PDR, and Myanmar, which are all classified as being among the least developed countries (LDCs). Furthermore, Myanmar illustrates a very authoritarian regime: "There is no regime within South-East Asia that has attracted as much international condemnation for its domestic practices and failures as Myanmar's ruling State Peace and Development Council" (SPDC) (Haacke 2010, p. 153). Naturally this assessment is not viewed positively by the other members of the GMS union of states, nor by the ADB, and, consequently, cooperation is affected. This explains the fact that in this regional association of states, each of the GMS member states has a different level of integration. The economic profile of Myanmar, which is examined in greater detail in this chapter, shows that a stronger integration of Myanmar in the GMS would clearly be conducive to economic growth.

The study of Myanmar's economic development reveals a multitude of problems. When viewed from an economic standpoint, the country is in a desolate state, especially with regard to its economic potential. The causes of this are at times the subject of controversial debate. In recent years, the responsibility for the unsatisfactory economic situation has consistently been placed on sanctions imposed by Western countries (North America and Europe). Cyclone Nargis can also be cited as a cause, as it has had a likewise negative effect on the country's economic situation (v. Hauff 2009, p. 40). In general, however, it can be said that while the sanctions and Cyclone Nargis have exacerbated the situation, they are not primarily to blame for the precarious economic situation. The purpose of this chapter is to identify and explain development trends in Myanmar's economic system.

In the years following its independence in 1948, Myanmar was economically one of the wealthiest countries in Southeast Asia. For many experts, the period between 1950 and 1962 was the country's "golden age" of the post-war era. "The eight-year 'Pyidawtha' Plan saw solid achievements in infrastructure, agriculture, and industry, despite failing to meet its ambitious targets because of the collapse in the price of rice after the Korean War" (Kyi et al. 2000, p. 2). Then, in 1962, the "Burmese Way of Socialism" began. This period has been analysed and differentiated in great detail, for example, by Perry (2007). In 1988, after twenty-six years of socialist rule, a military government came to power, known as the "State Law and Order Restoration Council (SLORC)". This military junta continues to govern the country to this day.

The military government initiated a transformation process to change the country from a planned economy to a market economy in the years after 1988. It has not yet been possible to conclude this process. From the perspective of the present, it occasionally appears as though the transformation process is still in its initial stages. First, reforms and liberalization policies were introduced after 1988, intended above all to ease the inflow of foreign investment and capital into the country. However, many of the announced reforms did not materialize or have not been implemented rigorously until now. For this reason, Myanmar is currently in a "double transition from underdevelopment and from socialism" (Andreff 1993, p. 515).

Rüland neatly sums up the initial situation: "It needs little foresight to forecast that Burma/Myanmar's transition is likely to take place under highly adverse and difficult circumstances. Most likely it is a transition paralleled by economic crises, at a low level of economic development accompanied by spells of violence and ethnic fragmentation. The long period of authoritarian rule further complicates a smooth transition as there is virtually no institutional base from which a new democratic government can be built" (Rüland 2002, p. 22).

Irrespective of this appraisal, it must be said — and here a remarkable contradiction becomes apparent — that Myanmar belongs to those countries that are rich in natural resources. Compared with many countries in the region, Myanmar has considerable deposits of minerals, natural gas, a great potential for an economically profitable timber industry, and large and fertile areas of land for agricultural use (Perry 2007, p. 13). Most economic experts agree, however, that the potential for economic development has been insufficiently exploited in Myanmar, at least in the past four decades. Compared in both absolute and relative terms with other developing countries in the region, Myanmar reveals a tendency to stagnate. Many experts even speak of economic and social regression as opposed to progress.

Although Myanmar is one of the richest countries in terms of raw materials, many indicators reveal that, economically at least, Myanmar is one of the least developed countries in the region. As an example, let us look at per capita income as an indicator of how Myanmar compares with other countries in the region. While per capita income was more or less the same in many countries in the region at the beginning of the 1950s, the differences between them have increased enormously since that time. This is especially true for Malaysia, but also applies to Thailand. At the other end of the spectrum, the per capita income of Myanmar first fell below that of Indonesia during the mid-1980s and has been losing considerable ground to the Philippines as well since that time. In 1998/99, the World Bank categorized Myanmar's per capita income of US$300 as one of the poorest among the developing countries (least developed countries — LDCs).

The economic development trends are identified here as the starting point. In doing this, the country's macroeconomic development trends are differentiated from structural development trends. Subsequent to this, development trends in foreign economies are identified. By doing this, it is possible to establish that foreign trade was definitively strained by the sanctions that were imposed. This is especially true of the garment sector. This, in turn, has had repercussions on the development of the larger domestic economy. Nevertheless, it remains to be established — and this is the principal thesis of this chapter — that the failures in economic development and the current economic misery can essentially be traced back to economic mismanagement by the military regime. An indicator of this is the "Index of Economic Freedom", according to which Myanmar was counted among the five most repressive economies in the world in the year 2007 (the other four are North Korea, Cuba, Libya, and Zimbabwe) (Alamgir 2008, p. 977).

MYANMAR'S ECONOMIC DEVELOPMENT

A comprehensive analysis of the economic growth and quality of life of the Burmese population is beyond the scope of this chapter (for a detailed discussion of economic and social development in Myanmar, see v. Hauff 2009). This analysis focuses on selected major economic trends and the development of the living standards of the population. Consequently, it is possible to recognize certain developmental trends and how they affect the lives of the population today.

Macroeconomic Trends

The following analysis of the development of the national economy places special attention on the 1990s and the early years of the new millennium. Conventional indicators will be used to analyse and assess macroeconomic trends. Over the long term, real gross domestic product (real GDP) shows a positive trend. While average GDP growth was 4.7 per cent in the 1970s, it fell back to 1.8 per cent in the 1980s. In the 1990s, average GDP growth reached a relatively high level of 5.8 per cent (World Bank 1999, p. 10). Looking more closely at the 1990s, we find it striking that the rate of growth was initially very low, at 2.8 per cent in 1990–91 and even –0.6 per cent in 1991–92. In 1992–93, there was then a huge jump to 9.7 per cent, but this rate declined, reaching 4.6 per cent by 1997/98.

Only in 2000–2001 was there again a slight increase in growth rate to 13.7 per cent, with a constant level of more than 10 per cent for the years 2001/02–2008/09. However, in this context, Set Aung has identified a significant problem with the calculation method: "GDP calculation in Myanmar is reportedly quite complicated, dealing both with official and parallel rates of exchange when converting some US$ dominated figures into local currency which results in inflated and misleading figures. Hence, it is neither easy nor appropriate to dollarize GDP data from local currency directly into US$ currency (Set Aung 2006)." There is no satisfactory answer to this problem.

In summary, Myanmar presented a relatively high level of economic growth in the 1990s, but this tended to decline in the years following 1994/95, levelling off at a rate of around 5 per cent until 1998/99, and increasing again until 2003/04 by more than 10 per cent. On the whole, this roughly corresponds with the development in other East Asian developing countries. However, in this regard it should also be pointed out that the Asian economic crisis of 1997 had only a minor effect on the economic growth in Myanmar due to the extremely dominant status of the agricultural sector and Myanmar's weak links with the global economy. The only appreciable effect of the crisis was a significant decrease in foreign investment. Several UN experts (e.g., United Nations Fund for Population Activities [UNFPA]) are of the opinion that the rate is actually much lower. The IMF estimates the current GDP per capita to be US$250, which is lower than that of Cambodia, Bangladesh, the Lao PDR, and Vietnam (Bünte 2004, p. 374).

Nevertheless, this permits only limited conclusions to be drawn from the general trends of economic growth in Myanmar. In a country in which the agricultural sector is extremely dominant, the growth rates in that sector are particularly relevant. The contribution of the agricultural sector as a share of GDP is nearly 60 per cent. An important feature is that, of the twenty-six million acres cultivated in 1995/96, nearly twenty million acres were planted with food crops whose yields have been stagnant or decreasing over the last decade. Only one in six acres had crops whose yields outpaced the growth of the population (Dapice 2003, p. 4). Over two thirds of all employed persons are working in agriculture endeavours, yet only one third of the population works on farms larger than three acres. This explains the widespread poverty that exists in the rural areas.

Many members of the labour force in the rural regions own no land of their own. According to estimates by UNDP, 40 per cent of the population does not own any agriculturally productive land. They work for daily wages. Beyond this, subsistence farming is common. Many of the small farmers face the additional problem of lacking access to financing, that is, they are unable to obtain loans. Another problem, especially for the small farmer,

FIGURE 4.1
Development of GDP from 1990 to 2009 (changes in %, in real terms)

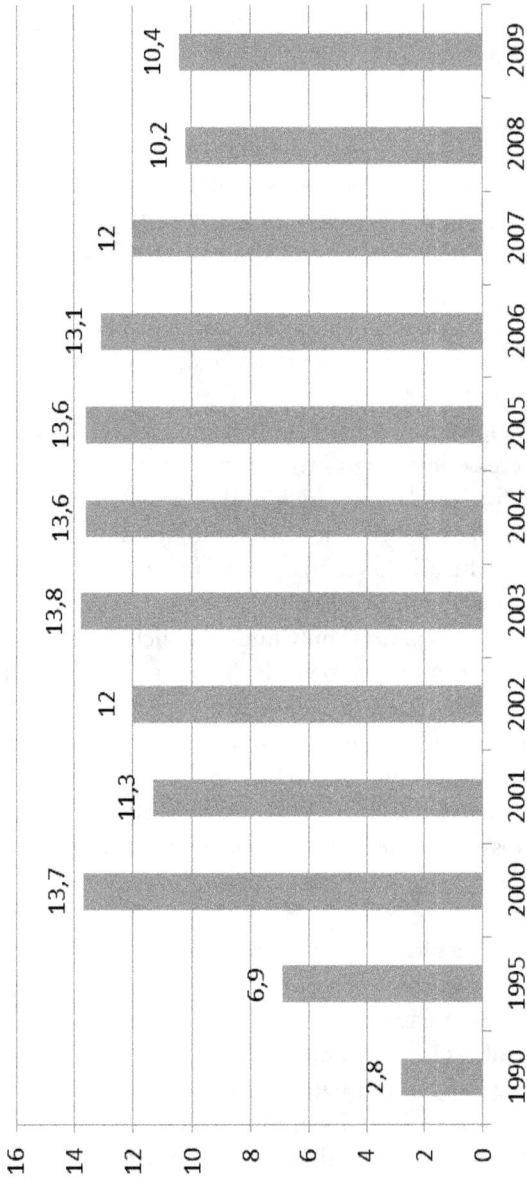

Source: Asian Development Bank 2010, p. 207.

is the fact that the prices for agricultural products are set artificially low by the government in order to prevent civil unrest in the cities. This in turn leads to low productivity, especially by the small farmers, who are unable to purchase farm equipment at an affordable price because of their low incomes.

The government price controls set below market value had a political objective and should have led to higher export earnings. The negative consequences were known and accepted by the government. In April 2003, the liberalization of the rice trade was attempted by allowing the price of rice to float, that is, state monopoly was ended (Bünte 2004, p. 275). However, the liberalization was short-lived. In 2004 the government ordered an export ban on rice to prevent a supply shortage at home. This resulted in a sharp price decline, thereby containing the inflation rate. These few examples demonstrate the inconsistency or impulsiveness of the agricultural policy, which did not contribute to a sustainable, positive expansion in this sector.

A further significant macroeconomic indicator for the assessment of economic development is the inflation rate. One peculiar feature of the way inflation is calculated in Myanmar is that, until 2000, it was restricted to a measurement of the consumer price index for Yangon, the capital. The market basket on which this was based originated in 1986 when the economy was still socialist in character. No inflation rates were measured to show price developments in the various provinces until the middle of 2000. Since 2000 the inflation rate — retrospectively also for recent years — has been measured for the country as a whole. If the available data are looked at in isolation, Myanmar has had extremely high inflation for many years. This had a particularly negative impact on the poorer population groups, as 70 per cent of their income is spent on the purchase of food.

It is difficult to assess the consequences of the high inflation rate. First — and Myanmar is not alone here — lower income groups (which form the clear majority in Myanmar) suffer the most from a high inflation rate, while the owners of real capital benefit from it. With respect to the price of rice, which is a particularly important product, urban workers have lost out as a result of inflation while the rural population benefits from inflation. In this context, it cannot generally be concluded that high rates of inflation exacerbate the impoverishment of the population. Yet there is still no doubt that people living on irregular income are particularly hard hit by inflation.

Here again a comparison between Myanmar and other countries in the region is interesting. As Figure 4.3 shows, the inflation rate has been significantly higher in Myanmar than in other East Asian countries since 1998.

FIGURE 4.2
Growth Rates of Consumer Price Index 1993–2009

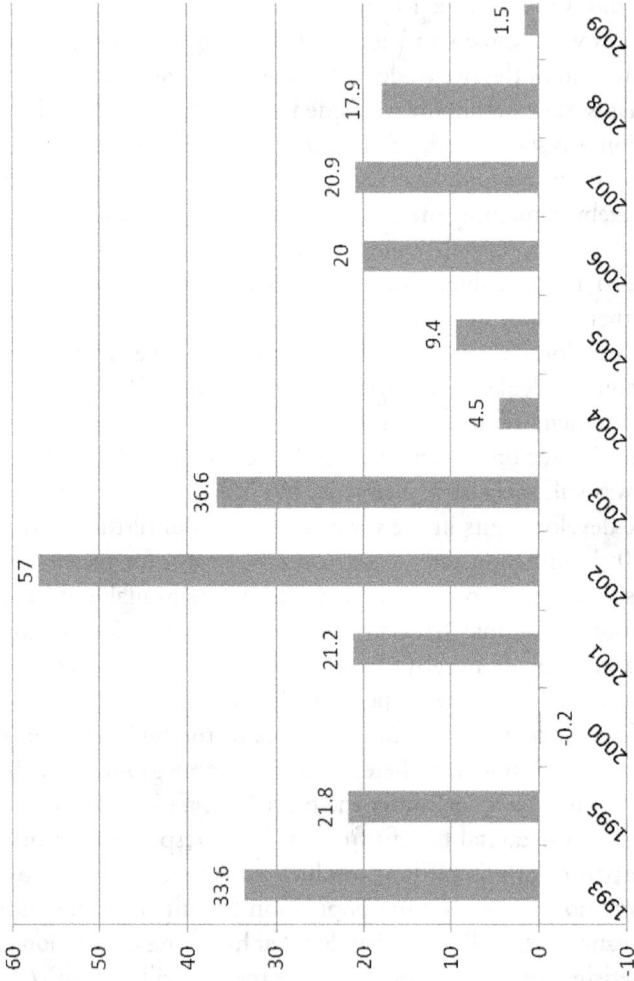

Source: Asian Development Bank 2010, p. 224.

FIGURE 4.3
East Asia CPI-Inflation, 1990–2009 (%)

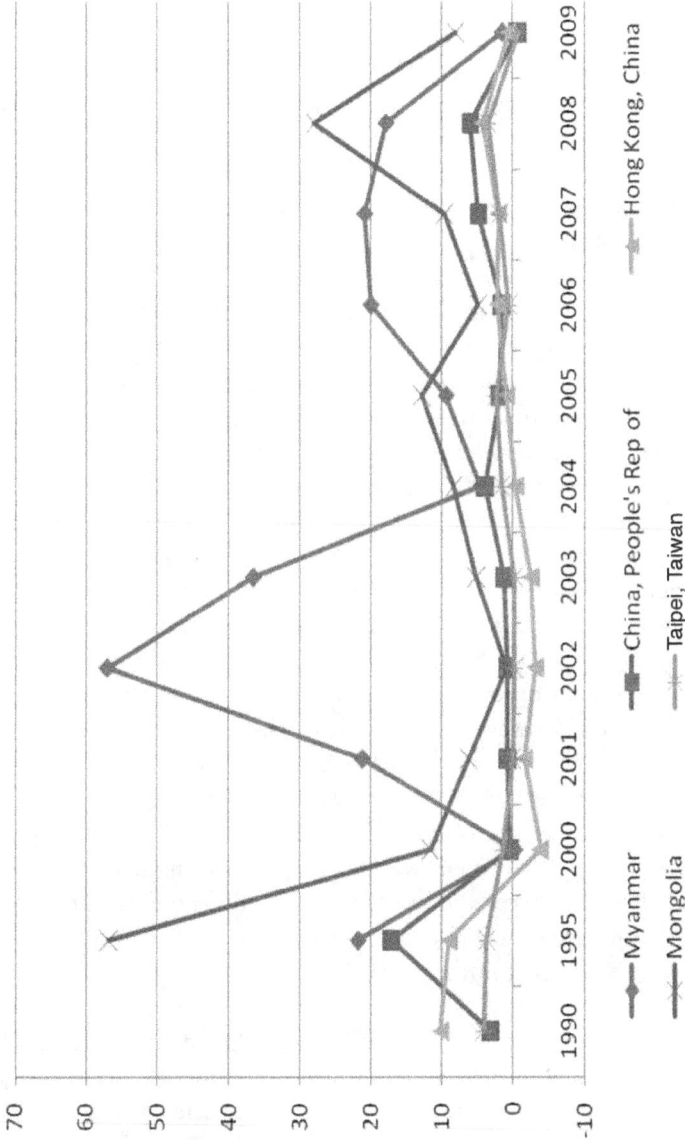

Source: Asian Development Bank 2010, p. 224.

The problem, as concerns the development of employment and wages, is that there is no official measurement of the unemployment rate in Myanmar. Let me illustrate this with an example. According to the official data for 1997/98, the potential number of gainfully employed people was 19.7 million out of a total population of 46.4 million. Of this potential figure, 18.3 million are currently employed. However, this figure does not include unpaid family members who are also employed. Consequently, the official unemployment figures do not stand up to scrutiny. The unemployment rate stated for 1992/93 was 5.3 per cent, while 5.8 per cent was reported for 1994/95, and 4.1 per cent for 1997/98 and 1998/99. The rate of increase in the number of employed people rose slightly in the 1990s. While this was 1.4 per cent in 1988/89, it rose by 2.9 per cent in 1992/93 and stood at roughly 2.1 per cent in the second half of the 1990s (ADB, 2001, vol. 2, p. 15). The official unemployment data fail to consider the problem of underemployment. Sanctions aggravate the problem of joblessness, for example, the closure of foreign textile manufacturing plants in the past led to between 50,000 and 60,000 textile workers losing their jobs. In this context, the situation in the job market is much more strained than the official unemployment data would indicate.

The growth of income shows relatively large fluctuations as income in the agricultural sector depends to a great extent on when the monsoon starts and how heavy it is. It is a different story for incomes in other sectors. At first glance, the public sector appears to be relatively stable although it is noticeable that incomes rose appreciably there after 1988/89 in the course of liberalization. However, when the high rate of inflation is considered, they rose by only 27.5 per cent in the period between 1988/89 and 2000. But in April 2000, government workers' wages were increased fivefold and other public-sector workers also received significant wage increases. By increasing these wages, the government was reacting to growing dissatisfaction among public-sector employees and, in this way, avoided potential political tension. This reaction is typical for a dictatorship. No reliable data are available for income developments in the private sector.

As one would expect, the wage increases in the public sector in 2000 and 2010 did not help to reduce the large budget deficit of the government. While the first half of the 1990s saw a dramatic increase in the budget deficit to 8 per cent of GDP, it dropped again to 5 per cent by 1999/2000, 5.8 per cent in 2001/02, 3.6 per cent in 2002/03, 4.9 per cent in 2003/04, 7.1 per cent in 2005/06 and, in the following years, went down to less than 1 per cent (ADB 2005, p. 321; ADB 2009, p. 2). "This is mainly due to several recent tax measures that are consistent with the bank's past advice. These include steps to improve tax administration, reduce tax evasion, raise the exchange rate used to value imports for tariff purposes, and, more recently, contributions from state economic enterprises (SEEs)" (IMF 2006, p. 6). It is also relevant in this context that the government financed about one third of it through issues of treasury securities.

One major reason for the continuing high level of debt until 2006 was the steady drop in the share of state revenue in GDP, from 17 per cent in 1981/82 to 7.9 per cent in 1992/93, to 6.4 per cent in 1995/96, and to 4.6 per cent in 2003/04. Only by drastically cutting spending could the budget deficit be reduced. Spending as a percentage of GDP fell quite considerably, from 7.2 per cent in 1998/99 to 4.9 per cent in 1999/2000. However, in 2003/04, expenditure again increased to 9.5 per cent of GDP. Myanmar is the only country in the region where the budget deficit is higher than the state revenue (4.6 per cent) as a percentage of GDP. Most of this spending is accounted for by economic services, followed by "other services", which include military spending. The share of the military in GDP is approximately 3.2 per cent, although experts assume that this share is considerably higher if the expansion and modernization of the army is considered. In other words, the military budget is probably by far the largest item in the Myanmar Government budget. The last available data are from 1992/93, when the military budget took up 43.8 per cent of the total government budget (ADB, 2001, vol. 2, p. 22).

By contrast, social spending fell in the 1990s from 1.8 per cent in 1992/93 to less than 1 per cent in 1999/2000. It should be mentioned that the deficits of the SEEs have increased substantially since the beginning of the 1990s. These deficits also present a great burden for the government budget. Greater stability in the value of money presupposes more autonomy for the Central Bank of Burma (CBM). Officially, the central bank is independent and should be able to control the money supply. In fact, however, it is very much held to the directions of the government, and therefore also obliged to print more money to cover the government's high deficits.

Trends of the Economic Structure

A brief introduction to the structure of Myanmar's economy is essential. This is necessary for an understanding of the contributions of the three sectors: agriculture, manufacturing, and services. A major characteristic of LDCs is their extremely one-sided economic structure. Myanmar's status as an LDC underlines this typical feature of its economy. The share of its industrial sector in GDP was only 9.2 per cent in 2002/03, and the entire secondary sector revealed a share of 13.6 per cent. Although the industrial sector has been at a constant level of less than 10 per cent ever since the end of the 1980s, the share of the secondary sector as a whole has risen somewhat since 2005. Figure 4.4 shows that overall economic development depends very significantly on the primary sector. Standing at 55.3 per cent in 1987, the primary sector's share achieved a slight increase to about 57.3 per cent in 2000 and then decreased after 2002. The tertiary sector also reveals a relatively stable share in GDP of 33 per cent until 2002 and has increased since 2003.

Agriculture contributes over 40 per cent and represents the most important sector of the economy, with about 60 to 70 per cent of the population dependent on it. This is a sign of low productivity and widespread subsistence farming. However, a positive assessment can be made for the rice production in 2004/05, which increased slightly to 24.5 million tonnes (prior year, 22.8 million tonnes). A new ban on exports is intended to keep the price stable for the public. The export of teak wood was also higher in 2004/05 at 12.8m cubic feet, which represents an increase of 13 per cent over the prior year. It is also assumed that a significant amount of illegal exports are shipped to China (Stärk 2006, p. 379).

In closing this section, it may be safely said that the overall economic situation is still desolate. Furthermore, it is evident that the overall economic situation is well below the level achievable given the economic potential of the country: the military regime has not been able to exploit this great economic potential, that is, it is incapable of planning for positive economic growth. The question now is how foreign trade developed during the last two decades.

Trends in Foreign Trade

The official trade analysis conceals several difficulties. The information in the official foreign trade statistics for Myanmar is to be understood as the lower limit for the actual trade. This is because three areas are not taken into account: the black market, arms imports, and the narcotics trade. In this chapter, we consider only the official trade volume since 1990, which can be established as a benchmark because that is when Myanmar began a transformational process from a socialist economic system to a market economy and world economic structures were undergoing a new development in the wake of the end of the Cold War.

FIGURE 4.4

Contribution of the Three Sectors to Real GDP, 1990–2009

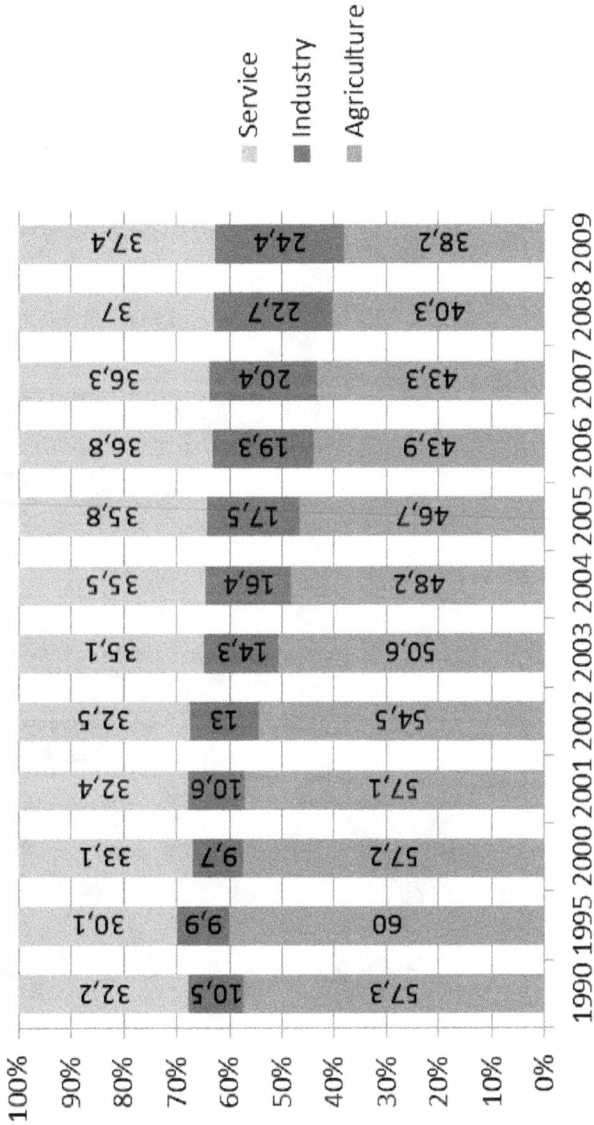

	Agriculture	Industry	Service
1990	57.3	10.5	32.2
1995	60	9.9	30.1
2000	57.2	9.7	33.1
2001	57.1	10.6	32.4
2002	54.5	13	32.5
2003	50.6	14.3	35.1
2004	48.2	16.4	35.5
2005	46.7	17.5	35.8
2006	43.9	19.3	36.8
2007	43.3	20.4	36.3
2008	40.3	22.7	37
2009	38.2	24.4	37.4

Source: Asian Development Bank 2010, pp. 160–62.

FIGURE 4.5
Myanmar's Official Trade Volume 1990–2009

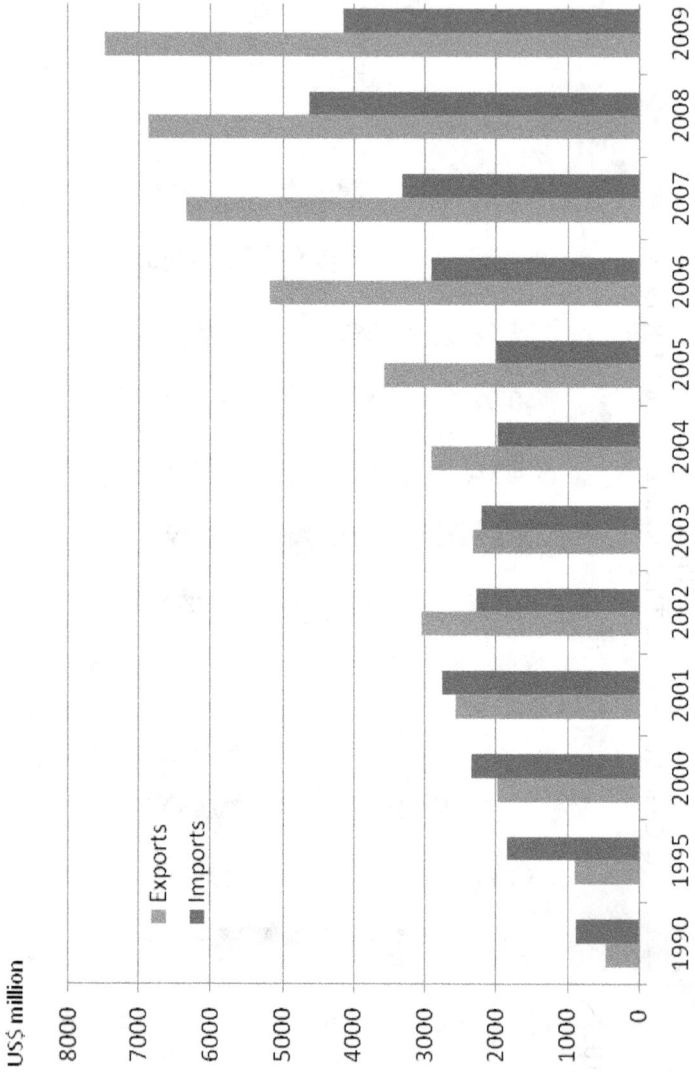

Source: Asian Development Bank 2010, pp. 215, 217.

The overview shows Myanmar's trade deficit from 1990 to 2001. A trade surplus occurred subsequent to that and, furthermore, it can be seen that imports reached a tentative high point in 2001 before subsequently declining by approximately 30 per cent. This can be explained by the reluctance of Western industrial nations to engage in trade with Myanmar. Here, the effect of the sanctions clearly emerges. In contrast, it is possible to establish that exports generally experienced a steady increase. Overall it can be established that trade experienced a yearly growth rate of a considerable 16 per cent from 1990 to 2003, which corresponds to that of the dynamic nations in the region.

An important export from Myanmar is gas. Myanmar began exporting gas in 1998, when its export revenue came up to US$1 million. In 2002, the value of gas exports already amounted to US$1.4 billion, accounting for more than 87 per cent of the trade surplus (Alamgir 2008, p. 981). The most important buyer nations are China and India. Notable in the entire export structure is the sharp increase in mineral fuels as the largest export-earning sector from 2000. An additional export sector that is of relatively significant importance is food and live animals. Although this sector was relatively stable from 1990 to 1999, with an export ratio of 38 per cent, it fell to 20 per cent from 2000 to 2004.

An important comparison indicator in international trade is the openness ratio. The matter at hand here is the relationship of foreign trade compared with the GDP (trade [exports + imports]/GDP). The higher this indicator is, the more open the economy. A comparison of Myanmar with its Southeast Asian neighbours provides compelling evidence as to where Myanmar stands. In 1990, Myanmar's ratio was 5.6 per cent compared with that of its neighbouring nations at 90.6 per cent. Even if one considers only the three other LDCs in the region, Cambodia, the Lao PDR, and Vietnam, those countries had a ratio of approximately 68 per cent. Myanmar's value sank to 0.6 per cent by 2004 while both other comparison groups increased by over 120 per cent. This clearly illustrates Myanmar is much more closed in comparison to its neighbours.

Finally Myanmar's most important trade partners should be identified. The ranking has not changed substantially over the past two decades. This applies at least until the time of the sanctions. Among the most important countries from which Myanmar drew its imports from 1990 to 1995, we find that imports came mainly from ten countries (81 per cent of the imports), and 76 per cent of all imports came from just five countries: China, Singapore, Japan, Malaysia, and Korea. From 2001 to 2005, Thailand replaced Japan in the group of five most important countries.

Myanmar's exports show a wider distribution. The ten most important countries to import goods from Myanmar account for 62 per cent of its exports (2001–5 the percentage was 77 per cent) and for the five most important countries, the percentage was 54 per cent (for 2001–5 this percentage was 64 per cent). Up until 2003, the United States was one of Myanmar's most important trade partners (in 1999 it was the most important importer of goods from Myanmar) (Alamgir 2008, p. 987). After the sanctions, Myanmar significantly expanded its trade with other authoritarian governments. The country's admission into ASEAN in 1997, by contrast, had a clearly insignificant effect on the trade structure (Bedfellows 2008, p. 935).

THE STANDARD OF LIVING

A regional comparison with respect to social and economic development in East Asia provides the first indication of Myanmar's ranking. What is striking about the region is the relatively large reduction in poverty and positive development in living conditions (human development) from the mid-1970s to the mid-1990s. GDP per capita grew by an impressive average of 7.2 per cent between 1985 and 1995 (World Bank 1999, p. 10). The number of people living in poverty fell from three fifths in 1975, to roughly one fifth in 1995, and then increased again until 2005 of about 32 per cent (Asian Development Bank 2009, p. 3). These overall positive developments in the 1990s suffered a severe setback as a result of the financial crisis at the end of the 1990s. We will have to wait and see how this develops in the long term.

At this point, the positive developments in Myanmar deserve to be mentioned. Living standards have improved in Myanmar to the extent that life expectancy has risen and the infant mortality rate has fallen. However, as shown in Table 4.1, the standard of living in most other countries in the region have risen far more and have shown greater improvement than in Myanmar over the past decades. Table 4.1 points out that Myanmar's childhood mortality rate is twice that of China and three times that of Vietnam. This is further evidenced by the fact that in Myanmar, according to data supplied by the World Bank at the end of the 1990s, malnutrition was seen in 39 per cent of all children under the age of five years and a third of these children were seriously undernourished (World Bank 1999).

The economic living standard of the population of Myanmar depends on a number of factors. The following discussion focuses on a few of these determinants. An initial evaluation of socio-economic living conditions can be found in the Human Development Index (HDI). A regional comparison shows that the HDI is higher in Myanmar than in Cambodia or the Lao

TABLE 4.1
Poverty and Human Development in Myanmar and East Asia

	Life expectancy at birth (years)						Infant mortality (per 1,000 live births)					Rate of economic growth (period average %)				
	1970	1993	2004	2005	2009	2010	1970	1993	2004	2005	2010	1970–1980	1981–1990	1990–2004	1990–2007	2010
China	62	69	72	73	73	74	85	31	30	23	17	7	9.2	8.5	8.9	9.6
Vietnam	49	65	71	74	74	75	55	41	19	16	22		4.6	5.9	6	6.7
Thailand	58	69	70	70	69	69	74	36	23	18	17	7.3	7.9	2.8	2.9	7
Cambodia		53	59	59	62	62			72	71	57			7.8	8.6	5
Lao PDR	40	51	55	63	65	66	145	95	82	62	61		11	3.7	4.2	7.4
Myanmar	50	60	61	61	61	63	122	79	76	75		4.7	1.8	5.6	6.8	5

Source: UNDP, Human Development Report 2009; CIA World Fact Book, World Bank Databank.

PDR because of Myanmar's better performance in the life expectancy and/or education index. Cambodia and the Lao PDR have a higher GDP index than Myanmar. In the six original ASEAN member countries plus Vietnam, it can be seen that social development is well correlated with overall economic performance (Thein and Nyo 1999, p. 395). In other words, the higher the GDP index, the higher the life expectancy and/or education index. Between 1992 and 2004, Myanmar's HDI was not stable. It should be remembered here that the way in which the HDI is calculated was modified after 1998, and the values for 1999 to 2004 are not comparable to those for prior years.

The striking fact here is that Myanmar fell from 111th to 138th place between 1992 and 2007. The living standard is also illustrated by the proportion of the population living below the poverty line and by the distribution of income. In this context, however, it should be emphasized that poverty is a very controversial topic for the Myanmar Government.

This also explains why the government has no official poverty line. Various sources disclose a poverty rate of roughly 32 per cent (Asian Development

TABLE 4.2
Human Development Index 1992–2010 for Myanmar

Year	HDI Rank	Life Expectancy Index	Education Index	GDP Index	HDI
1992	111	n/a	0.24	n/a	0.385*
1993	123	n/a	n/a	n/a	0.390*
1994	132	0.54	0.28	0.12	0.457*
1996	133	0.55	n/a	0.09	0.451*
1997	131	0.56	n/a	0.16	0.475*
1998	131	0.57	n/a	0.17	0.481*
1999	128	0.59	n/a	0.41	0.580
2000	125	0.59	0.32	0.41	0.585
2001	131	0.53	0.32	0.39	0.549
2002	132	0.54	0.33	0.39	0.551
2003	129	0.59	0.34	0.39	0.578
2004	130	0.59	0.35	0.39	0.581
2005	138	0.596	0.35	0.389	0.406
2007	138	0.603	0.37	0.368	n/a
2010	132	0.676	0.39	n/a	0.451

Note: *old formula
Source: UNDP, Human Development Report, 1992–2009.

Bank 2009) as mentioned before, while the United Nations estimates that over 50 per cent of the population is living below the poverty line. This presents a problem when attempting to make international comparisons as the wide discrepancy in figures may lead to a distorted view. Nevertheless, Table 4.3 is provided in an effort to convey some basis for orientation. It looks at the rural, urban, and total poverty rates in selected countries.

Compared with other countries in the region, Myanmar occupies a middle position in the ranking, with a poverty rate of 26.6 per cent. However, it should not be forgotten that the situation of the poor differs from country to country. Based on a poll of 300 households, for example, it can be stated that the situation of the poor in Myanmar in marginal urban areas is extremely desperate (Clawson and Keller 1999). The average income of men is roughly 100–200 kyats, while women earn as little as 50–200 kyats or less. Regular work is the exception for these people, and many people have to rely on casual or seasonal work.

This explains why the living conditions of these poor people are extremely critical. One further striking aspect is that poverty is distributed extremely irregularly between the various regions. The greatest difference in the Poverty Headcount Index is between the Tanintharyi Division (8.1 per cent) and the rural areas of Chin State (42.1 per cent). Here it has to be pointed out that the index in urban Chin State is only 19 per cent (and thus below the national average). The percentage of people living in poverty in rural areas

TABLE 4.3
Estimated Poverty for Rural and Urban Households (various years)

Country, year	National poverty line in %			Distribution of poor		
	Rural	Urban	Total	Rural	Urban	Total
Myanmar, 2001	28.4	20.7	26.6	68.5	31.5	100
China, 1998	4.6	2	4.6	82.1	17.9	100
Indonesia, 2005	34.1	8.8	n/a	96.9	3.1	100
Lao PDR, 2003	63.2	23.1	n/a	83.3	16.7	100
Malaysia, 1999	12.4	3.4	7.5	75	25	100
Mongolia	32.6	39.4	35.6	33.3	66.7	100
Philippines, 2003	44.5	11.6	30.4	n/a	n/a	100
Thailand, 2002	12.6	4	9.8	87.3	12.7	100
Vietnam, 2004	21.7	2.9	19.4	n/a	n/a	100

Source: Asian Development Bank 2004–2006, 2008.

is 47 per cent. There are many reasons for this uneven distribution of poor people in Myanmar. The concentration of people living in the poorer border regions is one of them.

An analysis of the distribution of income and property makes the standard of living even clearer. As a rule, distribution of income is measured by the Gini coefficient. While there are no reliable data for Myanmar for this purpose, at least some qualitative statements can be made. It can be assumed there is no great imbalance in income distribution in Myanmar. This is because of the largely homogeneous population. Burmese society "is not sharply divided into different classes or castes with unequal access to property or unequal levels of income" (Kyi et al. 1999, p. 130). In fact, the majority of the Burmese population has such a low level of income that one cannot identify any great differences among them.

During the socialist phase, the distribution of real property was limited to a maximum of nine to ten acres per landowner, which resulted in a drastic levelling of ownership wealth. Similar "levelling tendencies" were also manifested in the private sector, which is why only micro-enterprises and small business are privately owned still today. If Myanmar's economy were to open up, however, this might result in greater inequality in income and property distribution in the future, unless the state countered this development with some appropriate means. Currently the problem is rather that Myanmar has a very low average income level and widespread poverty.

A country's living standard is influenced by yet other determinants. Health status and education are particularly significant. After Myanmar's reorientation towards a market economy in 1998, it is interesting to note that the highest goal formulated by the State Peace and Development Council was in the social area: "To promote the health, fitness, and education level of the nation as well as to conserve the cultural heritage and the national character." This objective was to be supported through the creation of a national health committee, which was to be directed from the highest level of the office of the first secretary of the SPDC. In order to attain this goal, the government cooperated with international organizations such as the WHO, UNICEF, UNDP, UNFPA, and approximately twenty international NGOs (Bünte 2005, p. 11). In spite of these efforts, the health system in Myanmar still presents serious problems.

The health status is influenced to a great extent by the quantitative and qualitative dimensions of poverty and the resources of the health system. An accessible and well-equipped public health system is crucially important for the population of the poor. This is especially true for women and children. There is adequate proof that children living in poverty are very prone to disease and infection. Furthermore, there are some differences between the poor and non-poor in health status and access to services (World Bank 1999, p. 24). Those living in poverty usually have less access to health care facilities than those not living in poverty. This is the case, as can be empirically proved, for Myanmar.

Another crucial factor contributing to the state of the people's health is their access to drinking water. The following facts should be considered: (a) Myanmar has ample water resources. There are four main river systems covering most of the country. With seasonal variations, these rivers provide the population with an adequate quantity and quality of water. (b) Unlike other countries in the region, the relatively low level of industrialization and low level of motorization of the population have helped keep the country relatively free of any significant pollution up to this point. In principle, this is true for the water supply.

It is therefore surprising that, according to official statistics, an average of only 67.2 per cent of the population had access to safe drinking water in 2000. But here, too, there are huge regional differences. Yangon has the highest proportion of people (90.2 per cent) with access to safe drinking water. Chin, by contrast, has the lowest proportion of people with such access — only 44.5 per cent. In this context too it becomes clear that the population of border areas has the worst supply of drinking water.

Among other things, this results in a higher child mortality rate as mentioned earlier. In 1997 Myanmar had a slightly higher infant mortality rate (77 compared with an average of 68 per 1,000 live births in other Southeast Asian countries with comparable per capita GDP of between US$323 and US$396) and a significantly higher child mortality rate (113 compared with the average of 77 in these other countries). While infant mortality fell slightly in the 1990s, child mortality increased (International Monetary Fund 1999, p. 32). Widespread child malnutrition is given as a significant factor. In 1997, 39 per cent of the children under five years in Myanmar were regarded as malnourished. However, there are great differences here between different regions. From this, it may be concluded that living conditions in Myanmar are extremely poor. In principle, this should indicate a great level of dissatisfaction with the government, that is, the military regime.

THE NEED FOR REFORMS IN MYANMAR

The last two sections have shown the need for comprehensive economic and social reforms in Myanmar. A major deficit running throughout the years is due to the fact that Myanmar, to this day, has no clear economic model or economic plan. Officially, the military junta, following the 1988 coup, introduced a market economy to replace the socialist economic system. However, in principle there has actually been a state-regulated economy since 1989, specifically determined by state-owned enterprises.

An option for Myanmar in the future is to orient itself on the model of the social market economy. This, of course, presupposes a democratization of the economic system as well as the political system. The economic model of a social market economy includes a competitive order, a social security system, and a consistent legal framework for the economy (Körner 2007, p. 15ff., John 2007, p. 143ff.). The need for reform continues with the stabilization of macroeconomic development.

The government has in the last two decades not focused sufficiently on advancing the rate of growth. The overlapping problems of high budget deficits and the negative patterns displayed by many other indicators, such as the inflation rate and the desolate condition of the financial sector, are a significant burden to the development of a national economy. The need for reform can be clearly articulated based on an assessment of the problem situation. The major prerequisite for a well-functioning financial sector is a stable and independent central bank. The national currency must also be brought back to an exchange rate determined by the market and not defined by the state. A stable monetary value (a low inflation rate with little fluctuation) is an important condition of macroeconomic stability. An efficient financial sector additionally requires the existence of stable, private sector banks.

There are also numerous structural problems, such as the lack of efficiency or productivity in many state-run companies that require large subsidies to survive. The relative stagnation at low levels in many segments of the industrial sector is further evidence that the country's potential is nowhere near exhausted. This is particularly applicable in comparison to neighbouring countries in the region that have experienced dynamic industrial growth. Finally, the relatively low level of foreign direct investment, which can be explained by the political situation (sanctions) in the country, must be remembered.

As recent years clearly illustrate, those developing countries such as India, but also some of the GMS countries that have open economies, have experienced positive business growth (Holdefleiß 2004; ADB 2007). This implies that the economic isolation of Myanmar has produced the opposite effect — economic growth has been sharply impaired and the country has fallen behind other countries of the region.

The development of Myanmar's economy also depends to a large extent on the development of the education sector. Here again there is a great need for investment in schools and institutes of higher learning, in order for the country to return to the efficient education system that existed there in the 1950s. The current education system does not extend to a large percentage of the youth in rural areas, and the institutes of higher learning are inadequately equipped for the world today. In this respect, there is a need for a qualified and comprehensive study, above all, one that is independent of all political framework conditions.

The social sector in Myanmar finds itself in a problematic state as well. This is especially true in the area of health. The level of health among the population is not only strained by the widespread incidence of diseases such as malaria and HIV/AIDS, but also by the malnutrition of many children and the inadequate medical care available to the majority of the people. Health and education represent areas of significant deficiencies that can only be remedied by a reallocation of the national budget to the benefit of these two sectors. In this respect, as presented here in detail, there is still not enough attention being given in Myanmar to the close relationship between economic and social development. Finally, the need for reform of the labour market should be more closely examined.

In light of our analysis so far, the need for labour market reform in Myanmar can be subdivided into several areas. The deficiencies in the institutional conditions of the labour market lead to problems arising from a mismatch in the labour market. The chief phenomenon here is widespread underemployment, which is especially prevalent in the informal sector. There is also a gender gap in Myanmar, which can be broken down still further by region and ethnic origin.

The first remark to be made about the institutional conditions of the labour market is that they are centrally organized. As there are no autonomous or independent parties in the labour market (unions or employers' associations), the conditions are governed by the Labour Ministry policies. Moreover, the process of matching labour supply and labour demand is largely a responsibility assumed by the government. As a result of these relatively rigid structures, the labour market is inflexible, inefficient, and in need of reform. However, before this can happen, independent labour parties have to be integrated.

Placement efficiency must be improved and alternatives to state placement created. In addition, detailed empirical surveys are needed to expose the quality of state employment agencies and the success of their placement efforts. It is conceivable that the growth of the informal sector is evidence of evasive action by employees who do not wish to have their minds made up for them by the state.

Furthermore, an efficient matching process in the labour market calls above all for advice and support to be provided in places where there is a mismatch. Qualified advisory units, guided by supply and demand, are needed for the labour market. For this purpose, a detailed labour market policy tool has to be developed. Particular mention should be made of a qualified career advice and placement service. This requires:

- The availability of relevant labour market data (these have so far only been available in rudimentary form in Myanmar);
- Close and constructive cooperation between institutions and employers in the labour market; and
- The presence of an institutional superstructure — nationally, regionally, and locally.

Career guidance is essentially concerned with the advisee's choice of career and aptitude. The advice given must be guided strictly by the development of labour demand and the necessary qualifications of the people looking for work. The quality of advice depends greatly on how well future developments in the labour market can be forecast, which itself is crucially dependent on the availability of data. The significance of placement services is of growing importance in Myanmar, yet the quality and quantity of such services still leave much to be desired.

Vocational training and employment schemes are significant labour market policy tools. If it is assumed that structural changes in the economy will be implemented in Myanmar in the next few years, then it is essential that vocational training be geared to employers' requirements and economic demand, and the qualifications improved and diversified. However, the new labour market policy should only offer its own vocational training schemes if employees do not receive sufficient private vocational training. Equally, training needs in Myanmar have to be geared to the changing demands of the labour market. Here again, there is a pressing need for accurate labour market data.

Employment schemes have to be viewed as separate from the issues mentioned above. In developing countries, this is carried out in the form of job-creation schemes. In particular, these are schemes to reduce the poverty of specific risk groups. As a rule, the target groups are farmers with little agricultural land ownership, or unskilled workers in urban regions. Job creation schemes are primarily concerned with providing infrastructure and creating employment opportunities that may lead to income generation and thus poverty reduction. In rural areas, such schemes are frequently effective in compensating, at least in part, for seasonal fluctuations or lack of income and failed harvests. They can stabilize or increase income and improve purchasing power, thereby reducing the pressure for people to move away (rural exodus). These schemes should be made available to especially disadvantaged labour market groups, and this underlines their significance for Myanmar.

However, effective labour market reform and policy also depend on a stable or dynamic development of the national economy as a whole. Labour market development is one part of overall economic development and growth. For this reason, complementarities must be ensured between the conditions for the stability of the economy as a whole, and the needs of the labour market (v. Hauff and Kruse 1994, p. 24). Apart from a functioning, stable currency and financial market, this also requires stable commodity and service markets. This is highly relevant for the balanced or unbalanced development of the country's economic structure.

Moreover, the unequal distribution of income and wealth is also significant for the development of the labour market. Often raised in this context is the question of whether and when the redistribution of wealth and income will lead to a trade-off between efficiency targets on the one hand, and growth and distribution targets on the other (v. Hauff and Sauer 2003, p. 59ff). In answering this question, it is essential that increased productivity be the basis for a more equitable distribution, especially of labour.

The important premise here is that the potential and conditions for increased productivity actually exist. Land reform, for example, can be an important condition for the increased productivity of small farmers and small landholders, but this has often been denied in the past. It has also been shown that the introduction of an efficient system of social benefits can also lead to increased productivity. In this respect, if the creation of productive employment is to be a priority, a balance is desirable between the economic and social aims of the labour policies. The need for reform in Myanmar is great and the reforms are an important prerequisite for Myanmar's membership in the group of GMS states to strengthen positive economic growth and social development.

References

Alamgir, J. "Myanmar's Foreign Trade and its Political Consequences". In *Asian Survey* 48, no. 6 (2008): 977–96.

Andreff, W. "The Double Transition from Underdevelopment and from Socialism in Vietnam". *Journal of Contemporary Asia* (1993): 515–31.

Asian Development Bank. *Country Economic Report Myanmar*, vols. 1 and 2. Manila, 2001.

———. *Key Indicators 2005*. Manila, 2005.

————. *Key Indicators 2006*. Manila, 2006.

————. *The Mekong Region Trade: Trends, Patterns and Policies*. Manila, 2007.

————. *Key Indicators 2007*. Manila, 2007.

————. *Myanmar*. Manila, December 2009.

————. *Key Indicators 2010*. Manila, 2010.

Bedfellows, E. "Burma and ASEAN". *Asian Survey* 48, no. 6 (2008): 911–35.

Bünte, M. "Myanmar". In *Wirtschaftshandbuch Asien-Pazifik 2004/2005*, edited by Ostasiatischer Verein e. V. Hamburg, 2004.

————. "Dimensionen Sozialer Probleme in Myanmar — Ein Überblick". In *Armut im Land der goldenen Pagoden — Soziale Sicherheit, Gesundheit und Bildung in Burma*, edited by U. Bey. Essen, 2005.

Clawson, V., and D. Keller. "A Situation Analysis: Working and Out-of-School Children and Their Families in Hlaing Thar Yar Township, Ward 12, Yangon and Chan Mya Tharzi Township, Aung Pin Le Win, Mandalay". Yangon: World Vision Myanmar, 1999.

Dapice, D. "Current Economic Conditions in Myanmar and Options for Sustainable Growth". Global Development and Environment Institute Working Paper No. 03-04. Tufts University, Boston, 2003.

Durth, R., H. Körner, and K. Michaelowa. *Neue Entwicklungsökonomik*. Stuttgart, 2002.

Haake, J. "The Myanmar Imbroglio and ASEAN: Heading towards the 2010 Elections". *International Affairs* 86 (2010): 153–74.

v. Hauff, M. *Economic and Social Development in Burma/Myanmar*, 2nd ed. Marburg, 2009.

International Monetary Fund. *Myanmar: Recent Economic Developments*. Washington, 1999.

————. *Myanmar*. Washington, 2006.

Ishida, M. "Effectiveness and Challenges of Three Economic Corridors of Greater Mekong Sub-regions". In *IDA Discussion Paper, no. 35*, 2005.

Kyi, K.M. et al. *Economic Development of Burma — A Vision and a Strategy*. Singapore, 2000.

Perry, P.J. *Myanmar (Burma) Since 1962: The Failure of Development*. Burlington, 2007.

Rüland, J. "Political Transition in Southeast Asia — The Relevance of Burma". In *Shaping Concepts for Democratic Transition in Burma — Policies for Socially Responsible Development*, edited by Z. Oo. Washington, 2002.

Schmeier, S. "Regional Cooperation Efforts in the Mekong River Basin: Mitigating River-related Security Threats and Promoting Regional Development". *Austrian Journal of South-East Asian Studies* (2010): 28–52.

Set Aung, W. "Myanmar Economy, 2006". Unpublished manuscript.

Stärk, M. "Myanmar". In *Wirtschaftshandbuch Asien-Pazifik 2006/2007*, edited by Ostasiatischer Verein. Hamburg, 2006.

Stiglitz, J.E. "Some Lessons from the East Asian Miracle". *The World Bank Research Observer* 11, no. 2 (1996): 151–77.

Thein, M., K.M. Nyo. "Social Sector Development in Myanmar — The Role of the State". *ASEAN Economic Bulletin*, no. 12 (1999): 394–404.

UNDP. *Human Development Report 1992–2000, 2004, 2005, 2006, 2007, 2009.*

World Bank. *Myanmar: An Economic and Social Assessment.* Washington, 1999.

5

GMS CHALLENGES FOR THAILAND

Narongchai Akrasanee

The Association of Southeast Asian Nations (ASEAN) has progressed a lot and so has the Asia-Pacific Economic Cooperation (APEC), in terms of economic cooperation. Now we are moving on Greater Mekong Subregion (GMS) economic cooperation. The GMS started later than ASEAN and APEC, but it is catching up very quickly. Discussing the issues concerning GMS economic cooperation is therefore very timely.

This chapter is about the GMS from the perspective of Thailand. In order to understand the GMS we need to look at it from the perspective of different countries because they are different, and their perspectives need to be taken into consideration to promote the GMS.

Firstly, it is useful to go back a little in history — into the socio-political history of the GMS. It is important to understand this in order to appreciate how we see things differently. I will talk a bit about the diversity of the GMS and the attempts at connectivity. I will share with you my views of what Thailand thinks of the GMS and what it wants to do about the GMS.

I have been trying to come up with a phrase to capture my sentiment about the GMS. For the time being this phrase is — "from the same beginning, through different means, towards the same end". And that end is prosperity for the people in the area.

We can go as far back in history as we want, but what is important is our development just before and after the colonial period. I use the arrival of the Portuguese in Malacca before the sixteenth century as the beginning of the colonial era. At the time, Thailand was Siam, which was really a cultural entity — not an ethnic one — consisting of three major ethnic groups, viz., Thai-Lao, Mon-Khmer, and Java-Malay. We also had influences from China and India. This is obvious — two big countries next to us — there are lots of things we practise in Thailand that are of Indian or Chinese origin.

In the early colonial era, the Portuguese arrived in 1511, followed by the Spanish, the French, the Dutch, and later the British. During this early colonial period, Siam and the CMLV countries (Cambodia, Lao PDR, Myanmar, and Vietnam) were safe from colonization. The Spanish took over the Philippines; the Dutch took Indonesia. The French were more interested in religion at the time. They were trying to convert us to Christianity, but somehow did not colonize us.

The full colonial era was in the nineteenth century. The British and the French had their Industrial Revolution and most of us were colonized — Vietnam, Lao PDR, Cambodia by France; Myanmar by Britain. Siam remained independent. Somehow the British and the French could not decide who should take over Siam. So they took a part of each — one part in the north and northeast, and another in the south. We were offering Phuket to the British actually, but they wanted Penang. But what is important is that territorial issues had their origins during this period. Previously borders were not an issue. But when we had to give certain parts to the French and the British, suddenly territorial borders became an issue. Up to today, the border problems with Cambodia, the Lao PDR, and Myanmar are those that started when the British and the French tried to take over these lands.

During this period, Siam had very close relationships with rulers of Cambodia, the Lao PDR, and Vietnam. Although they became colonies, we kept good relations with them at the time.

What is pertinent is that after the end of World War II in 1945 came independence for CLMV: Cambodia in 1943; Lao PDR and Vietnam in 1945; Myanmar in 1948. Siam had become known as Thailand by then. It became Thailand in 1939. We had one prime minister who was nationalistic and thought we were of the Thai race, and more superior than any others. So he wanted to set up this so-called Thai country.

At the economic level, Thailand was not close to these countries after WWII because we had a different economic system. Thailand had a market economy particularly from 1960. We stopped state capitalism in 1960, partly to counter the expansion of communism at the time. CLMV followed socialism or state capitalism, depending on how you define it, until about 1990, when the Cold War started to end in 1989. China had already changed its regime before that when Mao Zedong passed away. So, all these countries had started to change in a significant way since 1990.

I think it is very important to think of 1989. Many things happened that year — the Berlin Wall fell, there was the Tiananmen incident, and the Vietnamese army left Cambodia — allowing the area to move towards a normal situation. That was the first time the Prime Minister of Thailand[1] came up with the phrase, "turning the battlefield into market place". We invited Prime Minister Hun Sen to visit Thailand in 1989.

After the Tiananmen incident, the system changed very fast. Deng Xiao Ping announced his market policies very strongly in 1990. So we became very much engaged with these countries only from 1990. It is important to understand this background. To Thailand, the GMS, economically speaking, is a recent phenomenon, unlike the United States and Europe.

The GMS as an economic development concept was launched by the Asian Development Bank (ADB) in 1992. The CLMV countries joined ASEAN at different times: Vietnam, 1995; Lao PDR and Myanmar, 1997; Cambodia, 1999. This aspect of ASEAN is important because it completed the mainland part of Southeast Asia. And having China in the GMS is also important. China has had a free trade agreement (FTA) with ASEAN from 2003 — another very important aspect. China also decided that the Guangxi region should be part of the GMS. Thirty per cent of the people in Guangxi are known to be from the Thai race, and many of them come to Thailand to study.

In terms of economic size, Thailand is the biggest in the GMS. In terms of population, Thailand is smaller than Vietnam. So there is big diversity within the GMS. There is also diversity in terms of per capita income.

Resources are a big issue for us. From Thailand's economic perspective, resources are the most important aspect of the GMS, followed by markets. We have exploited too much of our resources. Now we have to rely on the Lao PDR for electricity, Myanmar for natural gas, for instance. Our neighbouring countries have most of the resources we need. Of course land is an important resource as well. We have used up a lot of it in agriculture, so now we are interested in going into Cambodia, the Lao PDR, and Myanmar to grow crops and develop plantations.

As shown in Figure 5.1, we are most advanced economically. In terms of food security, we are very strong, stronger than the others. But we particularly

TABLE 5.1
GMS in 2009

	Population (millions)	GDP (US$ billion)	GDP per capita (Current US$)	GDP per capita at PPP (Current US$)
Thailand	67.0	264.0	3,940	8,051
Guangxi*	48.2	103.3	2,155	n/a
Yunnan*	45.4	82.1	1,812	n/a
Vietnam	87.2	93.2	1,068	2,942
Lao PDR	6.3	5.6	886	2,286
Cambodia	14.1	10.9	768	1,993
Myanmar	60.0	34.3	571	1,197

Note: * 2008 data.
Sources: International Monetary Fund, World Economic Outlook Database, October 2010 and National Bureau of Statistics of China.

FIGURE 5.1
Resources in GMS

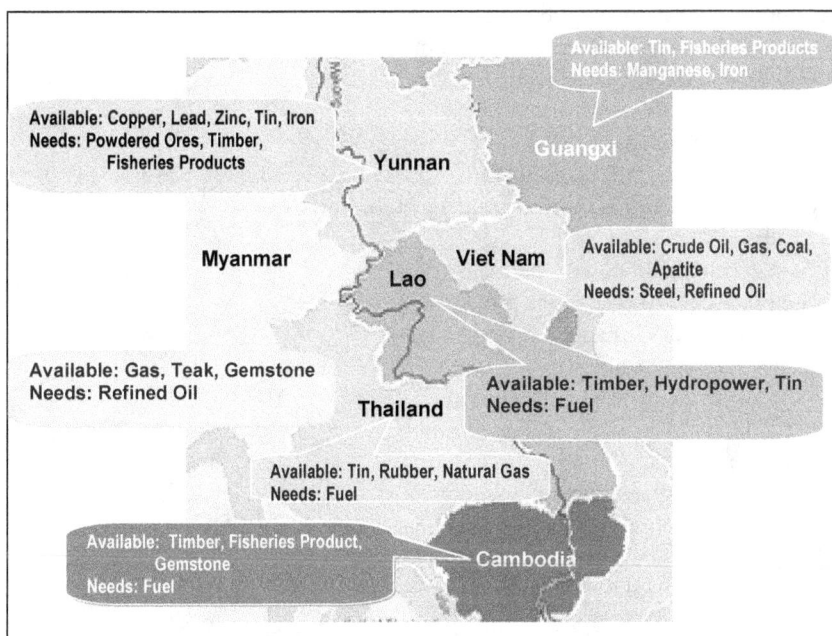

Available: Tin, Fisheries Products
Needs: Manganese, Iron

Available: Copper, Lead, Zinc, Tin, Iron
Needs: Powdered Ores, Timber, Fisheries Products

Yunnan

Guangxi

Myanmar

Viet Nam

Lao

Available: Crude Oil, Gas, Coal, Apatite
Needs: Steel, Refined Oil

Available: Gas, Teak, Gemstone
Needs: Refined Oil

Available: Timber, Hydropower, Tin
Needs: Fuel

Thailand

Available: Tin, Rubber, Natural Gas
Needs: Fuel

Available: Timber, Fisheries Product, Gemstone
Needs: Fuel

Cambodia

Source: Export–Import Bank of Thailand.

lack energy resources. I have to say that if ever we have a problem of our gas supply being stopped from Myanmar, we will be in trouble. Now this is already happening. In 2010, it happened twice, due to technical reasons. More and more we will be relying on the Lao PDR for hydropower energy.

Our central location is an advantage. This is all well documented in the ADB projects. We have a lot of ongoing and forthcoming projects, thanks to the ADB. They have put in a fantastic effort in developing a blueprint for infrastructure development in the GMS — energy, telecommunication projects, and transportation, which are some of the efforts being put in to tackle cross-border transactions, goods and services, and so on.

TABLE 5.2
Infrastructure Investment Plan in the GMS

Sector	No. of projects	Investment (US$ million)
Energy		
Ongoing projects		
• Hydropower plants in Lao PDR and China	2	2,400
• Improving/strengthening distribution/ transmission/interconnection systems in Cambodia, Vietnam, Thailand, and Lao PDR	6	900.7
Proposed projects		
• To construct/upgrade transmission/ distribution networks in Vietnam, Lao PDR, Thailand, Cambodia, China	13	Over 2,000
• To construct hydropower, thermal, combined cycle power plants mostly in Cambodia and Vietnam	7	Over 3,000
• Under feasibility studies		
– To construct hydropower plants and combined cycle power plants, mostly in Vietnam	10	
– To construct natural gas pipeline/power transmission lines/interconnection lines	3	
Telecommunications		
Ongoing project		
• Construction of Information Superhighway Network (ISN)	1	65.9

Proposed projects

• To construct new backbone/transmission networks in China, Myanmar, Vietnam, Cambodia, Thailand	3	Over 70
• To extend and increase access to ICT services in Myanmar, Cambodia	2	21
• Technical assistance study, e.g.,		
– Feasibility of applying unified tariff regime and numbering		
– Feasibility of a subregional synchronization network		

Transportation
Ongoing projects

• Construction/improving, upgrading		
– Road/highway/expressway	33	Over 3,000
– Port/container terminal	6	Over 600
– Airport	5	Over 10
– International bridge	2	128
– Railways, China	1	548
– Others	2	2,260

Proposed projects

• mostly on road/expressway construction	Over 100	Over 18,000

Source: GMS Development Matrix, ADB.

I would like to conclude here that connectivity has improved physically. But problems of cross-border rules and regulations remain. They are being resolved, but a lot still exist. There is also the difficulty of illegal migration. It is good to talk about cooperation, but cooperation also produces problems, particularly in the movement of people. And the most serious in this respect is at the border between Myanmar and Thailand. Because many of the people in Myanmar along the border are not happy with the Myanmar Government and vice versa, the easy solution for them is to come to Thailand. Now we have close to three million migrants from Myanmar working in Thailand, in all areas, including as housemaids. We also have many Cambodians crossing the border to work in construction. They have no unions; they are hard-working and not fussy about working conditions. Gambling is also an issue. It is illegal in Thailand. We have a lot of tour groups from Thailand going to casinos along the border. For us this is a social problem.

FIGURE 5.2
Growing Markets for Thai Exports

Thai Exports to GMS

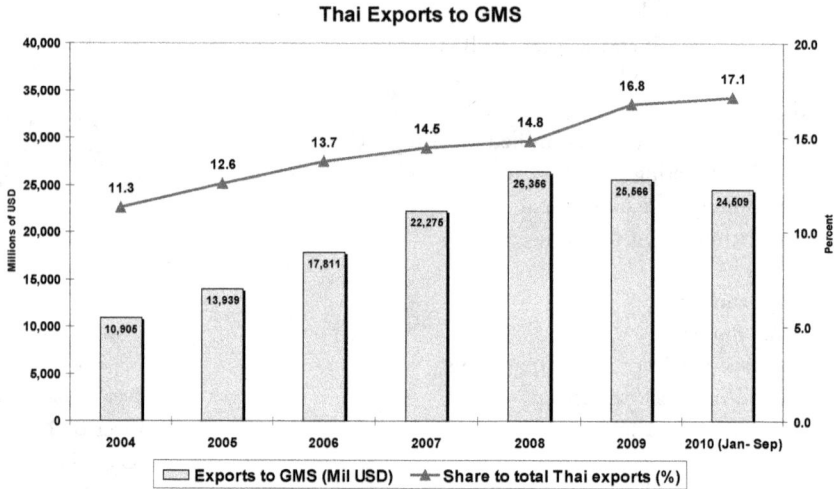

	Exports to GMS (Mil USD)	Share to total Thai exports (%)

Exports Structure (%)

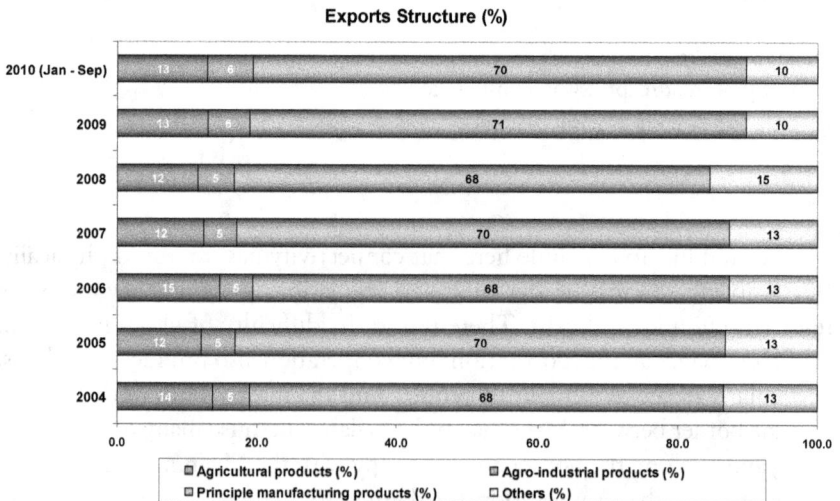

	Agricultural products (%)	Agro-industrial products (%)
	Principle manufacturing products (%)	Others (%)

Source: Ministry of Commerce, Thailand.

FIGURE 5.3
Sources of Raw Materials and Energy Supply

Thai Imports from GMS

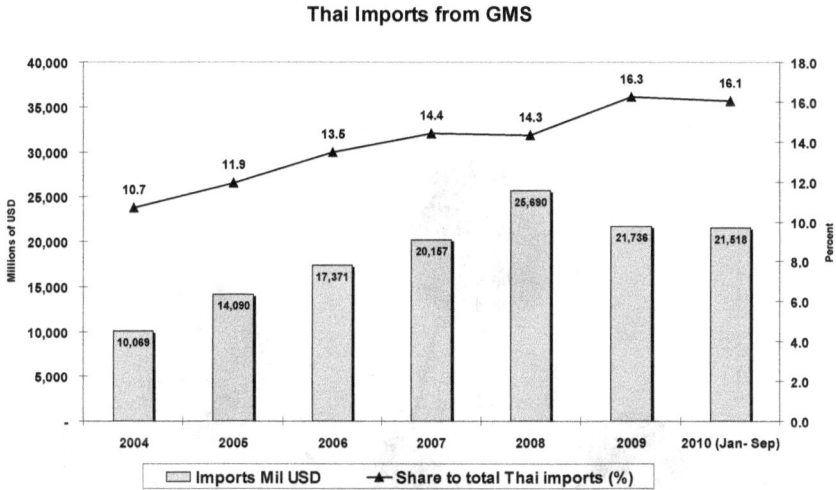

Imports Structure (%)

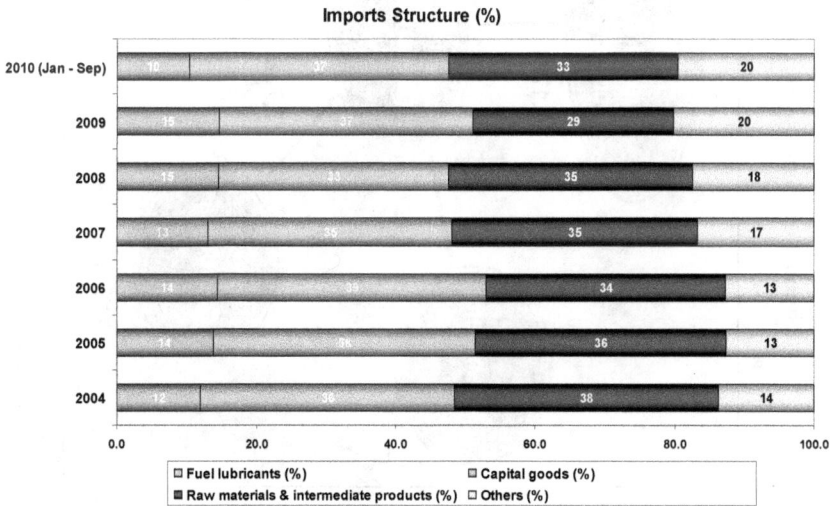

Source: Ministry of Commerce, Thailand.

FIGURE 5.4
Number of Flights Going In-Out to GMS Cities in 2009

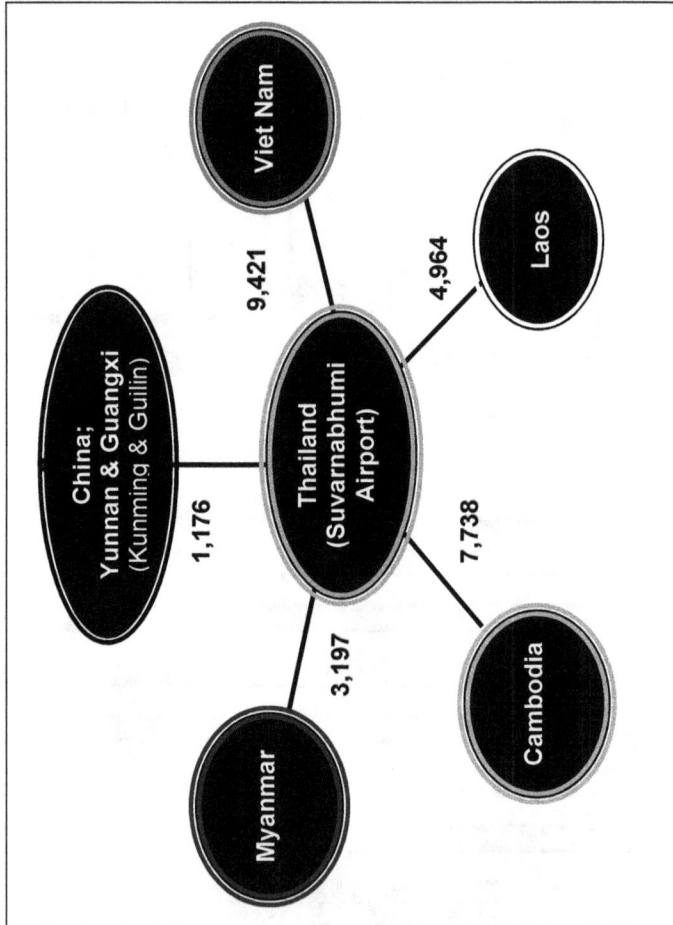

Source: Airports of Thailand Plc.

We benefit so much from the GMS through our exports because we are more advanced in terms of our consumer goods. If you go to the other GMS countries, you will see a lot of products made in Thailand. Many of the new hotels built in Angkor were built using materials from Thailand and things that they sell and use there are from Thailand. The development of the provinces along the border has been tremendous because of the development of Cambodia and the Lao PDR. You now see shopping malls coming up and departmental stores all over these border areas.

Logistics is also important for us (besides resources and markets). Statistics in 2009 show the number of flights from Thailand going in and out to other GMS countries — 9,421 to Vietnam, 3,197 to Myanmar, 7,738 to Cambodia, and 4,964 to the Lao PDR. That is why when the airport was closed due to our domestic political problems in 2008, the whole GMS suffered.

My conclusion is that the growth of the GMS is enhancing the growth of Thailand. That is definite. But when we look at the GMS, four areas capture the sentiments of the GMS and Thailand, and we must be mindful of them. We all say that the GMS has come a long way, but not evenly. Growth has been accelerating, but with serious concerns for ecology. Businesses want to do more, but face difficulties. GMS countries are in ASEAN and China, so they have to move quickly to keep up with China's high growth and the ASEAN Economic Community by 2015.

So how does the GMS adjust to these two huge forces? These are real challenges. Thailand, being an advanced economy, can give development assistance; negotiate cross-border trade investment facilitation; help in entrepreneurship development; and business promotion, in order to achieve prosperity for all.

It is difficult, but this will address the uneven development and cross-border issues. Ecology issues need to be looked into. And we can help facilitate the GMS in its contribution to ASEAN-China development. Since we are in the middle of the region, it is our role to do so.

Note

1. The seventeenth Prime Minister of Thailand (August 1988–February 1991), General Chatchai Choonhavan.

6

DEEPENING GMS COOPERATION IN A MORE INTEGRATED ASEAN AND EAST ASIA[1]

Vo Tri Thanh

Thanks to various measures for domestic economic reforms and regional economic integration, the East Asian economies in general, and the Association of Southeast Asian Nations (ASEAN) member economies in particular, have seen themselves becoming more deeply connected. Economic activities, particularly trade and investment activities, experienced a drastic increase in almost all sectors and all parts of the region. Cooperation between East Asian economies has also been enhanced, with the initial views to facilitating smoother flows of trade, investment, and labour, and eventually to joining hands in coping with more regionally common issues that arose in recent years.

In such a context, the Greater Mekong Subregion (GMS), with members Cambodia, the People's Republic of China (specifically Yunnan Province and Guangxi Zhuang Autonomous Region), the Lao People's Democratic Republic (PDR), Myanmar, Thailand, and Vietnam, is becoming an important and dynamic region. With assistance from the Asian Development Bank (ADB) in 1992, the six GMS countries launched a programme of subregional economic cooperation to enhance their economic relations, building on their shared histories and cultures, and covering priority sectors such as agriculture, human resource development, etc. Along with ASEAN integration and ASEAN-plus integration, economic integration under the GMS framework has also been rapid. This broadens the development opportunities for each member country while facilitating their joint efforts in a rising subregion with a relatively smaller development gap.

Nonetheless the GMS economies face a number of challenges in their integration and development processes. The challenge comes first from their low income levels, such as those prevailing in Cambodia, the Lao PDR, and Myanmar. Their economies also differ significantly in terms of labour and industrial structures. The gap in institutional settings across the GMS economies, which puts different constraints and presents various economic- and integration-facilitating ingredients, is another source of difference. In the new development context, GMS economies, as part of the dynamic East Asia, encounter to a larger extent non-traditional security issues, such as food security, climate change, among others. As these are major impediments to GMS cooperation, they necessitate bolder and more effective measures to resolve them.

This chapter attempts to discuss the context of, and policy recommendations for, deepening GMS cooperation. Apart from the introduction, it consists of four sections. The second section discusses the key objectives and policy ideas of GMS cooperation. The third section then reviews the socio-economic development progress in the GMS. Subsequently, the fourth section briefly refers to some new issues/challenges not fully taken into account by GMS Economic Partnership. Finally, the fifth section draws up some policy implications as to how GMS cooperation can be brought forward.

GMS COOPERATION: OBJECTIVES AND MAJOR PROJECTS/POLICY IDEAS

As part of the rapidly evolving East Asia, the GMS has huge potential for development. The subregion is a natural economic area with the Mekong River acting as the boundary between nations. The total area of the subregion is 2.6 million square kilometres, which provide habitation for a combined population of around 326 million. The subregion has flora and fauna expanding northward along the Malay Peninsula into Thailand, encroaching on the high mountains from the Himalayas, or advancing along the broad river valleys. In addition, after ten million years of changing sea levels, a rich legacy of unique life forms have evolved in isolation on the Cardamom and Annamite Mountains of Cambodia, the Lao PDR, Thailand, and Vietnam.

These are sources of agricultural income and subsistence for the majority of the people in the subregion.

Moreover, the land contains vast resources of timber, minerals, coal, and petroleum. The large number of rivers support water for agricultural and fishery production, and are also rich sources of energy in the form of hydropower. In addition, the subregion still possesses abundant coal reserves, while the oil and gas reserves are considerable. Most of these are in Myanmar, Thailand, and Vietnam. These abundant energy resources are still relatively underused.[2] Once they are properly and effectively used, they can facilitate rapid growth and development for the economies in possession of them.

Looking at another aspect, we see modernization and industrialization progressing quickly, helping to transform the GMS economies from subsistence farming to more diversified economies, based on more open, market-based systems. This process is accompanied by growing trade relations among the six GMS economies, particularly in terms of cross-border trade, investment, and labour mobility. Moreover, natural resources, particularly hydropower, are beginning to be developed and utilized on a subregional basis. This consolidates hope for further development in the subregion. With rich human and natural resource endowments and a low development level, the GMS has arguably the potential to be one of the world's fastest growing areas.[3]

Acknowledging that potential, the GMS economies formulated and implemented the Strategic Framework for 2002–12, which builds on accomplishments to date, lessons learned, and trends and challenges facing the subregion. Exhibited in the framework are a common vision, goal, and strategic thrusts for regional cooperation. As its objectives, the GMS Strategic Framework seeks to promote sustainable development and achieve a "GMS that is more integrated, prosperous and equitable" (ADB 2002, p. 22). Such objectives are to be realized via regional cooperation and through closer subregional economic linkages such as cross-border trade, investment, tourism, and other forms of economic cooperation. Notably, the objectives set out in the GMS Strategic Framework are very much in line with the ASEAN Vision, which is to transform ASEAN into a stable, prosperous, and highly competitive region with equitable economic development, and reduced poverty and socio-economic disparities.

Specifically, to realize its objectives, the GMS Strategic Framework is implemented through a set of activities with focus. The most important steps are to identify subregional projects that support the strategic thrusts with priorities; and to prepare a rolling investment and technical assistance programme for carrying out the projects. Thus, the GMS Programme focuses on eleven "flagship" programmes, namely: (i) North-South

Economic Corridor; (ii) East-West Economic Corridor; (iii) Southern Economic Corridor; (iv) Telecommunications Backbone; (v) Regional Power Interconnection and Trading Arrangements; (vi) Facilitating Cross-Border Trade and Investment; (vii) Enhancing Private-Sector Participation and Competitiveness; (viii) Developing Human Resources and Skills Competencies; (ix) Strategic Environment Framework; (x) Flood Control and Water Resource Management; and (xi) GMS Tourism Development. Underlying these "flagship" programmes is the shift in focus from (mainly) infrastructure to social, environment and trade, and development gap issues, and from mainly "hard" cooperation (that is, hard infrastructure) to "soft" cooperation (that is, soft infrastructure).

Narrowing the development gap within GMS economies is fundamental to realizing the goal of the GMS Strategic Framework in particular, and to inclusive growth of the subregion in general. There are two possible approaches to narrowing such a development gap. The first is to look at the key "gap indicators". Development gaps are multidimensional and interdisciplinary. Accordingly, various indicators can be used to measure them, and concentrated efforts can be directed to address the relevant aspects. For instance, Bui and Vo (2007) propose the "four-I" approach, which means viewing the development gap as a combination of income gap, infrastructure gap, integration gap, and institutional gap. Advantages to the approach include that it can be used for monitoring progress in reducing the development gap and can be employed for finding some (significant) causalities which, in turn, may indicate the areas/policies that need to be prioritized. But this approach also requires further analysis before suggestions can be made on institutional settings.

The second approach is a mix of reforms in each member country, intra-GMS cooperation, and external assistance. With this approach, reforms in each newer member country and associated lessons can be shared. But this approach requires a couple of considerations. First, the two major components of essential external assistance are special and differential treatment, and technical assistance in which institutional building is the key. The importance of these components can be seen more clearly through the existing problems of the IAI (Initative for ASEAN Integration), such as limited financial resources, capability, and collaboration/incorporation with other assistance programmes. Second, attaining efficiency and effectiveness of cooperation is easier said than done. At this stage, Cambodia, the Lao PDR, Myanmar, and Vietnam (CLMV) still suffer from the limited quality of human resources and limited financial resources. Moreover, they still have small market sizes, while their trade structures are more competitive than complementary. Facilitating economic cooperation via cross-border trade and investment can therefore be challenging. Yet CLMV can learn from, and talk with, one another at greater ease. To promote their development in particular, and GMS cooperation in general, China and Thailand should and can play more important roles.

SOCIO-ECONOMIC DEVELOPMENT PERFORMANCE OF GMS ECONOMIES

For the period of 2000–2009 as a whole, the average GDP growth rates of Cambodia, the Lao PDR, Myanmar, and Vietnam reached 8.0 per cent, 6.7 per cent, 9.5 per cent, and 7.2 per cent, respectively. Such growth rates were higher than those of other ASEAN member countries. In relative terms, there has been a tendency for income convergence between ASEAN-6 and CLMV. China, meanwhile, had the most rapid growth over the past decade. Table 6.1 indicates that the PPP-income gap between the CLV and the higher-income ASEAN members has generally been reduced between 2000 and 2008. Meanwhile, the income gaps between Cambodia and Vietnam, and between the Lao PDR and Vietnam, have been unchanged. Nonetheless, such an income convergence has been insufficient. The development gap in terms of PPP-income is still huge among CLMV, and between CLMV and Indonesia, the Philippines, Malaysia, and Singapore. In terms of the human development index (HDI), the gaps between CLMV and other ASEAN member countries are also substantial (Table 6.2).

The economic growth performance in GMS economies could be partly attributed to trade growth. In particular, intraregional trade made a significant

TABLE 6.1
PPP-income Gaps between Asian Countries

	2000	2005	2008
Cambodia	0.6	0.7	0.7
Indonesia	1.6	1.4	1.4
Lao PDR	0.8	0.8	0.8
Malaysia	6.0	5.3	5.1
Philippines	1.7	1.5	1.4
Singapore	23.7	19.9	17.8
Thailand	3.3	3.1	2.2
Vietnam	1.0	1.0	1.0
China	1.7	2.0	2.2

Note: Vietnam's PPP-income is set at unity.
Source: Ministry of Planning and Investment 2010.

TABLE 6.2
HDI of ASEAN Countries

		2000	2005	2007
		173	177	182
Brunei	Value	0.871	0.894	0.920
	Rank	32	30	30
Cambodia	Value	0.543	0.598	0.593
	Rank	130	131	137
Indonesia	Value	0.684	0.728	0.734
	Rank	110	107	111
Lao PDR	Value	0.485	0.601	0.619
	Rank	143	130	133
Malaysia	Value	0.782	0.811	0.829
	Rank	59	63	66
Myanmar	Value	0.552	0.583	0.586
	Rank	127	132	138
Philippines	Value	0.754	0.771	0.751
	Rank	77	90	105
Singapore	Value	0.885	0.922	0.944
	Rank	25	25	23
Thailand	Value	0.762	0.781	0.783
	Rank	70	78	87
Vietnam	Value	0.688	0.733	0.725
	Rank	109	105	116

Source: UNDP (various years).

contribution. At the ASEAN level, trade growth reached 1.3 per cent on annual average in 1995–2000, and 7.9 per cent per annum on average in 2000–2007. The corresponding figures are 0.9 per cent and 7.3 per cent for ASEAN-6, and 11.9 per cent and 16.5 per cent for CLMV. Intra-ASEAN trade growth was even faster, reaching 2.8 per cent per annum on average in 1995–2000, and 9.3 per cent per annum on average in 2000–2007. The respective figures for ASEAN-6 are 2.6 per cent and 8.9 per cent. However, intra-ASEAN trade growth for the CLMV averaged 6.7 per cent per annum and 16.0 per cent per annum for 1995–2000 and 2000–2007, respectively, which were smaller than theirs at the aggregate level. That is, the trade structures of CLMV are relatively less complementary within ASEAN.

Further insights can be drawn from the trade pattern of GMS countries in 2006 (Table 6.3). China saw rapid growth rates of both exports to and imports from the world, while their trade with GMS countries grew a bit more slowly. Yet China's imports from the GMS went up faster than that from ASEAN, indicating that the GMS is a more important source of inports for China. For Thailand, conversely, trade with the GMS economies rose more rapidly than that with ASEAN and with the world. This is also the observation for the case of Cambodia. The Lao PDR also focused more on trade with the GMS and ASEAN, though export (import) growth with the GMS economies was faster (slower) than that with ASEAN. Meanwhile, Vietnam tended to increase imports from GMS and ASEAN economies more rapidly, and made more effort to promote exports to the world outside of GMS and ASEAN.

Interesting observations can be made from the changes in ASEAN shares in CLMV's total trade. The Lao PDR and Myanmar saw their trade with ASEAN growing significantly, even in relative terms. The share of ASEAN in the total trade of the Lao PDR went up from 48.0 per cent on average in 1998–2000 to 62.3 per cent on average in 2001–3, and to 79.8 per cent in 2006. Similarly, in the case of Myanmar, the figure rose from 29.8 per cent in 1998–2000 to 41.2 per cent in 2001–3, and 59.0 per cent in 2006. That of Cambodia changed in the opposite direction, falling from 33.9 per cent on average in 1998–2000, to 30.1 per cent in 2001–3, and 19.1 per cent in 2006. For Vietnam, the share of ASEAN in total trade exhibited no unambiguous pattern, decreasing from 22.2 per cent on average in 1998–2000 to 20.2 per cent on average in 2001–3, then rising to 24.2 per cent in 2006, before falling to 20.7 per cent in 2008. Thus, even with the consensus on the importance of ASEAN, the CLMV are giving different emphases to this trade partner.

Figure 6.1 depicts the relative importance of GMS economies in intraregional trade in 2006. China reaped a big share of trade at this level, reaching around two fifths. Thailand followed, attaining 35 per cent. Again, as previously mentioned, Vietnam only accounted for a modest share of 16 per cent of GMS intraregional trade. This indicates the relatively lesser emphasis given by the country to GMS trade. Meanwhile, the Lao PDR, Cambodia, and Myanmar only had tiny shares in GMS intraregional trade. Thus, the development gaps amongst GMS economies somehow constrain their (relative) participation in intraregional trade.

But from Vietnam's perspective, trade with bordering (GMS) countries also went up in absolute terms (Table 6.4). Both export and import with Cambodia, the Lao PDR, and China went up in 2007–8. With the Lao PDR

TABLE 6.3
Growth Rates of Export, Import, and Total Trade of GMS Countries in 2006

	China	Cambodia	Lao PDR	Myanmar	Thailand	Vietnam
Trade with GMS						
Export growth (%, 2006)	28	24	57	n/a	29	6
Import growth (%, 2006)	23	28	37	n/a	23	26
Total trade growth (%, 2006)	26	28	42	n/a	26	19
Trade with ASEAN						
Export growth (%, 2006)	29	–18	62	38	14	12
Import growth (%, 2006)	19	9	21	31	10	35
Total trade growth (%, 2006)	23	6	32	35	12	26
Trade with the world						
Export growth (annual %, 2002–2006)	31	18	35	15	18	26
Import growth (annual %, 2002–2006)	28	19	25	7	20	23

Source: UNESCAP Trade and Investment Division 2008.

FIGURE 6.1
GMS Countries' Intraregional Trade, 2006

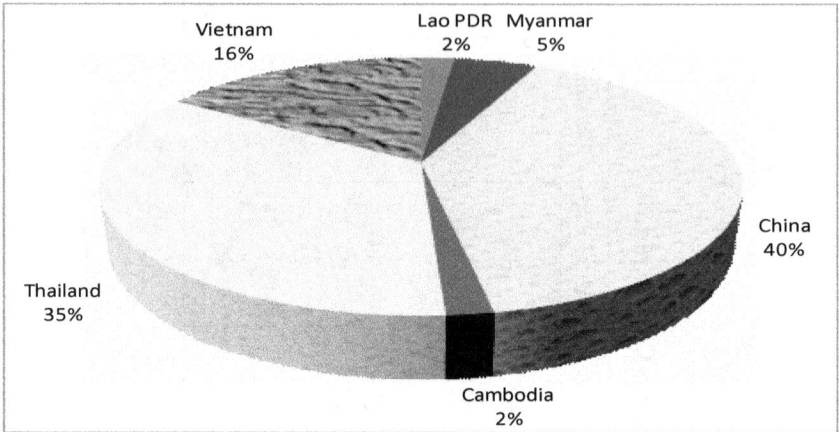

and Cambodia, Vietnam's exports seemed to increase faster than imports. But the reverse is observed in trade with China: Vietnam's imports from China went up drastically relative to what Vietnam could export to China. More importantly, Vietnam's trade deficit with China outweighed its trade surplus with Cambodia and the Lao PDR. A significant proportion of Vietnam's trade with Cambodia, China, and the Lao PDR was on a cross-border basis (Table 6.5). In the case of China, around one third of trade with Vietnam is cross-border. The figure for the Lao PDR is around 0.6 per cent, while all Cambodia's trade with Vietnam took place via the border.

ASEAN has also become a more attractive investment destination for investors. Foreign direct investment (FDI) into the region went up quite considerably during 2002–8. Between 2006 and 2008, FDI inflows to ASEAN countries went up by 8.6 per cent and intra-ASEAN FDI rose even faster, by 42.6 per cent. In 2008 alone, FDI into ASEAN reached almost US$59.7 billion, while intra-ASEAN FDI was equal to US$10.8 billion, or approximately 18.2 per cent of total FDI into ASEAN. This contributed significantly to trade between ASEAN members in particular, and to their stronger economic ties in general. From CLMV's perspective, China, Thailand, Singapore, and Malaysia are important investors.

After a long period of stagnation (1993–2003), FDI inflows to Vietnam started to increase. Such an increase can be seen in the number of new

TABLE 6.4
Trade of Vietnam with Bordering Countries (US$ million)

	2007				2008			
	Export	Import	Total	%	Export	Import	Total	%
Cambodia	991	202	1,193	27.7	1,431	210	1,641	37.6
Lao PDR	104	208	312	20.1	150	273	423	35.6
China	3,357	12,502	15,859	52.2	4,536	15,652	20,188	27.3

Source: Ministry of Industries and Trade of Vietnam. Department of Trade Statistics 2009.

TABLE 6.5
Border Trade between Vietnam and China, Lao PDR, and Cambodia
(US$ million)

	2007		2008	
	Trade turnover	Change %	Trade turnover	Change %
China	5,467.9	103.2	6,507.81	19.02
Lao PDR	312	20.1	423	35.6
Cambodia	772.06	12.1	1,077.15	39.5
Total	6,551.96	80.1	8,007.96	22.2

Source: Ministry of Industries and Trade of Vietnam. Department of Trade Statistics 2009.

projects, registered capital, as well as implemented capital. Recently the country promoted further FDI inflows from ASEAN countries. Accumulated (registered) FDI from ASEAN to Vietnam during 1990–2009 amounted to US$40 billion in 1,517 projects, which accounted for 26 per cent of total FDI and 13.8 per cent of FDI projects in Vietnam. At the same time, Vietnam also increased outward FDI to other ASEAN countries. By the end of 2009, Vietnam had 454 projects with a total registered capital of US$7.5 billion. Most of this outward FDI was concentrated in mining, energy, telecommunications, agriculture, and aquaculture, and placed mostly in Cambodia, the Lao PDR, and Myanmar.

Overall, there has been remarkable achievement in socio-economic development and the international integration of the GMS countries. Trade and investment linkages amongst GMS countries, and between the GMS and others, could be enhanced to a significantly larger extent than expected. However, there remain several issues that may constrain further enhancement of such linkages. First, major gaps still exist amongst the GMS countries, particularly in terms of income, human development, institutions, and infrastructure, etc. Second, significant progress has been achieved in establishing transportation corridors, but they (even completed ones) are far from being economic corridors with sufficient spillover impact on the livelihood of people in the concerned economies. Third, the issue of sustainability — particularly in terms of the environment — has not received sufficiently serious attention. Finally, although border trade has become a part of economic linkages and development with greater impact, it is also associated with a number of cross-border, non-traditional security issues. The resolution of these issues should be central to realizing the development potential of the GMS, not only at the country level, but also at the subregional level.

To achieve such a resolution, a comprehensive assessment of the implementation and associated impacts of the GMS Strategic Framework is necessary. However, to date most assessments of the impacts of the GMS Economic Partnership are partial and not comprehensive enough. Examples of such assessments with deficiencies are the findings on ADB RETAs (Regional Technical Assistance) or ADB-Funded Projects in the Mekong River Delta. Even the assessment of the CADP (Comprehensive Asia Development Plan) by the ERIA (Economic Research Institute) (2010) looks only at the economic impact of various corridors on the countries in the region, without consideration of impacts on other aspects such as the environment, social livelihood, etc. Still, some of the findings are remarkable. For instance, one important conclusion from ERIA (2010) and also from Kumagai et al. (2009) is that "border costs appear to play a big role in the allocation choice of populations and industries, and often [play a] more important role than physical infrastructures themselves". While failing to attain comprehensiveness, such findings deserve attention so that prompt policy efforts can be made.

ISSUES/CHALLENGES NOT FULLY TAKEN INTO ACCOUNT BY GMS STRATEGIC FRAMEWORK

Activities and "flagship" programmes under the GMS Strategic Framework led to significant socio-economic achievements in the GMS economies, particularly in terms of intraregional economic cooperation. Nevertheless, issues still remain for the continuing realization of the development potential in the subregion. This is partly due to the deficiencies within the GMS Strategic Framework itself, which fails to take into account several important issues and/or challenges. Within its limited scope, this section may only address some of them as follows.

First, the GMS Strategic Framework fails to reflect broader views/new ideas of development. In the new context, growth must be, on the one hand, inclusive. Such an inclusiveness can be realized through social protection and other (rational) public expenditures, through infrastructure investment on a network of secondary roads, water, and sanitation, etc., through support for SMEs so that they can be engaged in clustering and cooperation with large firms, and through innovations in microfinance. On the other hand, as the idea of green growth was not incorporated in the framework, subsidies and other distortions may lead to excessive consumption and production of energy and resources that is detrimental to the environment. This suggests the alternative use of a market-based approach in combination with cap and trade mechanisms and carbon emission taxes. Achieving green growth also requires technology transfer and research-and-development support. Additionally, other considerations include: (i) the distinction between commercial and non-commercial technologies, where the treatment of intellectual property rights is different; (ii) standards and conformity with the 3Rs; and (iii) the definition of "environmental" goods and services to promote green growth.

Second, the GMS Strategic Framework fails to consider the new role of East Asia and its new growth strategy. East Asia as a whole is becoming an important and dynamic region. Together, the East Asian countries (specifically ASEAN+3), have formed a large economic region, accounting for almost 30.6 per cent of the world population[4] and around one-fifth of world GDP (Vo and Nguyen 2010). East Asian economic integration has also been rapid, centring on the frameworks of ASEAN integration and ASEAN-plus integration. As a large production hub, East Asia benefits from wide and deep trade and investment relations with external countries, particularly the United States and the European Union. East Asia's exports to the two regions have been on a dramatic scale, made possible by the recently and rapidly established production networks at the regional level. The export-led growth strategy adopted by East Asian economies has also led to closer production linkages within the region, ultimately establishing a unique production network and stimulating agglomeration and fragmentation. Of equivalent importance for consideration is the drastically changing role of East Asia in the context of China and India emerging as major producers for the global economy.

Also, East Asia is in need of a new strategy that incorporates a greater element of growth rebalancing. Several elements of this strategy can be identified at this stage. The strategy must facilitate a more equitable process to address global macroeconomic imbalances. This in turn necessitates changes in the roles of East Asia, the United States, as well as other advanced economies. In another aspect, resources/savings in East Asia should be channeled for infrastructure development in the region. Also, countries such as Vietnam are enjoying a young demographic structure, but others such as Japan and China tend to encounter more problems with their ageing population. At the same time, the middle-income class is emerging in both scale and importance. Accordingly, this requires a revisiting of the role of social safety nets and changing demographic structures.

Third, attempts for regional economic integration should not stop only with trade and investment liberalization; instead, they should go even further to facilitation and connectivity. That is, effective trade liberalization and FTAs should be accompanied by, rather than separate from, trade and investment facilitation, as well as service-link cost reduction. In addition, challenges remain in ensuring interaction between the economic corridors and both agglomeration and fragmentation in a way that promotes economic growth and narrows the development gap. In fact, work in this direction has made some progress. This is seen in the establishment of several regional infrastructure development funds — such as those of the ADB, ASEAN, China-ASEAN, and the "Sub-Committee on Economic Cooperation" under the ASEAN-Japan Comprehensive Economic Partnership. In addition, "A Comprehensive Asia Development Plan" (CADP) was formulated by ERIA, while a new Master Plan for ASEAN Connectivity was developed to promote both physical connectivity and institutional connectivity (such as mutual recognition agreements, standards, single window, capacity building, etc.) as well as people-to-people connectivity. Yet challenges prevail in incorporating these elements in the GMS Strategic Framework, and in actually implementing them.

Finally, GMS integration is only a part of the more complex web of regional cooperation and stakeholders' engagement. Currently, there are a number of ODA (official development assistance) schemes, including loans, grants and technical cooperation, and various cooperation areas, with a number of donors. The donors are diverse, ranging from multilateral to bilateral donors, comprising both developed and developing countries. As a positive sign, issues of development sustainability and institutional reform are of more concern, while south-south cooperation has been strengthened. The scope for regional cooperation has been expanded (Table 6.6). The programmes with the widest scope are the East Asian Cooperation Work Plan and GMS development. East Asian development cooperation has been incorporated in several regional free trade agreements (FTAs), as well as new China-ASEAN cooperation initiatives such as China's "One Axis, Two Wings" and "Pan-Beibu Gulf Cooperation", and the "Two Corridors, One Belt" between China and Vietnam.

FIGURE 6.2
The Trade Chain

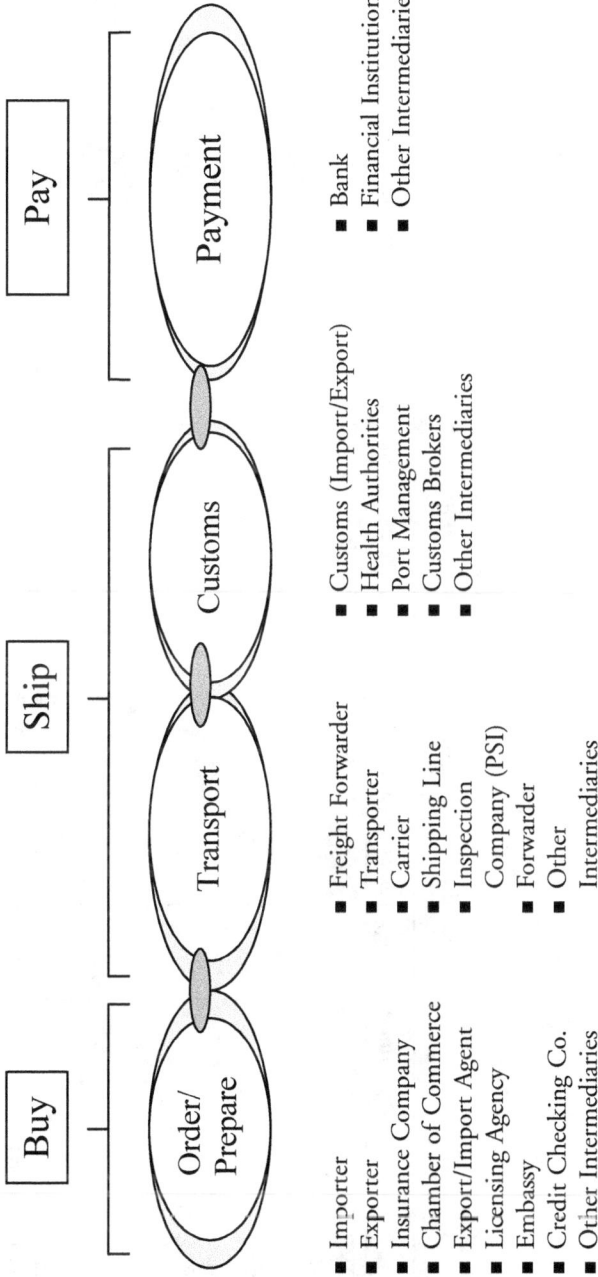

Buy

Order/Prepare
- Importer
- Exporter
- Insurance Company
- Chamber of Commerce
- Export/Import Agent
- Licensing Agency
- Embassy
- Credit Checking Co.
- Other Intermediaries

Ship

Transport
- Freight Forwarder
- Transporter
- Carrier
- Shipping Line
- Inspection Company (PSI)
- Forwarder
- Other Intermediaries

Customs
- Customs (Import/Export)
- Health Authorities
- Port Management
- Customs Brokers
- Other Intermediaries

Pay

Payment
- Bank
- Financial Institutions
- Other Intermediaries

TABLE 6.6
Regional and Subregional Development Cooperation Programmes

	Agriculture	Energy	Environment	HR	ICT	Transport	Tourism	Trade	Investment	Countries Involved
EACWP	x	x	x	x	x	x	x	x	x	ASEAN, China, Japan, Korea
IAI		x		x	x	x				ASEAN
GMS	x	x	x	x	x	x	x	x	x	CLMV, Thailand, China
AKBDC	x	x		x	x	x	x	x	x	ASEAN, China
ACPMECS	x			x		x	x	x	x	CLMV, Thailand
BIMP- EAGA	x						x			Brunei, Indonesia, Malaysia, Philippines
IMT-GT		x		x	x	x	x	x	x	Indonesia, Thailand, Malaysia

Source: Joint Expert Group on EAFTA Phase II Study 2009.

Nevertheless, many ongoing cooperation programmes still overlap and have not been implemented yet. At the same time, they are too spatially and sectorally widespread, leading to the dispersion of efforts and resources. This is not to mention the possible lack of complementarity of various development cooperation programmes in the same sector, which may eventually cause development cooperation programmes to be less than meaningful (Joint Expert Group on EAFTA Phase II Study 2009).

POLICY IMPLICATIONS

The GMS economies have made drastic efforts, as well as significant achievements, in regional integration and cooperation. With political will and the institutionalization of subregional integration, particularly along with ASEAN and East Asian integration, the economies involved are getting closer. Subregional trade and investment have tended to go up drastically. In line with this, with external assistance, the subregional economies have designed and implemented various development cooperation programmes, with different scopes. Continuing progress in GMS integration, however, requires further cooperation attempts in addressing common issues to regional development, particularly in the new context of East Asian integration and development. The contents in this chapter show several policy implications for the GMS economies in the forthcoming years.

First, the Strategic Framework for GMS integration and development should be put in a broader framework of development concept and regional integration and cooperation schemes. The institutionalized process for East Asian integration cannot succeed without the strengthening of ASEAN integration. In turn, ASEAN integration would not produce the desired outcomes if the development gap continued to widen. Besides, East Asia may need to establish regular "dialogue fora"/mechanisms for building regional mutual trust/credibility and studying new development paradigms. In doing so, East Asian and other donors may also talk about the needs for and/or design of assistance programmes, so that such programmes can be incorporated and coordinated effectively. Additionally, along with this process, the interests of and costs-benefits to GMS members, especially CLMV, must be taken into account in any regional initiative/arrangement.

Second, all stakeholders should cooperate to make the regional cooperation and assistance master plans more effective. They should assess and monitor the progress of GMS/CLMV integration and reduction of the development gap, by developing and using a set of appropriate quantitative and qualitative indicators. In doing so, the four-I approach proposed by Bui and Vo (2007) may be useful. To ensure the effectiveness of such a monitoring process, the stakeholders should also improve the economic statistics/database and, at the same time, strengthen information sharing. To ensure the relevant outcome of regional cooperation and assistance master plans, comprehensive assessment should be made of the socio-economic and environmental impacts. Moreover, successful regional cooperation and assistance master plans must involve consultation with each CLMV country to understand their reform processes and situations better, so that assistance programmes may better complement their needs. In particular, as CLMV countries are mainly at a low-development level, assistance programmes should focus more on building institutions and capacity, as well as the development of soft infrastructure. After the consultations with CLMV, it is essential to make the regional master plans in tandem with national strategies, in terms of developing networks of national primary and secondary transportation, corridor towns, and industrial zones.

Finally, stakeholders should set up institutions for implementation and resource mobilization. Specifically, more appropriate regional institutions should be established. This can be done by supporting the establishment of the AEC (ASEAN Economic Community) by 2015, and by building effective surveillance/monitoring and dispute settlement mechanisms. In connection with the previous implication, the cooperation of international institutions/donors for development assistance should be strengthened. The question that arises is whether the Initiative for ASEAN Integration (IAI) should be transformed into Initiative for East Asian Integration (IEAI) for implementation at a broader level, including the coordination of various development funds.

There are various possible approaches for resource mobilization to support GMS integration. Among them is the "2 plus 1" cooperation scheme, that is, the cooperation between two or more low-income countries while receiving the financial support from a more advanced country or an international institution. This approach allows for better ownership of low-income countries and makes the financial support of donors relevant to their needs. Other existing schemes of importance should also be exploited more effectively. Public-private partnerships (PPP) are currently employed to varying extents, but still require further efforts to develop best practices. In a more specific aspect, the Master Plans for ASEAN Connectivity have been prepared, but will only come into effect with the establishment of a High Level Task Force for implementation in tandem with CADP and China-ASEAN infrastructure development schemes. Last, but not least, attention should be paid to the interaction between "top-down" and "bottom up" policy processes, which should involve the effective participation of politicians/policymakers, experts, and the business community.

To repeat, closer GMS cooperation is critical to ASEAN, ASEAN-China, and East Asia integration. Current convenience and the completed aspects in the process may solidify the hopes for the GMS itself and for subsequent work to be built on success so far. However, such hopes and their realization are by no means unconditional. In fact, they can become true for the development of GMS economies only as long as the underlying vision can be reinforced in such a way that ensures the fair distribution of benefits to the countries involved.

Notes

1. Paper presented at the conference "GMS: From Geographical Corridor to Socio-economic Corridor", 18–19 October 2010, ISEAS, Singapore.
2. These details are from the ADB website.
3. See ADB website.
4. As of 2010. Data for ASEAN+3 only.

References

ADB. *Building on Success: A Strategic Framework for the Next Ten Years of the Greater Mekong Subregion Economic Cooperation Program*, 2002.

Asian Policy Forum (APF). "Recommendations to Asian Leaders of Policy Responses to Secure Balanced and Sustainable Growth in Asia". ADBI, Tokyo, September (draft), 2010.

Bhattacharyay, Biswa Nath. "Infrastructure for ASEAN Connectivity and Integration". *ASEAN Economic Bulletin* 27, no. 2 (August 2010).

Bui, T.G. and T.T. Vo. "Approach to Development Gaps in ASEAN: A Vietnamese Perspective". *ASEAN Economic Bulletin* 24, no. 1 (April 2007).

Chia Siow Yue. "ASEAN Economic Integration — Development and Challenges". Paper presented at the AEPR conference on "The ASEAN Economy: Diversity, Disparities and Dynamics", Tokyo, 1 October 2010.

Economic Research Institute for ASEAN and East Asia (ERIA). *Comprehensive Asia Development Plan*. ERIA, August 2010.

Joint Expert Group on EAFTA Phase II Study. "Desirable and Feasible Option for an East Asia FTA". Final Report on EAFTA Phase II Study, 2009.

Kawai, M., and Wignaraja. "Free Trade Agreements in East Asia: A Way toward Trade Liberalization?". ADBI Brief, no. 1, June 2010.

Lord, Montague. "The Strategic Role of Corridor Towns in the Development of GMS Economic Corridors". 5th GMS Development Dialogue, 20 November 2010.

MPI. "Vietnam's Socio-Economic Development Strategy 2011–2020" (Draft in Vietnamese). Hanoi, April 2010.

Satoru Kumagai et al. "Predicting Long-term Effects of Infrastructure Development Projects in Continental South East Asia: IDE Geographical Simulation Model". ERIA Discussion Paper Series, ERIA, December 2008.

Trade and Investment Division (UNESCAP). "Economic Cooperation and Regional Integration in the Greater Mekong Sub-region". Staff Working Paper 02/08, September 2008.

Vo, T.T. "Achieving an Efficient AEC by 2015: A Perspective from Vietnam". Paper presented at the ASEAN Roundtable 2010 on "Achieving the AEC 2015: Challenges for Member Countries". Singapore, 29 April 2010.

————. "Nanning- Singapore Economic Corridor: Bridging ACFTA-based Regional Development". A presentation at the 5th Pan-Beibu Gulf Economic Cooperation Forum, Nanning, China, 12–13 August 2010.

Vo, T.T. and A.D. Nguyen. "Development Cooperation in East Asia". Paper presented at the conference on "East Asia Economic Integration in the Wake of Global Financial Crisis", Seoul, Korea, 7 July 2010.

7

CHINA (YUNNAN)–GMS ECONOMIC COOPERATION
New Development and New Problems

Guangsheng Lu

DEVELOPMENT AND CURRENT SITUATION

Yunnan and GMS: A Survey

Located in southwest China, Yunnan is the country's eighth biggest province in terms of size (394,100 km²) and population (45.53 million, 2008). Besides the Han people, there are twenty-five ethnic minority groups, seventeen of them transnational. Yunnan shares a 4,060-km common border with Myanmar, the Lao PDR, and Vietnam and is close to Thailand, Cambodia, India, and Bangladesh. It has about 600 rivers which belong to six different river systems. Major rivers are the Dulongjiang, the headwaters of the Irrawaddy; the Nujiang, which is the upper reaches of the Salween; the Lancangjiang, known as the Mekong in the Lao PDR and Vietnam; the Red River which empties into the Gulf of Tonkin (Beibuwan in Chinese) through Vietnam. The strategic location of Yunnan does have great geopolitical and geo-economical significance, and its multinational water issues are complicated and sensitive. (See Table 7.1 for Yunnan's economic indicators.)

TABLE 7.1
Key Economic Indicators in Yunnan, 2009

	GDP (billion yuan) and ranking	Government revenue (billion yuan) and ranking	Per capita income (yuan) and ranking
Yunnan	616.8 (24)	149.0 (17)	8,686 (14)
Guangxi	770.0 (18)	96.6 (21)	9,116 (12)
Guangdong	3,908.1 (1)	862.0 (1)	13,405 (4)
China	33,535.3 (n/a)	6,847.7 (n/a)	N.A. (n/a)

Note: 1. Numbers in parentheses show domestic rankings.
      2. N.A. = not available; n/a = not applicable.
Source: National Bureau of Statistics of China.

Yunnan was one of the earliest provinces in China to be engaged in regional economic cooperation with neighbouring countries. In the early 1990s, after the Cold War, Yunnan joined the Greater Mekong Subregion (GMS) which was proposed and financially supported by the Asian Development Bank (ADB). The GMS is a regional economic cooperation mechanism within the Langcang-Mekong River Basin. It comprises the six countries of Cambodia, China, the Lao PDR, Myanmar, Thailand, and Vietnam. In 1992, with ADB's assistance, the six countries entered into a programme of subregional economic cooperation designed to enhance economic relations among them. Yunnan was the only Chinese province to participate in the GMS at the time, and Guangxi followed suit in 2005 when the second GMS Summit was held in Kunming. There are eleven sectors for cooperation in the GMS, namely, agriculture, energy, the environment, human resource development, investment, telecommunications, tourism, trade, transportation, multisector, and the development of economic corridors. Over the past two decades, the GMS is the important reason for, and the highlight of, Yunnan's opening up and its regional economic cooperation with the GMS countries.

Trade, Investment, and Aid between Yunnan and the GMS

In recent years, Yunnan's trade with ASEAN and the GMS grew quickly. Between 2005 and 2009, Yunnan's total trade with the GMS reached US$93.38 billion and the country maintained a positive trade balance with the other GMS countries all these years (Table 7.2). The main goods Yunnan exported to the GMS were phosphorus chemicals, non-ferrous metal, mechanical and

TABLE 7.2
Yunnan's Imports from and Exports to GMS Countries
in 2005–9 (US$ million)

From	Import and Export	Export	Import	Balance
Myanmar	4,617.39	3,075.19	1,542.20	1,532.99
Vietnam	3,236.93	2,570.65	666.27	1,904.38
Lao PDR	459.62	230.83	228.79	2.04
Thailand	987.76	827.27	160.48	666.79
Cambodia	37.01	36.26	0.75	35.51
Total	9,338	6,740	2,598	4,142

Source: Author's calculations based on data from the website of the National Bureau of Statistics, the Ministry of Commerce, the Department of Commerce of Yunnan Province, and the Nanning Customs Office.

TABLE 7.3
China's Trade with ASEAN and the GMS in 2009 (US$ million)

	Import + Export		Imports		Exports	
	ASEAN	GMS	ASEAN	GMS	ASEAN	GMS
China	213,000	63,847	106,710	30,694	106,300	33,153
Yunnan	3,151	2,411	1,052	695	2,099	1,716
Guangxi	4,950	4,175	1,330	954	3,620	3,221
Guangdong	63,310	2,861	36,480	1,831	26,830	1,030

Source: Author's calculations based on data from the website of the National Bureau of Statistics, the Ministry of Commerce, the Department of Commerce of Yunnan Province, and the Nanning Customs Office.

electrical products, and textiles. Goods imported from the GMS into Yunnan were metallic mineral ore, semi-manufactured non-ferrous metal, rubber, and agricultural products.

In 2009 the trade volume between Yunnan and ASEAN was US$3.15 billion, US$2.1 billion for exports from Yunnan to ASEAN, and US$1.05 billion for imports from ASEAN to Yunnan. Trade with ASEAN accounted for almost 40 per cent of Yunnan's total foreign trade, and trade with the GMS at US$2.41 billion accounted for 30 per cent (Table 7.3). The trade volume of Yunnan with Myanmar, Vietnam, Indonesia, Thailand, Malaysia, the Lao PDR, and Singapore is more than US$100 million each. Trade with Myanmar, the biggest partner, reached US$1.227 billion, accounting for 15.3 per cent of Yunnan's total foreign trade, and the corresponding figures for Vietnam are US$0.79 billion and 9.9 per cent respectively.[1]

Yunnan's outbound investment has been on the rise in recent years. Despite the global financial crisis since 2008, Yunnan's actual outbound investment managed to reach US$683 million from January to November 2009, 1.8 times that of the previous year; this investment sum was the tenth highest nationwide, and the first among the western provinces of China.[2]

From January to November 2009, Yunnan set up forty-four new enterprises in Myanmar, the Lao PDR, and Vietnam, with a committed investment volume of US$376 million, which accounted for 76 per cent of total outbound investment. In the first half of 2009, with a total investment volume of US$1.078 billion, Yunnan set up 166 enterprises in the three countries, which were oriented mainly towards hydroelectric development, mineral exploration, electricity, the processing trade, machinery, and building materials. Of all the investment involved, 70 per cent came from private enterprises.[3]

Energy, which is one of the areas of cooperation between China and the GMS, has raised some international concerns in recent years. China, the world's second-largest oil user, sees the use of oil pipelines as a way of getting over the "Strait of Malacca dilemma". Bringing energy supplies through Myanmar via the pipeline is a handy way to circumvent the Strait of Malacca, as an effort to diversify supply routes.

On 21 December 2009, the China National Petroleum Corp (CNPC) signed an agreement with the Myanmar Energy Ministry to receive exclusive rights to build and operate the China-Myanmar crude oil and gas pipeline. The construction formally began when Premier Wen Jiabao made a visit to Myanmar on 3 June 2010. It was reported that this oil-gas pipeline can deliver 22 million tonnes of oil, approximately 400 thousand barrels per day, and 12 billion cubic metres of gas to China every year[4] (see Figure 7.1).

In 2009, the Opium Substitute Plantation (OSP),[5] a project initiated by Yunnan and approved by Beijing, had almost 200 enterprises from Yunnan developing their OSP projects in northern Myanmar and the Lao PDR. These OSP projects have achieved an accumulative total investment of RMB1 billion.[6] The area of opium plantation had been reduced from 156,465 acres in 2004 to 4,5951 acres in 2007, decreasing by 70 per cent. China's central government has implemented favourable policies for these OSP projects, including a development fund of RMB50 million (approximately US$7.35 million) per year, exit and entry facilitation, import quotas, and taxation deductions and exemptions.[7]

FIGURE 7.1
Map of China's oil pipeline from Bay of Bengal

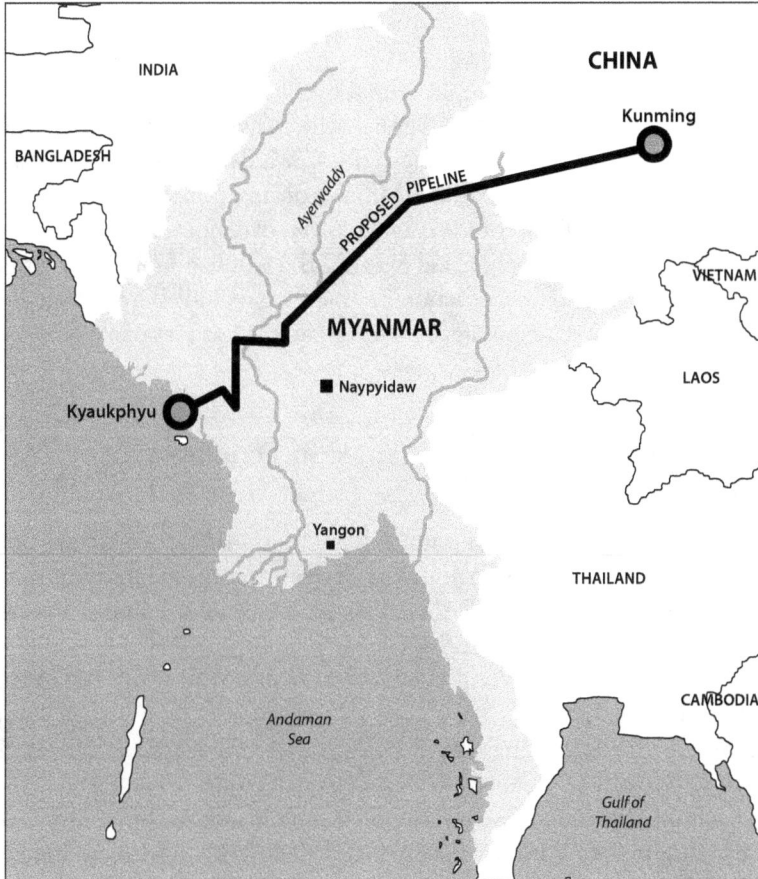

Source: <http://my.reset.jp/~adachihayao/indexE090826.htm>.

Aid is another important form in China-GMS economic relations. It is unclear how much aid was provided because China never publishes its foreign aid in detail. However, it is believed that China's aid to the GMS, especially to Myanmar, the Lao PDR, and Cambodia, has kept growing in recent years, and it has become one of the biggest donors in the GMS. On 12 April 2009, China suggested that a US$10 billion ASEAN-China investment fund be established to provide funding for infrastructure and logistic development projects. In addition, China also proposed the setting up of a US$15 billion

ASEAN-China lending fund to provide soft loans to member countries of ASEAN to develop their trade mechanisms. In addition, China announced that a special aid fund of RMB270 million would be granted to Cambodia, the Lao PDR, and Myanmar in 2009 to help these three countries overcome their difficulties in the financial crisis.[8]

Aid projects are usually implemented by Chinese companies on the basis of tendering and bidding. Some Yunnan enterprises have undertaken some foreign-aid projects, mainly in terms of non-rewarded assistance, interest-free loans, and discount loans for the GMS. According to the annual report for revenues and expenditure of China's Ministry of Commerce in 2010, that year's total volume of foreign aid was RMB13,085 billion.[9] Aid projects undertaken by Yunnan Construction Engineering include the construction of the Cambodian Government office building and the Lao National Gymnasium for the 2009 Southeast Asia Games.

Yunnan is Lagging behind Guangxi in Economic Cooperation with the GMS

The Guangxi Zhuang Autonomous Region, sharing a common border with Vietnam, is similar to Yunnan in having the geographical advantage of connecting China and ASEAN. With both earnestly longing to play an important role in the China-ASEAN Free Trade Area (CAFTA), Yunnan and Guangxi are vying for economic cooperation with ASEAN and the GMS and for a favourable policy from China's central government. Before 2004, Yunnan took the lead in cooperating with the GMS, with more trade and investment volume and regional cooperation mechanisms. Things changed after 2004: Beijing chose Nanning, the capital of Guangxi Zhuang Autonomous Region, as the venue for the CHINA–ASEAN EXPO in 2004; Guangxi joined the GMS in 2005 at the second GMS Summit held in Kunming; in 2008, China's State Council designated Guangxi the major player in developing the Beibuwan Economic Zone. In China, it is believed that regional economic development depends on "who gets the policy, rather than who gets the talents". It is not surprising that many Yunnanese attribute Yunnan's lagging behind Guangxi in the opening up towards Southeast Asia in recent years to its lack of a favourable regional development strategy[10] from Beijing. "Yunnan got little from Beijing", they said.

From 2005 to 2009, Guangxi's trade with the GMS was more active than Yunnan's with the GMS (Table 7.4). In 2009, Guangxi had a much bigger trade volume both with ASEAN and the GMS than Yunnan did (Table 7.3). In 2009, trade with Vietnam accounted for 80 per cent of Guangxi-ASEAN

TABLE 7.4
China's Trade with the GMS between 2005 and 2009 (US$ million)

	Import + Export	Imports	Exports
Yunnan	9,338	2,598	6,740
Guangxi	12,604	6,121	6,483
China	253,788	125,571	12,8217

Source: Author's calculations based on data from the website of National Bureau of Statistics, the Ministry of Commerce, the Department of Commerce of Yunnan Province, and the Nanning Customs Office.

trade, which makes Vietnam Guangxi's biggest trade partner.[11] There are also differences in regional cooperative approaches with Yunnan focusing on the GMS, and Guangxi, a member of the GMS after 2005, shifting much of its attention to the Pan Beibu Gulf (PGB) economic cooperation after 2008.

A NEW OPPORTUNITY FOR YUNNAN–GMS ECONOMIC COOPERATION

China is Pursuing a "Bridgehead Strategy" Southwestward

On 27 July 2009, in a speech at the end of his visit to Yunnan, China's President Hu Jintao said that Yunnan could be an important connector in bridging China with not only South Asia, but also Southeast Asia, especially the GMS countries. President Hu said: "[Yunnan] needs to use advantages of the main land passages connecting China with Southeast and South Asia, strengthen the communication and cooperation with Southeast Asian, South Asian and GMS countries, enhance the quality and level of [the] border area's opening-up to build Yunnan into an important bridgehead for China's Opening-up towards Southwest".[12]

However, it was not the first time that President Hu proposed the concept of "bridgehead". Yunnan was named the third "bridgehead" after Xinjiang (Uygur Autonomous Region) became a bridgehead and hub for China's westward opening up in September 2006, and Heilongjiang a bridgehead and hub in China's opening along the northeastern border areas in June 2006.

What is the "Bridgehead Strategy"?

The concept of "bridgehead" is somehow vague and obscure. It is derived from a military term meaning a fortress that controls the bridge and wharf from the front line of a battle. China prefers to use the term "bridgehead" as a hub in regional economic integration, which has a strong converging and radiating effect on the factors of production. This hub will have a ripple effect that is able to promote regional economic integration. Apparently, China has been using the "bridgehead" concept more frequently in the context of regional economic cooperation.

As for the so-called "bridgehead strategy toward[s] [the] southwest", the word "southwest" does not merely refer to the southwest region of China, but includes an even wider scope reaching out to Southeast Asia and South Asia, and even the Indian Ocean to some extent. It is noteworthy that China has always avoided open discussions on such issues as "China's Indian Ocean Strategy".

Why Was the "Bridgehead Strategy" Proposed?

Before his inspection visit to Yunnan, President Hu pointed out that the main diplomatic emphasis of China, at the time and in the near future, was to realize and deepen the surrounding geostrategy work for consolidating the fundamental positions which emerging neighbouring countries have been enjoying in China's overall diplomatic settings.[13] This may be an indication that China would pay more attention to its diplomacy with its neighbouring countries and raise its strategy from "To be a good neighbour and partner" to "To build strategic backing".

There are also other interpretations for the "bridgehead" strategy. One is that China is searching for new land channels to connect itself with its neighbouring countries. The "bridgeheads" in Xinjiang, Heilongjiang, and Yunnan point in the direction of northeast, northwest, and southwest respectively. This may be due to China's rise from a regional power to a global power. Land channels are really supplementary to the sea channels in China's "Peaceful Development" strategy.

The bridgehead strategy can be seen as a new notion that the Chinese central government is putting forth in the development of the west regions. Although 2010 marked the tenth anniversary of China's massive campaign for developing its western regions, the absolute development gap between the west and the east regions have enlarged rather than narrowed.[14] The bridgehead strategy has been mooted as a new strategy for developing west China.[15] One of the most important measures is to grant the western provinces preferential policies in the name of "national strategy".[16] In China, a regional development plan can be called a "national development strategy" if it is approved by the State Council (sometimes it is published by the National

Development and Reform Commission). This kind of national development strategy means a very favourable policy and financial support. Although no one knows exactly how a "national development strategy" can push forward local economic and social development, all provincial governments earnestly long for it, and regard it as a key factor in their competition with different provinces.

Yunnan's Role in the Bridgehead Strategy

As China seems to be pursuing a bridgehead strategy in promoting its relations with its mainland neighbours, Yunnan has become a key player in China's opening up towards its southwest region. Yunnan constitutes the most convenient land passageway to both Southeast and South Asia from China.[17] The bridgehead strategy is also a response to the security concerns around its surroundings. With four fifths of China's foreign energy supply passing through the Strait of Malacca, China is constantly seeking to diversify its foreign energy supply. Thus, the China-Myanmar oil and gas pipeline, proposed in 2004, officially began construction in June 2010[18] as an attempt to diversify its supply channel via the southwest region. China's oil imports from the Middle East and Africa (accounting for 56 per cent and 30 per cent of its total respectively) pass through the Indian Ocean.[19] It is of vital importance for China to approach the Indian Ocean via Yunnan.

Regional economic cooperation will be the main means for China to implement the bridgehead strategy. Bilateral and multilateral economic cooperation, including the China-ASEAN Free Trade Agreement (CAFTA), the GMS, and BCIM,[20] will reduce the sensitivity of international politics.

From the second half of 2009, Yunnan is taking the bridgehead strategy as its largest development opportunity. Since President Hu's speech in July 2009, Yunnan has done much to prepare for the implementation of the strategy. On the basis of extensive research and opinion soliciting to work out blueprints and development plans, Yunnan hopes that it can be granted some kind of "national strategy" within the framework or in the name of the bridgehead strategy.

It is reported that the Yunnan provincial government has listed eight priority areas[21] within the framework of the bridgehead strategy. They are: (1) infrastructure development, especially in transportation, communications, and as a power grid hub; (2) logistics; (3) energy, especially new and renewable energy to enhance its energy security; (4) tourism; (5) formulating new industrial bases on its competitive advantage; (6) a financial hub with renminbi settlement; (7) a platform to speed up cross-border cooperation and foster regional economic cooperation with India, Myanmar, Bangladesh, and the

GMS; and (8) educational and cultural exchanges and cooperation. If all, or some, of the above listed can be put on the nation's Twelfth Five-Year Plan, it would mean that favourable policies and financial support will be granted to it by Beijing. It is estimated that economic cooperation between Yunnan and the GMS will spell a bright future.

PROBLEMS IN THE YUNNAN–GMS ECONOMIC COOPERATION

There are various limitations and constraints in the current and future economic cooperation between China (Yunnan) and the GMS: different domestic and international development levels, political, economic, and even social factors, hardware and software, etc., all of which are multidimensional and complicated.

Low Economic Development Level

With the low economic development level of both GMS members and Yunnan, limited market capacity, shortage of funds, and insufficient complementarities of industrial cooperation are the biggest challenges to further regional cooperation. All members of the GMS are relatively poor, with a small capacity for consumption and severe shortages of funds. Yunnan, benefiting from China's rapid economic growth, is still one of the laggard provinces in China. Cambodia, Myanmar, and the Lao PDR are each listed among the forty-nine least-developed countries (LDC) in the world. It is unrealistic to expect these problems to be solved in the near future. In addition, in the past years, the ADB, the major source of funding, has reduced its financial support to the GMS. These factors pose the biggest difficulty for GMS economic cooperation.

What Follows the Improvement of Infrastructure?

In the last decade, although there has been substantial improvement in the transport infrastructure connecting Yunnan and the GMS, problems still remain. Transportation continues to be a bottleneck that hamstrings regional cooperation. In the early years of the 1990s, Yunnan prioritized the programme of "building an international pathway towards Southeast and South Asia". The Kunming-Bangkok Highway,[22] completed in April 2008, was regarded as a landmark. Although Yunnan province places high hopes on this highway, its current traffic is much lower than predicted. Cited as the main cause for this is the lack of transportation facilitation between Yunnan, the Lao PDR, and Thailand in the areas of exit and entry procedures, quarantine inspection, road toll collection, and transportation regulations. At present China is still working out several transportation construction programmes in regional cooperation, such as highways or high-speed railways (Kunming-Rangoon, Kunming-Kyaukpyu [Myanmar], Nanning-Bangkok-Singapore, and Mohan [Yunnan]-Vientiane, etc.).[23] As such, China and the GMS countries need to pay more attention to both hardware and software in advance.

Uncertainties of Regional Cooperation Mechanisms

The GMS is currently facing a development bottleneck. Firstly, capital investment in GMS projects, e.g., the Kunming–Bangkok Highway mentioned above is not receiving the returns expected and, as a result, further investment will be obstructed. Secondly, the governments of all the GMS members and the ADB are facing a dilemma. If there is no persistent and large investment, there will be no fundamental improvement in GMS infrastructure building. And without this improvement, there would be no foundation for further economic development and regional cooperation. Thirdly, for GMS cooperation, while infrastructure is still a priority, it is equally important to address the "software" aspects, particularly those that can enhance competitiveness, reduce the negative effects of connectivity, and ensure sustainability of development.[24]

There are also uncertainties in free trade between China (Yunnan) and the GMS under CAFTA. According to CAFTA, since 1 January 2010, import tariffs for more than 93 per cent of goods traded between China and the ASEAN-6[25] have been zero. For the new four members, namely Cambodia, Myanmar, the Lao PDR, and Vietnam, zero tariffs will not happen until 2015. It is estimated that of all the Chinese enterprises that export to ASEAN, only 1 per cent of the enterprises outside Yunnan and 5.5 per cent inside Yunnan are now enjoying the zero-tariff benefit. The main reason is that the enterprises know little about zero tariff of CAFTA and the application procedures are rather complicated.[26] Prior to 2010, trading between China and ASEAN took advantage of Yunnan as a land pathway, sometimes enjoying the benefit of lower import and export tariffs in the name of border trade. Yunnan is now worried that its transition role in China-ASEAN trade is likely to become less important because goods that go directly to ASEAN-6 will enjoy zero tariff.

Domestic Divergences

Domestic divergences between different levels and departments have a negative impact on Yunnan-GMS economic cooperation. Firstly, although the Central government has the final say over its good "neighbourhood" policy with the GMS countries and over the stabilization of the border area, local governments have their own stakes over economic development. Yunnan pays much attention to exploiting the GMS markets and resources to meet its demands. But Beijing, prioritizing harmonious relations with the GMS countries, does not want to see any investment from China doing harm to these relations. Secondly, governmental departments urge investors to pay attention to environmental and social issues with which investors usually do not concern themselves. It is hard for the Chinese Government to take effective actions against bad operating activities, such as deforestation and mining pollution. Thirdly, there is more competition than collaboration between the two governments of Yunnan and Guangxi in the economic cooperation with the GMS and in seeking favourable policies from the central government. The most important mechanism for Yunnan is the GMS, whereas for Guangxi it is the Pan Beibu Gulf Economic Cooperation (PGB), which received the go-ahead from Beijing in February 2008. It creates some confusion among the GMS countries and mobilizes limited resources for regional cooperation.

Environmental and Social Problems

There have been negative environmental impacts due to Chinese investment in the GMS. There are three main reasons for these: (1) Chinese investments focus on mining and hydropower development, which easily harm the environment; (2) Some Chinese investors, many being small or medium scale private enterprises, fail to pay enough attention to environmental protection as required by local environmental laws and regulations; (3) There is a lack of laws and regulations regarding environmental protection in the host countries and, when there are any, the enforcement is weak due to corruption, such as in the case of Myanmar and the Lao PDR.

In recent years, some international non-governmental organizations have been paying close attention to these issues, and attribute much of the environmental degradation to the Chinese investments, especially in mining and dam-building projects on the upper reaches of the Mekong River in Yunnan. In March 2010, four GMS countries in the lower reaches of the river, namely Cambodia, the Lao PDR, Thailand, and Vietnam, lodged a formal complaint with China for building too many dams in the upper stream of the Mekong River. China refused to accept this complaint and ascribed the drought to extreme dry weather in Southwest China. Song Tao, Chinese Vice-Foreign Minister, argued that "the runoff volume of Lancang River accounts for only 13.5 percent of that of the Mekong River".

It is unfair to put all the blame on Chinese investments and neglect their contribution to local economic development. Any investment in mining, hydropower development, and in almost any other industries, regardless of its source, will lead to some extent of environmental impact. There is a strange phenomenon: NGOs are inclined to blame and distrust China, while China dislikes and rejects NGOs. If this problem cannot be solved, it will be hard to balance economic development and environmental protection.

There are also some social problems linked to these Chinese investments in the GMS. Some investors and Chinese workers do not understand local values and cultures, and are not paying enough attention to their corporate social responsibility (CSR). Bribery is rampant and some Chinese investors are used to getting things done by illegal means and taking advantage of legal loopholes. Chinese investors tend to prefer their own Chinese workers rather than the locals.

Factors of International Politics

China's bridgehead strategy also arouses concerns and worries from the Southeast Asian countries, especially the GMS ones, South Asian countries, and Western powers and international organizations. As such, China avoids using the term, bridgehead strategy, in the international media and has not, at least till now, explained the strategy to its neighbouring countries and other parties. China also avoids using the term when seeking transnational cooperation with its neighbouring countries. It is obvious that "bridgehead" cannot be achieved and the Yunnan–GMS economic cooperation will not have a bright future without understanding and support from neighbouring countries.

International political factors also affect the Yunnan-GMS economic cooperation. On the one hand, some GMS countries still have a mixed and uneasy feeling over China's rising influence. On the other hand, India is always vigilant about China's movement towards the Indian Ocean. India is not likely to accept China's entry into BIMSTEC, the Bay of Bengal Initiative for Multi-Sectoral Technical and Economic Cooperation. It will not be surprising to see a trans-regional economic cooperation initiative from China (Yunnan) in future with the aim to connect Southeast Asia and South Asia.

AN OUTLOOK FOR YUNNAN–GMS
ECONOMIC COOPERATION

Economic cooperation is the main engine for China to open up its southwest regions. Although there are geopolitical and geo-economical tensions between Yunnan and the GMS countries with the implementation of China's bridgehead strategy, the prospects for economic cooperation remain positive.

If Yunnan is granted a "national" development plan by the central government, a series of favourable polices and financial support initiatives are expected to come along, which will lead to a new wave of intensive investment in Yunnan. The bridgehead strategy will be the biggest opportunity for Yunnan's development in forthcoming years.

There are four possible channels through which Yunnan can cooperate with the GMS. Firstly, under the framework of CAFTA, tariffs can be lowered. Non-tariff barriers can be eliminated and trade can be facilitated with the gradual use of the renminbi as the settlement currency in trade with ASEAN. Secondly, cooperation in investment with the GMS should be strengthened. The China-ASEAN Investment Agreement was signed in the middle of 2009 and bilateral investment agreements with the GMS countries are now on China's agenda. Thirdly, regional economic cooperation could be unfolded under the GMS framework. Besides infrastructure building, more attention should be paid to the environment and mechanism building. Fourthly, China should increase its aid to the GMS and the aid should be dispersed in more flexible ways.

There are still some obstacles to be overcome in Yunnan-GMS economic cooperation. If they are not dealt with properly, they could hinder the development of further regional cooperation, which will have a negative impact on China's new diplomatic policy for neighbouring countries. China has made arrangements to handle the problems arising from such economic cooperation, by strengthening its regulations and guidelines for Chinese GMS investors to follow in exercising environmental protection and corporate social responsibilities. It is reported that China's Ministry of Environmental Protection is drafting guidelines for Chinese investment overseas.[27] China is also paying close attention to its soft power and image to avoid its image being tarnished. Last, but not the least, China is adopting a more open and transparent attitude towards regional environmental cooperation.

Notes

1. Statistics are taken from the National Bureau of Statistics, the Ministry of Commerce, Department of Commerce of Yunnan Province, and the Nanning Customs Office.

2. Xinhua Net, 7 January 2010 <http://www.yn.xinhuanet.com/newscenter/2010-01/07/content_18706638.htm>.

3. Xinhua Net?6 January 2010 <http://www.yn.xinhuanet.com/topic/2010-01/06/content_18699612.htm>.

4. 6 May 2010 <http://news.sina.com.cn/c/2010-06-05/080617613917s.shtml>.

5. Opium Substitute Plantation (OSP) is a project initiated by Yunnan to plant economic crops, such as rubber trees, sugarcane, paddy, corn, cassava, and tropical fruit in fields formerly used to plant opium poppies. The plantation is located in the area of the notorious "Golden Triangle", and the gains are mostly exported to China. There are three objectives for OSP. Firstly, to reduce, if not eliminate the planting of opium poppy. Secondly, to provide local people with work opportunities and income, and thirdly, to supply agricultural products for the Chinese domestic market.

6. 17 July 2009 <http://www.yunnan.cn/html/2009-07/17/content_683327.htm>.

7. 24 September 2008 <http://www.dh.gov.cn/ycic/5766859322847920128/20080924/207882.html>.

8. 17 April 2009 <http://business.sohu.com/20090414/n263370487.shtml>.

9. 6 April 2010 <http://file.mofcom.gov.cn/moffile/search/pages/detail.jsp?seqno=15555>.

10. In China, this kind of regional development plan can be called a "national development strategy" if it is approved by the State Council (sometimes it is published by the National Development and Reform Commission). This kind of national development strategy means very favourable policy and financial support.

11. 18 January 2010 <http://www.asean35.com/news/12838.html>.

12. Hu Jintao: "A Speech at the end of Inspection Visit to Yunnan" <http://www.dehong.gov.cn/goverment/voice/2009/0821/goverment-26143.html>.

13. *People's Daily*, 21 July 2009 <http://politics.people.com.cn/GB/1024/9687405.html>.

14. *China Daily*, 27 March 2010 <http://www.chinadaily.com.cn/micro-reading/china/2010-03-27/84609.html>.

15. 19 January 2010 <http://www.huaxia.com/tslj/rdqy/xb/2010/01/1722944.html>.

16. In China, many people believe that local economic development depends on "policy firstly, and cadre secondly". It is not surprising that many Yunnanese ascribe Yunnan's lagging behind Guangxi in opening up towards Southeast Asia in recent years to her not being granted such a national development strategy from Beijing. Guangxi was given two important shows of support from Beijing recently: one, Beijing decided that the China–ASEAN Expo be located in Nanning, the capital of Guangxi Zhuang Autonomous Region in 2004, and two, the State Council approved the Development Plan of Beibuwan Economic Zone in Guangxi in 2008. But Yunnan got nothing, they said.

17. The distance from Kunming, the principal capital of Yunnan, via Lashio, a city in north Myanmar, to the coast of the Indian Ocean in west Myanmar, is only

about 2,000 km, which is more than 3,000 km shorter than from Kunming via the Malacca Strait to the coast of the Indian Ocean.

18. "China-Myanmar Oil and Gas Pipeline Project Underway", *People's Daily Online*, 7 June 2010 <http://english.people.com.cn/90001/90778/90861/7015958. html>.

19. WANG Dehua? "On China's Strategy of 'Harmonious Indian Ocean'", *Journal of Social Sciences* 12 (2008): 30–39.

20. BCIM is a transregional and track II cooperation mechanism among Bangladesh, China, India, and Myanmar.

21. 9 June 2010 <http://yn.wenweipo.com/whshidian/ShowArticle.asp?ArticleID =4679>.

22. The Kunming-Bangkok Highway, completed in April 2008, is an 1,807-km highway. It shortens the travel time from forty-eight hours to twenty hours from Kunming, Yunnan, via the Lao PDR, to Bangkok, Thailand.

23. In a speech, Professor Wang Meng-shu from the Beijing-Jiaotong University, revealed that China has planned the domestic construction of high-speed railways so that by 2025 China will be connected by rail with seventeen countries, which includes the Southeast Asian route, starting from Kunming, which will go through Vietnam, Cambodia, Thailand (or from Kunming through Myanmar to Thailand), Malaysia, and Singapore. See <http://www.chinawuliu.com.cn/cflp/newss/content/201003/652_116974.html>.

24. Arjun Goswami, "Greater Mekong Subregion (GMS) 2020: Issues, Prospects and Challenges" <http://www.afdc.org.cn/afdc/UploadFile/2009111336517029. pdf>.

25. The ASEAN-6 members are Brunei, Indonesia, Myanmar, the Philippines, Singapore, and Thailand.

26. 16 March 2010 <http://asean.yunnan.cn/html/2010-03/16/content_1106151. htm>.

27. 20 May 2009 <http://fec.mofcom.gov.cn/zlyj/dywz/260080.shtml>.

8

TRADE AND INVESTMENT IN THE GREATER MEKONG SUBREGION
Remaining Challenges and the Unfinished Policy Agenda*

Jayant Menon and
Anna Cassandra Melendez

The Greater Mekong Subregion (GMS) is often described as one of the most successful stories of economic transition and integration among developing countries.[1] For much of the 1970s and early 1980s, while the rest of Asia was busy growing and integrating with the global economy, the GMS remained extremely poor and isolated — the outcome of years of conflict and central planning in Cambodia, the Lao People's Democratic Republic (Lao PDR), Myanmar, and Vietnam (CLMV). Beginning in the mid-1980s, however, these countries began a gradual process of reform and liberalization.

The CLMV countries' transition towards a market-based system has allowed the GMS to reinvent itself as one of the most dynamic subregions in the world. In the last twenty years, the GMS has grown at a faster pace than the whole of developing East Asia and the Pacific, with much of this growth coming from the CLMV countries. While Thailand and the rest of Asia reeled from the impact of the 1997/98 Asian financial crisis, the CLMV countries continued to post positive growth, given their limited connection to global financial markets at the time (Figure 8.1). While these countries were not as immune to the more recent global financial crisis (GFC), with sharp drops in growth that have begun to reverse only recently, this underlies a decade of growing openness and integration with the global economy. The sustained economic growth leading up to the GFC has been accompanied by a gradual shift away from agriculture, which has traditionally accounted for the biggest share of value added in the CLMV countries. Across the subregion, industry, manufacturing, and services now account for a bigger share of value added (Table 8.1).

This economic progress has translated into marked improvements in human development outcomes across the subregion (Table 8.2). GDP per capita in constant 2000 U.S. dollars has more than doubled in Cambodia, Lao PDR, and Vietnam since the early 1990s. Infant mortality rates have declined rapidly in the last fifteen years, while literacy rates have shown gradual improvements since the beginning of the decade. Perhaps more importantly, poverty rates (that is, the poverty headcount ratio at $1.25 a day, PPP) have fallen dramatically across the subregion. In Cambodia and Thailand, poverty rates have declined by roughly half in just a little over a decade; meanwhile, in Vietnam, poverty rates fell from 63.7 per cent of the population in 1993, to 21.5 per cent of the population in 2006.

Strong rates of economic growth have been fuelled in part by increased trade and investment in the subregion. Since the beginning of the 1990s, increased trade has played a huge part in spurring growth in the GMS, with exports playing a critical role in the subregion's recovery after the 1997/98 crisis. Just as trade has increased throughout the region, foreign direct investment (FDI) inflows have also risen dramatically over the last two decades.

These positive developments notwithstanding, a number of critical challenges continue to limit the subregion's potential to reap gains from trade and investment. This chapter explores these challenges and identifies key elements of the unfinished policy agenda, which need to be addressed going forward.

The chapter is organized in five sections. Following the introduction, the next section looks at the evolution of trade and investment policy and economic cooperation in the GMS countries, highlighting policy changes that have helped spur trade and investment growth. The third section brings together available data to examine the changing structure of trade and investment in the GMS. The following section examines remaining challenges and identifies key elements of the unfinished policy agenda. A final section concludes.

FIGURE 8.1
GDP Growth in GMS Countries, 1990–2009

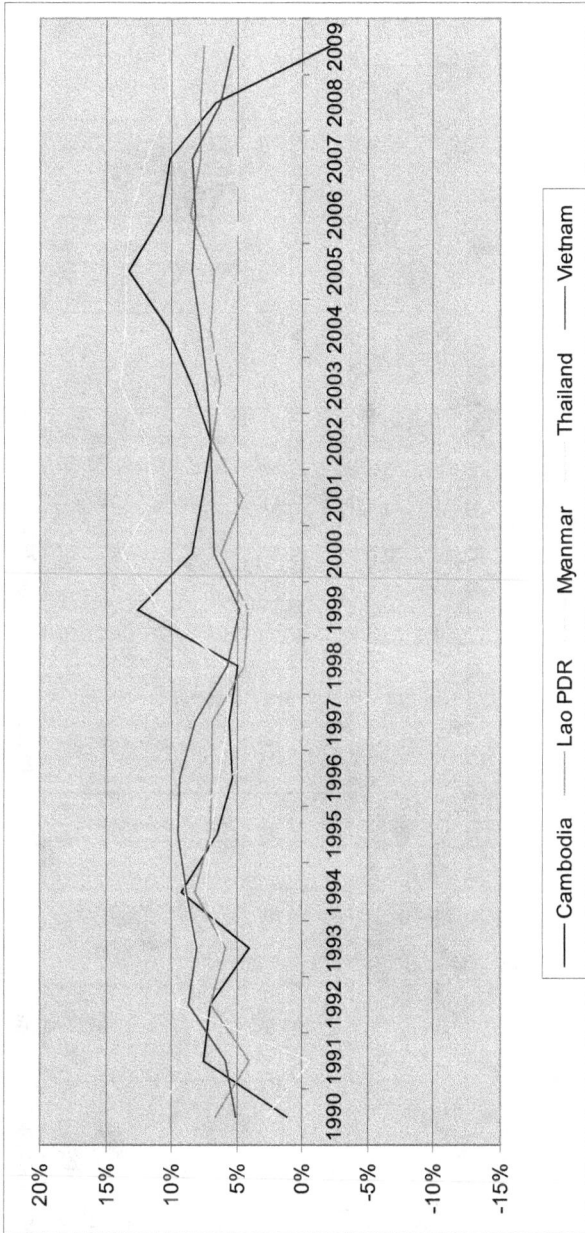

Cambodia — Lao PDR — Myanmar — Thailand — Vietnam

Source: Asian Development Bank Statistical Database System (SDBS).

TABLE 8.1
Economic Growth and Restructuring in the GMS

Country/Region	Real GDP growth (%) (in constant 2000 US$)				Value Added as a % of GDP							
					Agriculture		Industry		Manufacturing		Services	
	1990 1994	1995 1999	2000 2004	2005 2008	1995	2008	1995	2008	1995	2008	1995	2008
Cambodia	—	6.9	8.5	9.9	49.6	34.6	14.8	23.9	9.5	16.4	35.6	41.5
Lao PDR	6.1	6.4	6.0	7.7	55.7	34.7	19.2	28.2	14.3	9.3	25.1	37.1
Myanmar	5.07	7.2	12.9	13.2	60.0	48.3	9.9	16.2	6.9	11.6	30.1	35.4
Thailand	9.01	1.5	5.1	4.3	9.5	11.6	40.7	44.2	29.9	34.9	49.7	44.2
Vietnam	7.32	7.5	7.2	7.8	27.2	22.1	28.8	39.7	15.0	21.1	44.1	38.2
East Asia & Pacific	9.45	3.6	4.1	5.2	19.3	12.2	44.3	47.0	30.9	32.8	36.5	40.9

Source: World Bank World Trade Indicators 2009/10 and World Development Indicators 2010.

TABLE 8.2

Socioeconomic and Poverty Indicators in the GMS Region, 1990–2008

Country/Region	GDP per capita (constant 2000 US$)		Infant mortality rate (per 1,000 live births)		Literacy rate, adult total (% of people aged 15 and above)		Poverty headcount ratio at $1.25 a day (PPP) (% of population)	
	1990	2008	1995	2008				
Cambodia	206[1]	511	86.3	69.3	67.3 (1998)	77.0 (2008)	48.6 (1994)	25.8 (2007)
Lao PDR	227	475	81.5	47.5	60.3 (1995)	72.7 (2005)	55.7 (1992)	44.0 (2002)
Myanmar	—	—	80.6	70.6	89.9 (2000)	91.9 (2008)	—	—
Thailand	1,400	2,640	21.1	12.5	92.7 (2000)	93.5 (2005)	5.5 (1992)	2.0 (2004)
Vietnam	227	647	32.9	11.8	90.3 (1999)	92.5 (2008)	63.7 (1993)	21.5 (2006)
Developing East Asia and the Pacific	481	1,760	38.9	23.1	90.6 (2000)	93.1 (2008)	50.8 (1993)	16.8 (2005)

Notes: 1. Cambodia data for 1993
2. For Lao PDR, the poverty headcount ratio based on $1 a day (unadjusted) declined from 46.3 per cent in 1992 to 33.5 per cent in 2002 to 27.6 per cent by 2007.
Source: World Bank World Trade Indicators Online, 2009/10, World Bank Development Indicators 2010.

EVOLUTION OF TRADE AND INVESTMENT POLICY AND ECONOMIC COOPERATION IN GMS COUNTRIES

With the exception of Thailand, the other GMS countries had been closed to external markets up until the late 1980s. Trade and investment reforms were an integral part of the CLMV's efforts to move away from central planning towards a market-based economy. The trade and investment regimes of the three countries have gone through several changes as an integral part of the ongoing policy of transition towards market-oriented economies. The GMS has also been quick to seize opportunities for economic cooperation and has been actively engaged in negotiations of preferential trade agreements.

Trade and Investment Policy: Early Unilateral Reforms

The opening up of Cambodia, the Lao PDR, and Vietnam to trade and investment occurred almost concurrently in the late 1980s. Cambodia's government was the first to embark on a market-oriented reform process in 1985. The Cambodian Government abolished the state monopoly for foreign trade in 1987 and allowed the private sector to engage in foreign trade in 1989 (ADB 2006). The government also promulgated a liberal foreign investment code in July 1989 and a National Investment Council was set up in 1991 with the task of reviewing all foreign investment applications.

The outcome of these reforms was somewhat lacklustre, however, and perhaps unsurprising, given the continuing warfare within the country. As an outcome of the UN-led peace process, elections were held in July 1993 and a multi-party democratic government was established in September 1993. This helped accelerate the process of economic reform in Cambodia. The foreign investment regime in Cambodia underwent an overhaul in 2003. The revised Law on Investment came into force on 27 September 2005 and represented a major attempt to equalize incentives for foreign and local investors, achieve greater transparency in incentives provided, and minimize distortions and delays arising from policymaker discretion. Meanwhile, quantitative restrictions on trade were abolished and import tariffs were progressively streamlined.

In the Lao PDR, the process of transition to a market-oriented economy began in 1986 with the implementation of the New Economic Mechanism, a major programme of economic reforms. Tariffs were lowered soon after the reforms were adopted and a major reduction was implemented in 1995 when a complex multiple tariff rate system with a 150 per cent maximum rate was replaced by a simpler six-band structure (ADB 2006). A Foreign Investment Code was passed in July 1988 and the Foreign Investment Management Committee (FIMC) was set up under the direct purview of the Prime Minister to act as the apex agency that approves, monitors, and promotes FDI. At the initial stage, the prime objective of the FDI policy in the Lao PDR was to engage foreign investor participation in restructuring state-owned enterprises (SOEs). The Investment Code was supplanted by the Law on Promotion and Management of Foreign Investment in July 1994, which was again substantially revised in October 2004.

Foreign investment is permitted in all business sectors, with 100 per cent ownership allowed in most sectors, except in mining and energy projects, in which the government contributes to share capital or retains the right to buy a pre-agreed share of equity. In joint ventures, foreign equity participation is required to be at least 30 per cent of total invested capital.

The opening of the economy to FDI was part of Vietnam's "renovation" (*doi moi*) reforms initiated in 1986. Procedures for the approval of investment projects were streamlined and fresh investment incentives were granted under a new Law on Foreign Investment enacted in 1996.

Meanwhile, in the area of trade reform, Vietnam enacted the Law on Import and Export Duties in 1988 and replaced the original import tariff schedule in 1992 with a detailed, consolidated schedule based on the Harmonized System of tariff nomenclature. The tariff structure was progressively fine-tuned and the maximum tariff rate was reduced from 200 per cent in 1997 to 113 per cent in 2004. Vietnam also abolished quantitative restrictions and converted to tariff rate quotas for some products (ADB 2006).

Membership in Economic Cooperation and Trade Agreements

The adoption of these unilateral policy reforms set the stage for increased trade and investment in the GMS. However, recognition of the fact that these unilateral efforts could only achieve so much provided an important impetus for the GMS countries to engage in economic cooperation agreements. These agreements have increasingly been used as a tool for overcoming constraints in infrastructure development and trade facilitation, as well as providing leverage for pursuing further economic reforms.

The GMS Programme

The earliest of these agreements was the GMS Economic Programme initiated by the Asian Development Bank (ADB) in 1992. The original members of the GMS programme were Cambodia, the Lao PDR, Myanmar, Thailand, Vietnam, and Yunnan Province of the People's Republic of China (PRC). In 2004 Guangxi Zhuang Autonomous Region of the PRC also joined the GMS.

The GMS programme is a classic case of *market* as opposed to *institutional* integration. While institutional integration is characterized by legal agreements and institutional arrangements that promote preferential trade among members of the agreement, market integration relies on non-official institutions that provide public and quasi-public goods that reduce transaction costs associated with the international movement of goods, services, and other production factors.

As a programme of market-based integration, the GMS agenda has concentrated on the provision of physical infrastructure that has public good characteristics, e.g., cross-border infrastructure. Indeed, essential infrastructure of all types remains underdeveloped in most of the GMS economies, and the GMS programme has focused on overcoming this constraint. Initiatives such as the east-west, north-south, and southern economic corridors are creating a network of roads that connect the region, reducing the cost of transporting goods and people from one corner of the region to the other. Options for interconnections for power transmission and the development of fibre optic transmission links — both covered through the GMS flagship programmes on power and telecommunications — also fall within the geographic scope of these corridors.

Apart from "hardware" in the form of physical infrastructure, the GMS programme has also tried to address complementary "software" issues. A key initiative towards this end is the Cross-Border Transport Agreement, a comprehensive multilateral instrument that supports a range of measures to facilitate trade and investment that are designed to promote integration. These include:

(i)   one-stop customs inspection;
(ii) cross-border movement of persons (e.g., visas for persons engaged in transport operations);
(iii) transit traffic regimes, including exemptions from physical customs inspection, bond deposit, escort, and phytosanitary and veterinary inspection;
(iv) eligibility requirements for road vehicle cross-border traffic;
(v)   exchange of commercial traffic rights; and
(vi) infrastructure, including road and bridge design standards, road signs, and signals (ADB 2009*a*).

Emerging transport networks and economic corridors are transforming the economic geography of the region. Enhanced connectivity, along with cooperation in transport and trade facilitation, has been associated with an elevenfold increase in intraregional trade since the programme's inception in 1992. Priority infrastructure projects worth around US$10 billion have either been completed or are being implemented. As connectivity between the GMS countries improves, their linkage with the region as a whole is also enhanced. For example, when the economic corridors are completed, it should be technically feasible for goods to be transported by land from Singapore through Malaysia to anywhere in the subregion.

While the availability of cheap and trainable labour in the GMS has been a key factor in promoting trade and FDI, it is not the only determining factor. The availability of a wider array of complementary inputs, including better trade facilitation and high-quality infrastructure and logistics, are critical in making the trade and investment environment efficient by world standards.

Despite the achievements of the GMS programme in this area, a lot more remains to be done. Tables 8.3 and 8.4 reveal considerable variations in trade facilitation and logistical performance across the GMS countries, with Thailand and Vietnam performing better than the CLM countries.

Membership in ASEAN, WTO, and PTAs

Soon after the launch of the GMS programme, the CLMV countries sought membership in the Association of Southeast Asian Nations (ASEAN) and the World Trade Organization (WTO).[2] Vietnam became a member of ASEAN in 1995, the Lao PDR and Myanmar joined in 1997, and Cambodia joined

TABLE 8.3

Export and Import Costs and Documentary Requirements, 2005–8

Indicator	Country	2005	2006	2007	2008
Cost to export	Cambodia	736	722	722	732
(US$ per container)	Lao PDR	1,420	1,420	1,750	1,860
	Myanmar	—	—	—	—
	Thailand	848	848	615	625
	Vietnam	669	669	669	734
Cost to import	Cambodia	816	852	852	872
(US$ per container)	Lao PDR	1,690	1,690	1,930	2,040
	Myanmar	—	—	—	—
	Thailand	1,042	1,042	786	795
	Vietnam	881	881	881	901
Documents to export	Cambodia	8	11	11	11
(number)	Lao PDR	11	11	9	9
	Myanmar	—	—	—	—
	Thailand	9	9	7	4
	Vietnam	6	6	6	6
Documents to import	Cambodia	12	11	11	11
(number)	Lao PDR	15	15	10	10
	Myanmar	—	—	—	—
	Thailand	12	12	9	3
	Vietnam	8	8	8	8

Source: World Bank World Development Indicators 2009/10.

TABLE 8.4
Logistical Performance Index of GMS Countries, 2006

Indicator	Country	Rating
Logistics performance index: Ability to track and trace consignments (1=low to 5=high)	Cambodia	2.53
	Lao PDR	1.89
	Myanmar	1.57
	Thailand	3.25
	Vietnam	2.9
Logistics performance index: Competence and quality of logistics services (1=low to 5=high)	Cambodia	2.47
	Lao PDR	2.29
	Myanmar	2
	Thailand	3.31
	Vietnam	2.8
Logistics performance index: Ease of arranging competitively priced shipments (1=low to 5=high)	Cambodia	2.47
	Lao PDR	2.4
	Myanmar	1.73
	Thailand	3.24
	Vietnam	3
Logistics performance index: Efficiency of customs clearance process (1=low to 5=high)	Cambodia	2.19
	Lao PDR	2.08
	Myanmar	2.07
	Thailand	3.03
	Vietnam	2.89
Logistics performance index: Frequency with which shipments reach consignee within scheduled or expected time (1=low to 5=high)	Cambodia	3.05
	Lao PDR	2.83
	Myanmar	2.08
	Thailand	3.91
	Vietnam	3.22
Logistics performance index: Overall (1=low to 5=high)	Cambodia	2.5
	Lao PDR	2.25
	Myanmar	1.86
	Thailand	3.31
	Vietnam	2.89
Logistics performance index: Quality of trade and transport-related infrastructure (1=low to 5=high)	Cambodia	2.3
	Lao PDR	2
	Myanmar	1.69
	Thailand	3.16
	Vietnam	2.5

Source: World Bank World Trade Indicators 2009/10.

in 1999. Myanmar, Cambodia, and Vietnam became members of the WTO in 1995, 2004, and 2007 respectively, and the Lao PDR is at an advanced stage in negotiations for WTO accession.

As members of ASEAN, the GMS countries are also parties to the ASEAN Free Trade Agreement (AFTA). Unlike the GMS programme, AFTA is designed to pursue institutional as opposed to market integration. In essence, AFTA is a preferential trading arrangement (PTA) based on a legal agreement that prescribes tariff reductions on a purely discriminatory basis. The centrepiece of the AFTA proposal is the common effective preferential tariff (CEPT). It differs from the PTA in that its approach is essentially by sectors, making it more comprehensive and less cumbersome than the item-by-item approach of the PTA. The objective of the CEPT scheme is to lay the foundation for the creation of a single ASEAN market. Under the revised AFTA plan, tariffs of products in the CEPT Inclusion List[3] were to be reduced to 20 per cent within a time frame of five to eight years (beginning in January 1993) before they were cut to 0–5 per cent. This target has already been virtually realized for the six original members of ASEAN, including Thailand.

The CLMV countries are also far along in the implementation of their CEPT commitments, with almost 80 per cent of their products having been moved into their respective CEPT Inclusion Lists. Of these items, about 66 per cent already have tariffs within the 0–5 per cent tariff band (ASEAN 2010). The CLMV countries were granted extensions on phasing in sensitive products. All quantitative restrictions on sensitive products must be eliminated by 1 January 2013 in Vietnam, 1 January 2015 in Lao PDR and Myanmar, and 1 January 2017 in Cambodia (ASEAN 1999).

In addition to the AFTA, the GMS countries are also increasingly becoming parties to bilateral trade agreements, which have risen as multilateral trade talks at the WTO have stalled. Table 8.5 provides a summary of each GMS country's PTAs as of July 2010. As expected, Thailand has been the most active in pursuing PTAs among the GMS countries, with twenty-four in total, eleven of which are currently in effect. Vietnam follows with thirteen PTAs, seven of which are in effect. Thailand's PTAs involve a more diverse mix of trading partners, while the CMLV countries' PTAs mainly involve countries within the Asia-Pacific region (Table 8.6; see Annex A for a full list of PTAs). Table 8.6 presents a summary of the major PTAs to which the GMS countries are signatories, primarily as members of ASEAN.

TABLE 8.5
PTAs by GMS Country, as of July 2010

	Concluded	Under Negotiation	Proposed	Total	Of which inside Asia and the Pacific only
Cambodia	6	1	2	9	8
Lao PDR	8	1	2	11	10
Myanmar	6	2	2	10	9
Thailand	11	7	6	24	17
Vietnam	7	3	3	13	11

Source: ADB Asian Regional Integration Center (ARIC) Free Trade Agreement Database for Asia.

CHANGING PATTERNS OF TRADE AND INVESTMENT IN THE GMS

Overall Trends in Trade and Changing Structure of Exports

Although trade growth contracted in real terms in 2008 and 2009 as a result of the GFC, in general, unilateral policy reforms and greater economic cooperation have led to positive trade growth in the GMS. This is true particularly for Cambodia and Vietnam, where real trade growth has been higher than the average growth of trade for developing East Asia and the Pacific. The Lao PDR's trade contracted in real terms in 2000–2002, but rebounded in 2004 (Figure 8.2). With the exception of Myanmar, trade openness has increased throughout the region, with trade as a percentage of GDP above 100 per cent in Cambodia, Thailand, and Vietnam (Figure 8.3).

The direction of trade over the past two decades suggests a marked expansion in GMS countries' trade not only with the world, but more particularly among themselves (Figure 8.4). Cambodia's direction of trade would be the only exception to this general trend. In the 1990s, Cambodia's trade with the subregion accounted for about a third of its total trade, on account of log and timber exports. However, this share has since declined, largely as a result of a ban on log exports and the growing importance of the United States and the European Union as export destinations. The PRC is also fast emerging as a major source of imports.

The larger GMS countries, Thailand and Vietnam, have shown modest increases in subregional trade over the last two decades, but, as would be expected, these countries trade predominantly with the rest of the world and

TABLE 8.6
Summary of Major PTAs to which GMS Countries are Signatories

	ASEAN FTA	ASEAN-PRC FTA	ASEAN-Korea FTA	ASEAN-Japan EPA	ASEAN-INDIA FTA	ASEAN-CER (Australia and New Zealand)
Date in Effect	1 January 1993	1 July 2005	1 June 2007	1 December 2008	1 January 2010	1 January 2010
Date Signed	28 January 1992	21 November 2004	24 August 2006	14 April 2008	13 August 2009	27 February 2009
Time to negotiate (start of formal negotiations to FTA signing)	2–3 years (Oct 1990–Jan 1993)	2–3 years (Nov 2002–Nov 2004)	1–2 years (Feb 2005–Aug 2006)	4–5 years (Oct 2003–Apr 2008)	5–6 years (Oct 2003–Aug 2009)	4 years (Feb 2005–Feb 2009)
Trade in Goods Liberalization	**Inclusion list:** 99% of tariff lines at 0–5% (of which 60% are duty-free) for ASEAN-6 by 2010; 88% for CLMV by 2015. **Sensitive track:** 0.2% of tariff lines remaining among ASEAN-6 (Philippines and Indonesia).	**Normal track:** Tariff elimination on 90% of products for ASEAN-6 and PRC by 2010 (flexibility up to CLMV 2012); for CLMV by 2015 (flexibility up to 2018). **Sensitive track:** Tariff reduced to 0–5% by 2018 for ASEAN-6 and PRC; 2020 for CMLV. **Highly sensitive track:** Tariff rate reduced to below	**Normal track:** Tariff elimination on 95% of products by 2010 (flexibility for 5% of tariff lines for the Philippines and Indonesia up to 2012). **Sensitive track:** maximum of 10% of tariff lines where tariff reduced to 0–5% by 2016.	**Normal track:** tariff elimination within 10 years upon entry into force. **Sensitive track:** tariff reduction to 0–5% in 10 years.	**Normal Track:** coverage: 80% of tariff lines (NT1/NT2) by 2013/2016 for ASEAN-5 and India; 2018/2019 for the Philippines and India; 2018/2021 for CMLV. **Sensitive Track:** 10% of tariff lines. At least 50 tariff lines at MFN 5% will be at a standstill; reduction to 4.5% from entry	**Normal track:** Tariff elimination on 90% of products by 2013 for Australia, New Zealand, and ASEAN-6 (with flexibility for Indonesia and Thailand). **SL1:** 6% of tariff lines by 2020. **SL2:** 3% of tariff lines with 20% margin of preference by 2020. **Longer tariff elimination:**

continued on next page

TABLE 8.6 — cont'd

	ASEAN FTA	ASEAN-PRC FTA	ASEAN-Korea FTA	ASEAN-Japan EPA	ASEAN-INDIA FTA	ASEAN-CER (Australia and New Zealand)
		50% by 2015 for ASEAN-6 and PRC and 2018 for CMLV.			to 4% by 2016 for ASEAN-6 and India (special arrangements for Indonesia and Thailand; and 2019 for the Philippines). India identified crude and refined palm oil, coffee, black tea and pepper as Highly Sensitive.	Cambodia, Lao PDR, Myanmar, and Vietnam (2020–24).
Notes	ASEAN Economic Community Blueprint in November 2007 sets out concrete steps for services by 2015. ASEAN has concluded 7 (seven) Mutual Recognition Agreements (MRAs) in **Services**. The Comprehensive **Investment** Agreement was signed on 26 February 2009.	**Services** agreement came into force in July 2007 (first package of services liberalization). Agreement in trade in services in effect as of July 2007 and on investment signed in August 2009.	**Services** agreement signed in November 2007. **Investment** agreement signed 2 June 2009. Thailand signed the AKFTA on 27 February 2009.	Bilateral EPAs and BITs commitments will apply. As of Feb 2009, 7 countries (Japan, Singapore, Malaysia, Brunei, Vietnam, Lao PDR, and Myanmar) have implemented the AJCEP. To negotiate liberalization on services and investments.	Negotiations in Trade in Services and Investment are under way and are targeted to be concluded by August 2010. The AIFTA Trade In Goods (TIG) Agreement was signed on the 13 August 2009. As of 1 January 2010, India, Singapore, & Malaysia have implemented the Agreement.	**Services** and **investments** agreement included. AANZFTA is the most comprehensive FTA ASEAN has concluded at a single undertaking. In force on 1 January 2010 for Australia, New Zealand, Brunei, Malaysia, Myanmar, Philippines, Singapore, and Vietnam.

Source: ADB Asian Regional Integration Center (ARIC)

FIGURE 8.2
Real Trade Growth in GMS Countries, 1995–2009
(constant 2000 prices)

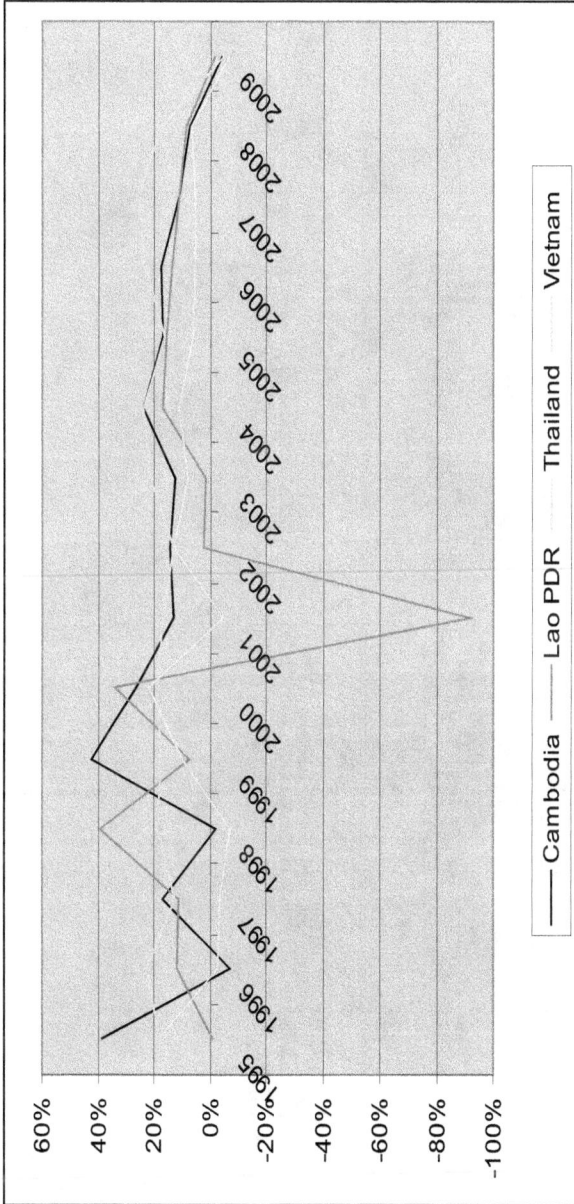

Cambodia ——— Lao PDR ········ Thailand ——— Vietnam

Note: Data unavailable for Myanmar.
Source: World Bank World Trade Indicators, 2009/10

FIGURE 8.3
Total Trade and Trade Openness in GMS Countries, 1990–2008 (bar and line)
(in current US$ million and % of total GDP)

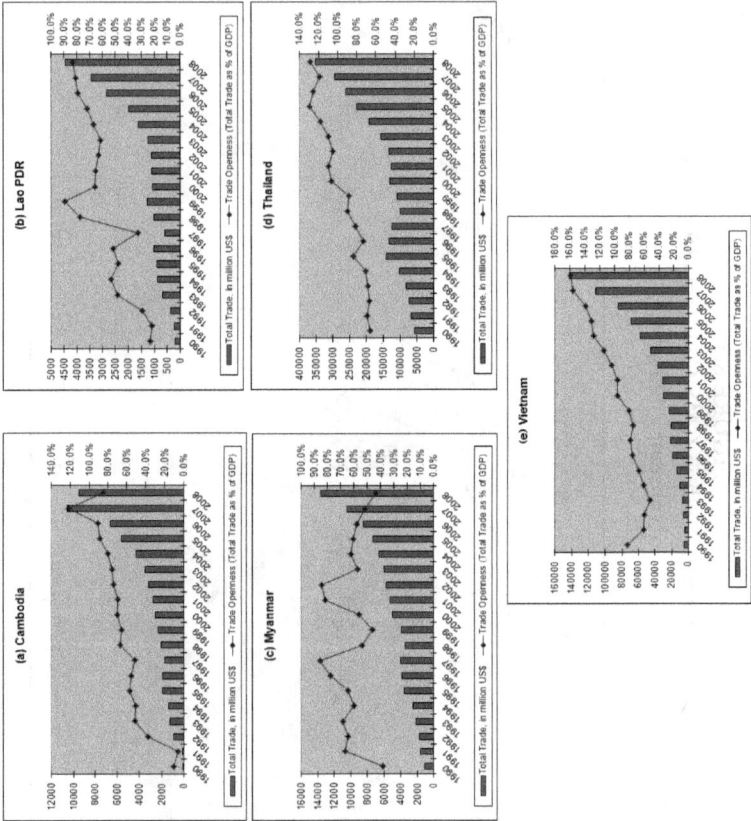

Sources: IMF Direction of Trade Statistics 2010; IMF World Economic Outlook database.

FIGURE 8.4
Direction of Trade, 1990–2008

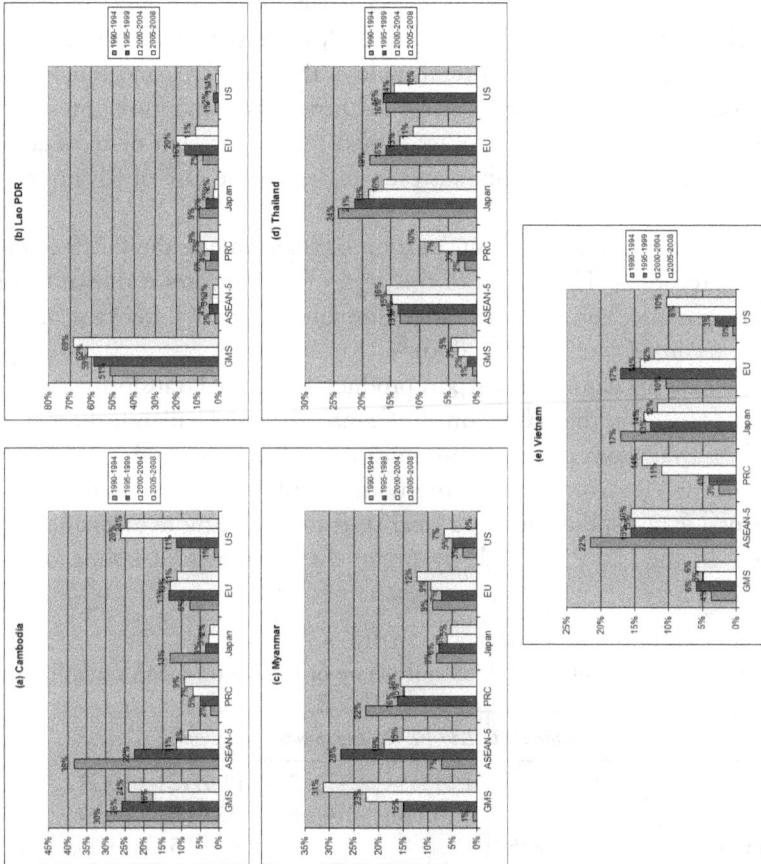

Source: IMF Direction of Trade Statistics, 2010.

have more diversified partners. In Thailand, Japan continues to be the biggest trading partner, although Japan's share has been steadily declining in recent years and is likely to be overtaken by the PRC soon. The PRC is already Vietnam's second-biggest trading partner, accounting for 14 per cent of trade in 2005–8.

The share of intra-GMS trade in total trade has been higher for the smaller countries, Lao PDR and Myanmar, reflecting both trans-shipment arrangements and limited commercial penetration beyond the immediate neighborhood. Between 2005 and 2008, trade within the subregion made up more than two thirds of total trade in the Lao PDR, and roughly a third of total trade in Myanmar. These countries trade the most intensely with Thailand. In 2008 Thailand accounted for 86 per cent of the Lao PDR's total intra-GMS trade; this was even higher in the case of Myanmar, at 98 per cent (Table 8.7).

Nonetheless, a significant portion of trade among the GMS economies is not recorded. The nature of this type of trade makes it difficult to know its magnitude, but estimates range from about 30 to 50 per cent or more of total recorded trade (ADB 2006).

Changing demand for export products has helped transform the structure of exports from the subregion. In Cambodia and Thailand, there has been a shift away from primary commodities to labour-intensive manufactured goods. In Vietnam, primary commodities still make up close to 40 per cent of total exports, but there is a clear shift towards a more diversified exports base. In the Lao PDR and Myanmar, there was a similar shift away from

TABLE 8.7
Intra-GMS Flows in 2008, US$ mil (share of total Intra-GMS trade in brackets)

	Cambodia	Lao PDR	Myanmar	Thailand	Vietnam	Total
Cambodia		0.952554	1.412439	710.4912	640.312	1353.168
		(0.1%)	(0.1%)	(52.5%)	(47.3%)	
Lao PDR	1.026259		0	2501.375	413.053	2915.454
	(0.0%)		(0%)	(85.8%)	(14.2%)	
Myanmar	1.550298	0		4895.21	104.5873	5001.348
	(0.0%)	(0.0%)		(97.9%)	(2.1%)	
Thailand	2109.06	2382.558	5108.16		6330.89	15930.67
	(13.2%)	(15.0%)	(32.1%)		(39.7%)	
Vietnam	1640.7	422.9	108.2	6254.5		8426.3
	(19.5%)	(5.0%)	(1.3%)	(74.2%)		

Source: IMF Direction of Trade Statistics, 2010.

primary commodities in 2000. However, this trend has since been reversed due to increased external demand for primary commodities, particularly ores and metals in the case of the Lao PDR, and natural gas in the case of Myanmar (Figures 8.5 and 8.6). Thailand has made up the bulk of this demand, importing around 61 per cent of the Lao PDR's ore and metal exports and 98 per cent of Myanmar's total fuel exports in 2008.

The shift towards manufactured export products has been most pronounced in Cambodia, where textiles and garments quotas from the United States and the European Union led to the emergence of an extremely narrow export base dominated by clothing and footwear. In 2008, clothing and footwear accounted for 88 per cent of Cambodia's total exports (Figure 8.7), with the bulk of this going to the U.S. and EU markets (these two markets accounted for roughly 87 per cent of Cambodia's total exports of clothing and footwear in 2008).

In Thailand, trade in machinery and other equipment comprised almost half of total exports in 2008. Production fragmentation trade has become a critical part of Thailand's export dynamism, and there are indications that Vietnam is following suit, as the share of machinery and equipment in Vietnam's total exports rose to 12 per cent in 2008. At present, however, clothing and footwear continues to make up the bulk of Vietnam's manufactured exports, accounting for 27 per cent of total exports in 2008 (Figure 8.7).

Overall Trends in Foreign Direct Investment

Along with trade, FDI to the subregion has also risen over the last two decades. In 2008 total FDI stock amounted to US$153 billion, or 37 per cent of total GDP. Cambodia and Vietnam have FDI stock to GDP ratios well above the subregional average, with Thailand just slightly below it. In contrast, Myanmar's openness to FDI has declined since 1998. Historically, Thailand has been the largest FDI recipient in the region, but Vietnam has been catching up in the last couple of years (Figure 8.8).

The source country composition of FDI to GMS countries is characterized by a clear regional bias (Figure 8.9). Investors are predominantly from ASEAN, Japan, the PRC, and the Asian newly industrialized economies. In Cambodia, the Lao PDR, and Thailand, intra-ASEAN FDI flows made up roughly a fourth of total flows between 2000 and 2008. Despite the predominance of ASEAN investors, however, the European Union has also been an important source of capital for the Lao PDR (23 per cent), Myanmar (33 per cent), and Vietnam (18 per cent).

FIGURE 8.5

Composition of GMS Exports, 1990, 2000, and 2008

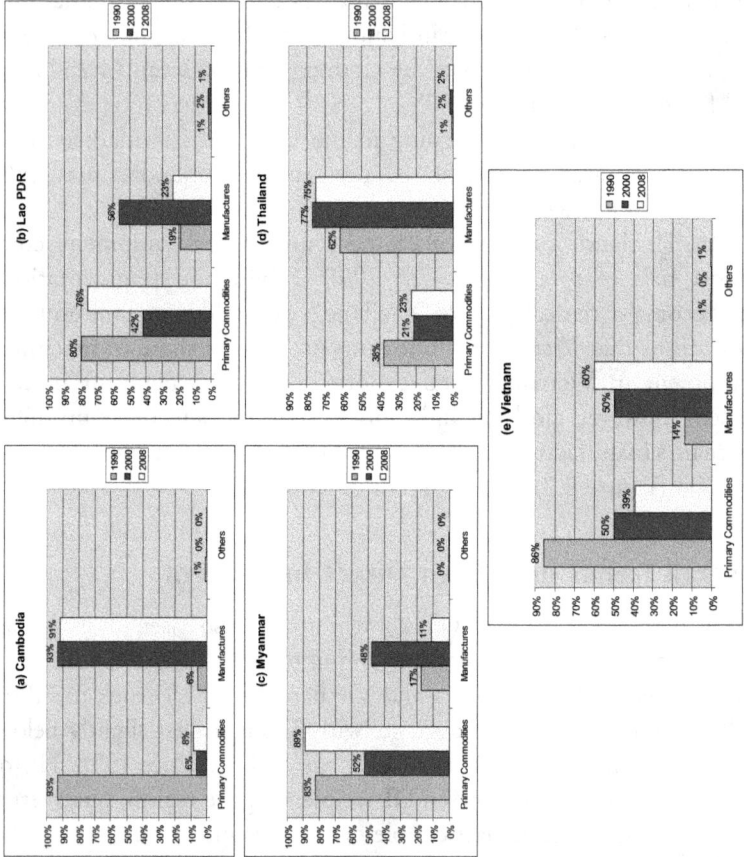

Source: UNCTAD COMTRADE database.

FIGURE 8.6

Major Primary Commodities in Total Exports of Lao PDR and Myanmar.

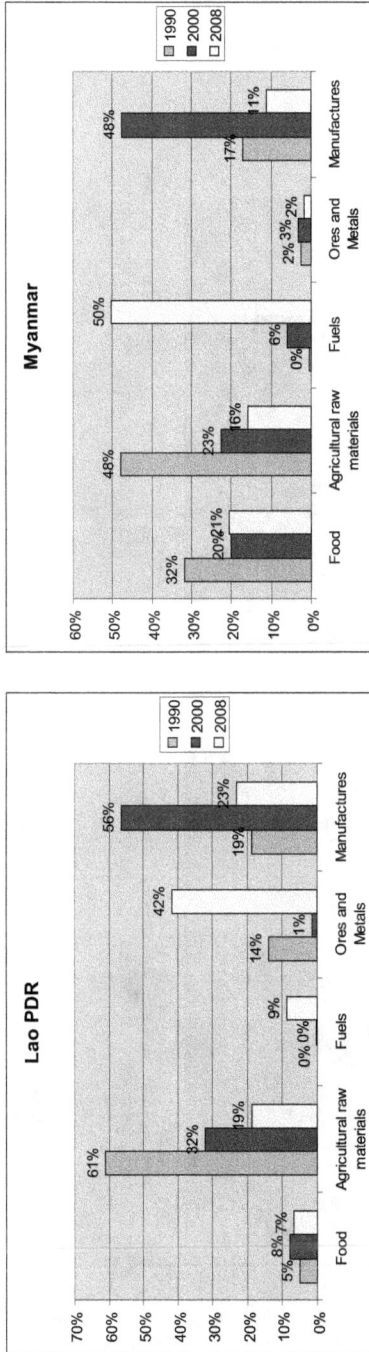

Source: UNCTAD COMTRADE database.

FIGURE 8.7
Major Manufactured Products in the Total Exports of Cambodia, Thailand, and Vietnam, 1990, 2000, and 2008

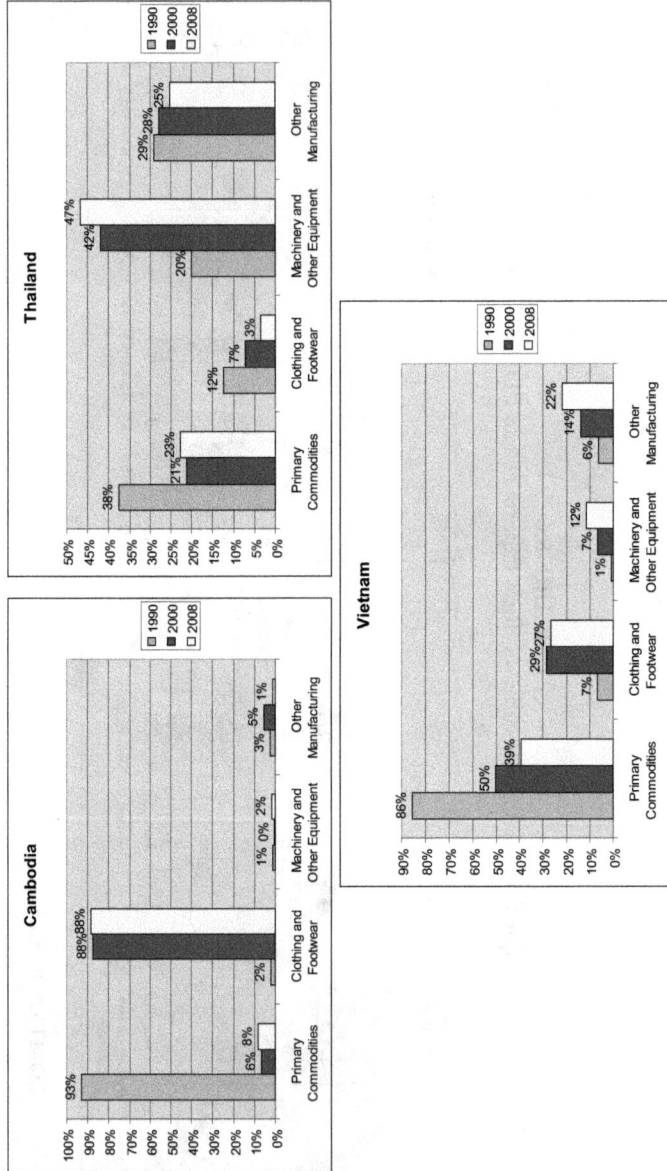

Source: UNCTAD COMTRADE database.

FIGURE 8.8
FDI and FDI Openness in GMS, 1990–2008

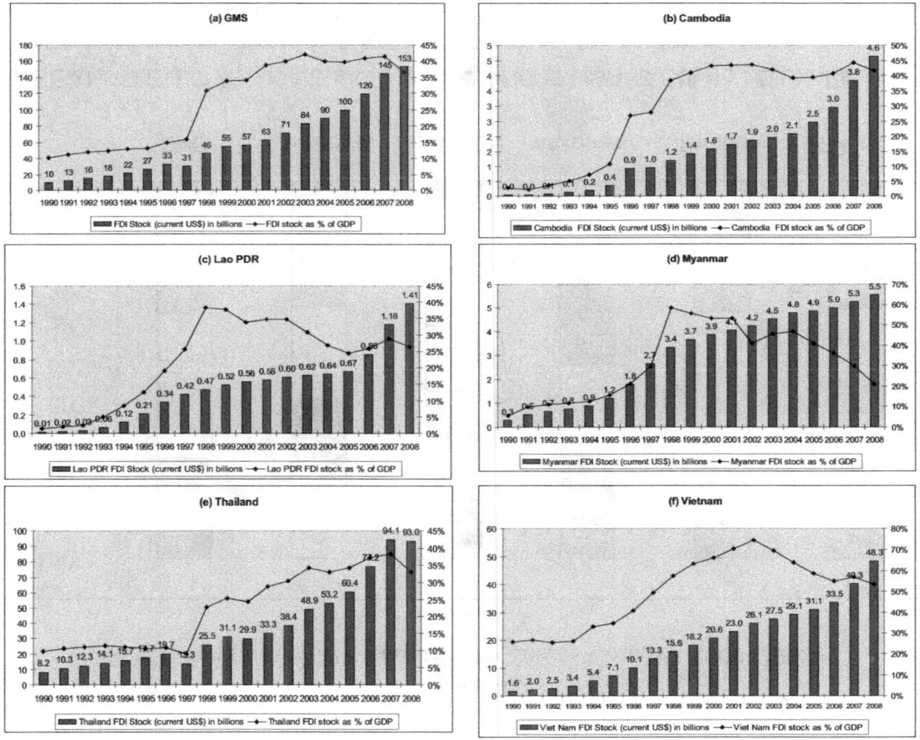

Source: UNCTAD World Investment Report 2010.

FIGURE 8.9
FDI Inflows into GMS Countries by Source Country, 2000–2008

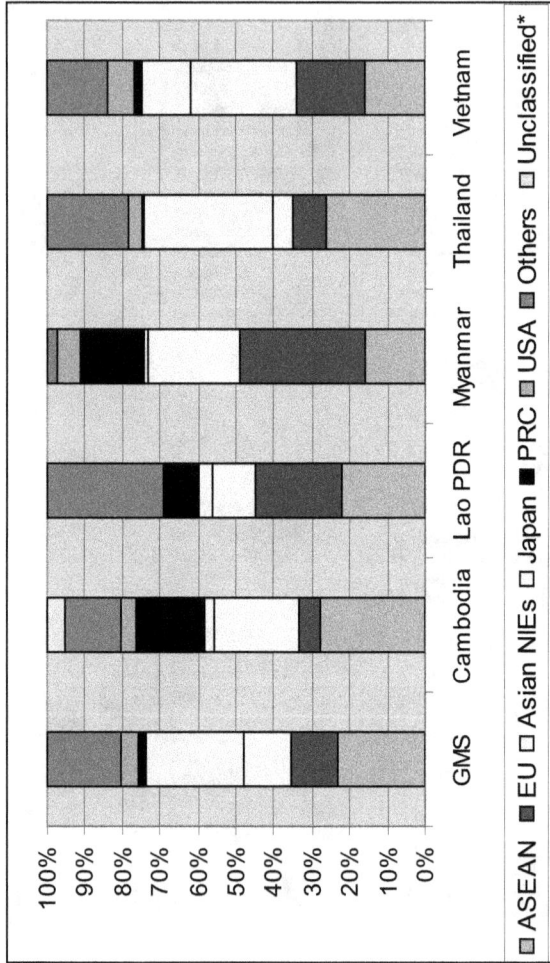

Source: ASEAN Statistical Yearbook 2008.

As for intra-GMS FDI flows, data for 1995–2005 suggest that these have been important sources of capital for the smaller GMS countries, particularly the Lao PDR, where they accounted for about a third of total FDI flows, originating mostly from Thailand (Figure 8.10).

That trade and investment are growing hand in hand in the subregion is no coincidence. Early signs of a trade-investment nexus are emerging whereby trade not only encourages investment, but investment, in turn, encourages trade. For instance, FDI in agriculture and forestry, and in mining and hydropower projects, have contributed significantly to export growth in the Lao PDR, while FDI in garments have helped strengthen Cambodia's clothing and footwear exports (ADB 2006). This is a virtuous circle that links back to economic growth.

REMAINING CHALLENGES AND THE UNFINISHED POLICY AGENDA

The foregoing discussion has highlighted considerable progress in enhancing trade and investment policies and outcomes in the GMS. These gains notwithstanding, a number of critical challenges continue to limit the subregion's potential for reaping further gains from trade and investment. Furthermore, we have seen the countries of the region subject to several external shocks, the latest being the GFC. How can these countries reduce their vulnerability and increase their resilience to such shocks?

Further Rationalizing Tariff Rate Structures

The biggest challenge facing the GMS countries in improving their trade performance relate to accelerating trade facilitation reforms and dealing with a wide range of non-tariff barriers that continue to interfere with trade flows. The need to deal with these issues and reduce trade costs is now widely acknowledged, and measures are being put in place in order to address them. Nevertheless, we should not neglect the traditional area of tariff liberalization as the reform process is far from complete. Furthermore, the increasing presence of FTAs present new challenges in rationalizing tariff structures, and creating a trade regime that ensures that distortions do not peter away the gains from trade.

The opening up of the CLMV countries in the 1990s has led to significant tariff cuts. Table 8.8 presents the average CEPT and MFN tariffs, and the difference between the two (margin of preference, or MoP), since the year the CLMV countries entered AFTA.[4] The data clearly show a general trend

FIGURE 8.10
Share of Intra-GMS Inflows in Total FDI, 1995–2005

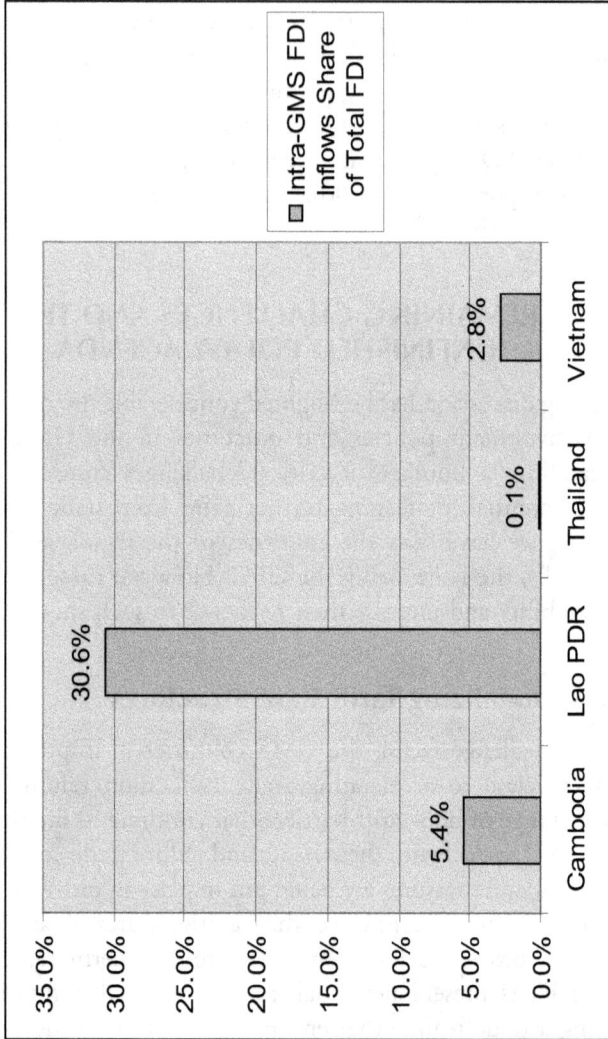

Source: ASEAN 2006. Statistics of Foreign Direct Investment in ASEAN, Eighth Edition.

TABLE 8.8
MFN and Preferential Tariffs in the CLMV Countries, 1998–2007

		1998	1999	2000	2002	2003	2004	2005	2006	2007
Cambodia	MFN			16.46	16.41	16.41	15.81	14.26	14.25	14.18
	CEPT				8.87	7.83		9.08		6.85
	MoP				7.54	8.58		5.18		7.33
Lao PDR	MFN	10.34	10.33	10.33	10.34		10.33	9.71	9.71	9.71
	CEPT			7.21	6.70		6.15	3.88		1.57
	MoP			3.12	3.64		4.18	5.83		8.14
Myanmar	MFN	5.54	5.51	5.49	5.51	5.51	5.51	5.6	5.6	5.6
	CEPT				4.81	4.81	4.26	4.29		3.36
	MoP				0.71	0.7	1.25	1.31		2.24
Vietnam	MFN	4.47	12.43	13.08	15.80	16.03	16.81	16.81	16.81	16.81
	CEPT	3.71	7.39	7.54	6.86	6.57	5.5	4.08	2.27	2.35
	MoP	0.76	5.04	5.54	9.06	9.46	11.31	12.73	14.54	14.46

Note: Blank spaces reflect missing data.
Source: Calvo-Pardo, Freund, and Ornelas, 2009.

of declining MFN and preferential rates, although reductions in the average MFN tariffs seem to have stalled across all four countries since 2005. With the exception of Myanmar, MFN tariff rates in the GMS in 2007 were higher than the average for developing East Asia and the Pacific of 9.6 per cent. The MFN tariff rates in Cambodia and Vietnam were higher than the average for low-income countries of 12.5 per cent.

With CEPT rates continuing to fall in line with AFTA commitments, their respective MoPs have increased since 2005. The MoP in 2007 is almost 15 per cent in Vietnam, and around 7–8 per cent in Cambodia and the Lao PDR. Thus, the newer members of ASEAN have chosen to operate a two-tier tariff system, with two rates for each tariff line.

This contrasts with the approach taken by the original members of ASEAN, which have opted to multilateralize the CEPT preferences for a large share of their tariff lines (Menon 2007). For Singapore, Malaysia, and Brunei, more than 80 per cent of tariff lines had been fully multilateralized as early as 2002. Indonesia and the Philippines had fully multilateralized more than 60 per cent of their tariff lines by 2002. For the remaining tariff lines, the MoP was less than 10 per cent in all of these countries (see Feridhanusetyawan 2005). In a comparison with external tariffs of major FTAs, the World Bank (2005) finds that only the North American Free Trade Agreement (NAFTA) has lower external tariffs than AFTA. The low MoPs are confirmed by the low utilization rate of preferences. A survey by the Japan External Trade Organization (JETRO; 2003) found that in 2002, the rate was only 4 per cent for Malaysia, and 11 per cent for Thailand.[5]

Why have the original member countries been multilateralizing most of their CEPT concessions? The main reason would relate to the desire to minimize trade diversion. When preferences are fully multilateralized, the MoP is zero as is the potential for trade diversion. Even if it is not zero, the lower the MoP, the lower the potential for trade diversion. This approach also reflects the long-standing commitment of the original ASEAN members to the concept of open regionalism.

Emulation of the approach taken by the original members would be in the interest of the new members of ASEAN. Indeed they will need to emulate this approach if they are not to be left behind, and if they are to succeed in deepening regional integration. Regionalism through ASEAN membership could then provide the GMS economies with an opportunity to pursue multilateralism aggressively and thus allow regionalism through AFTA to be a building block, rather than a stumbling block, towards free and open trade. This applies equally to the other ASEAN+1 FTAs that the GMS members of ASEAN will participate in (Table 8.6), as well as the individual bilateral FTAs being pursued by each country (Annex A).

There are reasons apart from minimizing trade diversion for the new member countries to emulate their predecessors in concurrently bringing down external tariffs. The freedom of members of an FTA to set their own barriers against trade with non-members raises the possibility of trade, production, and investment *deflection*. Trade deflection occurs when imports enter the FTA via the member country with the lowest tariff on non-member trade. Trade deflection distorts the region's trading patterns with the rest of the world and deprives the member country that eventually consumes the import of tariff revenue. In the case of the GMS and ASEAN, revenue is likely to be lost to a member such as Singapore, which is virtually a free-trade port.

Production deflection will occur if the manufacture of products containing imported inputs shifts to countries that have lower tariffs on the inputs because differences in tariffs outweigh differences in production costs. This is detrimental to economic efficiency and welfare since the pattern of productive activity will be based on differences in duties rather than on comparative advantage. The deflection of production may also affect the pattern of international investment. If differences in tariffs outweigh differences in production costs, tariffs will dictate investment decisions. Investment deflection will reinforce detrimental effects on welfare and efficiency associated with production deflection. Although the GMS economies may not currently be subject to much production or investment deflection because most are still not developed enough to compete with the other ASEAN members for the same types of investments, they could avoid it in the future by multilateralizing their AFTA tariff preferences.

To deal with potential trade, production, and investment deflection, AFTA imposes "domestic ASEAN content" requirements, based on rules of origin (RoO). These rules limit regional trade preferences to commodities that incorporate a minimum of 40 per cent domestic ASEAN content. Other ASEAN+1 FTAs would have their own RoOs, as would other individual country bilateral FTAs. These different RoOs, combined with other FTA-specific requirements, such as differing inclusion, exclusion, and sensitive lists, underlie the costs associated with the spaghetti bowl effect. Furthermore, the application of these rules can only limit, but not eliminate, trade, production, and investment deflection in AFTA. Krueger (1995) goes further to suggest that these rules can lead to the "export" of protection. This occurs when a member country deliberately purchases a higher-cost input from another member rather than a lower-cost alternative from a non-member in order to satisfy rules of origin requirements and gain duty-free access for its end-product exports.

RoOs are also notoriously difficult to police and the administrative burden can be substantial. Not only is the origin of a product difficult to determine in this era of increasing internationalization of production, but the transaction costs resulting from the extensive documentation associated with this cumbersome process could nullify any benefits coming from freer intraregional trade. In many of the GMS economies, the administrative costs associated with implementing RoOs or measuring domestic content could be crippling.

Adoption of the non-discriminatory approach to regionalism by the new member countries would maximize the extent and pace of their integration with the global economy. It would also simplify implementation of the tariff reduction component of the various pending "ASEAN+1" PTAs (Table 8.6) and the other PTAs that GMS countries have been pursuing (Annex A). This is underlined by the fact that the completion dates vary across the various FTAs. For instance, the CLMV countries have to complete their tariff reductions by 2015 for the ASEAN-PRC FTA, 2016 for the ASEAN-India FTA, 2018 for the ASEAN-Korea FTA, 2017 for the ASEAN-Japan FTA, and 2020 for the ASEAN-CER FTA (Table 8.6). Apart from avoiding trade diversion and deflection, the multilateralization approach would untangle them from the spaghetti bowl by doing away with the tedious and costly tasks of implementing RoOs and measuring domestic content of their imports. This would be the best option.

So, why have the new member countries of ASEAN resisted the multilateralization approach? It appears that the main reason may relate to concerns over potential loss in government revenue. Indeed, the concern over loss of government revenue is perhaps the most significant issue associated with participating in AFTA for the new ASEAN member countries. This is because these countries continue to derive a significant share of government revenue from trade taxes.

Retaining a multiple rate tariff regime is being pursued in an attempt to offset, or mitigate, the anticipated revenue losses associated with AFTA, as well as ASEAN+1 FTAs and other bilateral FTAs. What are the likely revenue impacts of the multiple-rate system compared with the one-rate system? To answer this question, we need to look at: (i) the costs associated with administering each system; and (ii) the likely change in tariff revenue collections associated with each system. We need to consider both the costs of administration and the change in tariff collections because the relevant variable is the change in government revenue (not just the change in tariff revenue) associated with each system.

The costs associated with administering the multiple-rate system are clearly going to be higher than with the one-rate system. If the multiple-rate system is going to be effective in practice, then customs authorities in new ASEAN member countries will have to measure the domestic content of all of their imports in order to determine which rate should apply. As we have already argued, measuring domestic content with accuracy is very difficult for any country, and it will be close to impossible for the new ASEAN members.

Additional tariff revenue will only be collected if non-member country imports are levied at the higher MFN rate. If there is a significant difference between the two rates, there will be a strong incentive for trade deflection. With trade deflection, imports from outside ASEAN will enter new ASEAN member countries through a low tariff country, such as Singapore.

Creating a system whereby six or more tariff rates can apply to each tariff line, depending on the source, also increases the potential for rent-seeking behaviour. It is an open secret that some portion of revenue associated with trade taxes is collected privately rather than publicly in these countries. A higher MFN rate compared with the many preferential rates will provide a new avenue through which private rents are extracted, with no change to public customs revenue collection.

In conclusion, the multiple-rate system is a second-rate system compared with the one-rate system because it is more costly to administer, is economically distortionary, and is unlikely to produce a significant increase in government tariff revenue collections. It could also lead to increased rent-seeking behaviour. Without a significant increase in tariff revenue collection, the increased costs of administration and the economic costs associated with trade diversion will produce an outcome that is inferior in welfare terms compared with the one-tariff rate system.

Moreover, tariff escalation remains higher than the regional average for agricultural goods in the case of Cambodia and Vietnam, and non-agricultural goods in the case of Cambodia, Thailand, and Vietnam (Table 8.9). This creates an anti-export bias by raising the effective rate of protection on final goods produced for the domestic market.

In sum, there is an urgent need to rationalize tariff structures in order to address tariff dispersion as a result of the various FTAs so that trade diversion can be minimized.

Reducing Vulnerability to External Shocks: Issues of Diversification and Rebalancing

There is a widespread perception among government officials and policymakers that the GMS countries remain highly vulnerable to external shocks. This concern manifests itself in calls for diversification of the export commodity base and export markets and, more recently, growth rebalancing. The GFC has simply hastened such calls. What, if anything, should the CLMV countries do to reduce this vulnerability? How valid are the proposals on diversification and rebalancing being put forward, and how should the region respond?

It is true that exports from the CLMV countries are still concentrated in a small number of goods and markets. The data on the composition of exports presented earlier and in Table 8.10 bear this out. It is also true that these make these countries highly vulnerable to sudden changes in external demand, as the recent GFC has demonstrated. Therefore, the increasing calls to diversify the economy and therefore reduce reliance on a narrow range of export commodities and markets are not surprising. But how should the GMS countries go about diversifying their economies? First, how should countries go about diversifying their export commodity base? In answering this question, it is useful to distinguish between intrasectoral versus intersectoral specialization. In other words, should the diversification take place by shifting resources towards new activities within sectors, or through intersectoral resource movements? Intersectoral diversification would involve changes to the percentage of GDP accounted for by the key sectors — agriculture,

TABLE 8.9
Average Applied Tariffs and Tariff Dispersion, various years

Indicators	Cambodia		Lao PDR		Myanmar		Thailand			Vietnam			Developing East Asia-Pacific		
	2000–2004	2005–2008	2000–2004	2005–2008	2000–2004	2005–2008	1995–1999	2000–2004	2005–2008	1995–1999	2000–2004	2005–2008	1995–1999	2000–2004	2005–2008
MFN Applied Tariff — Simple Average — All Goods (%)	16.40	14.25	9.59	9.70	5.51	5.60	23.05	16.65	9.53	16.52	16.63	16.81	19.09	10.95	9.39
MFN Applied Tariff — Simple Average — Agricultural (AoA) Goods (%)	19.44	18.10	18.99	19.46	8.51	8.66	38.48	31.04	19.91	23.05	23.71	24.15	25.08	15.89	12.40
MFN Applied Tariff — Simple Average — Non-Agricultural Goods (%)	15.93	13.66	8.17	8.22	5.05	5.14	20.81	14.57	8.59	15.52	15.56	15.70	18.21	10.22	8.97
MFN Applied Tariff — Dispersion — All Goods (%)	0.83	0.76	0.83	0.84	1.15	1.12	0.73	0.89	1.26	1.13	1.25	1.12	1.27	1.29	1.04
MFN Applied Tariff Escalation (diff, finished-raw) — All Goods (%)	—	7.57	—	-2.68	—	1.39	—	6.42	0.79	—	—	7.54	—	2.22	1.84

Indicators	Cambodia		Lao PDR		Myanmar		Thailand			Vietnam			East Asia-Pacific		
	2000–2004	2005–2008	2000–2004	2005–2008	2000–2004	2005–2008	1995–1999	2000–2004	2005–2008	1995–1999	2000–2004	2005–2008	1995–1999	2000–2004	2005–2008
MFN Applied Tariff Escalation (diff, finished-raw) — Agricultural (AoA) Goods (%)	—	14.01	—	1.61	3.50	5.48	—	11.37	2.97	—	—	16.10	—	4.99	9.69
MFN Applied Tariff Escalation (diff, finished-raw) — Non-Agricultural Goods (%)	—	6.74	—	2.08	1.80	1.54	—	9.20	9.32	—	—	9.27	—	3.24	2.51
MFN Applied Tariff Escalation (% change, finished-raw) — All Goods (%)	—	69.39	—	-20.56	—	26.02	—	81.88	6.71	—	—	55.83	—	46.92	21.96
MFN Applied Tariff Escalation (% change, finished-raw) — Agricultural (AoA) Goods (%)	—	128.8	—	8.30	47.30	89.25	—	82.63	13.19	—	—	95.48	—	80.72	80.81
MFN Applied Tariff Escalation (% change, finished-raw) — Non-Agricultural Goods (%)	—	61.50	—	30.04	42.86	33.69	—	221.3	250.5	—	—	90.06	—	78.68	66.97

Source: World Bank World Trade Indicators 2009/10.

manufacturing, and services — while intrasectoral diversification could leave these proportions relatively unchanged.

In this context, it is important to recognize that there is a gradual process of diversification at the macro level that is already taking place naturally as part of the process of economic development. This is evidenced by the changing share of GDP accounted for by the three key sectors over time, particularly the reduction in the share accounted for by agriculture and the increase in share of manufacturing and services (see Table 8.1). The question then is the extent to which government policy should intervene to control or direct this process, or hasten it. In this regard, pursuing intersectoral diversification would require a greater level of government intervention — in the form of subsidies as part of a package of industry policy incentives — than intrasectoral diversification. This is because the artificial relative price changes required to induce resources to shift across sectors would be larger than those required for intrasectoral reallocations.

There are a number of reasons that intrasectoral specialization is to be preferred if pursuing a policy of diversification. First, the adjustment cost associated with intrasectoral specialization is likely to be much lower than intersectoral specialization (see Menon and Dixon 1997). This is because intrasectoral specialization does not require intersectoral factor movements. It is likely that factors of production can be moved more easily across activities within a sector, with greater similarity in factor intensities, than they can across sectors, where factor intensities are likely to vary more widely. Trade expansion through intersectoral specialization is more likely to require factor transfer from export-oriented industries to import-competing industries, whereas trade expansion through intrasectoral specialization may only require factor transfer within export-oriented industries.

This is already being recognized by leaders and policymakers in the region. In an interview, former Prime Minister Abhisit Vejjajiva of Thailand highlighted the need for intrasectoral specialization within agriculture and services, downplaying calls to diversify into heavy industry, stating that "[t]he strengths of our economy lie in agriculture and the country's beauty, which attracts tourism". He added that "it is [not] necessary that the country has everything from upstream to downstream industries. Some people say the automobile industry will have a problem if we don't have a steel industry. But I don't think this holds true, given the benefits of ASEAN cooperation."[6] In short, there is room to diversify into a range of activities related to traditional sectors that should be pursued first. That is, it would be more sensible economically to consider activities related to agro-processing such as rice milling, for instance, before venturing into the manufacture of automobiles or airplanes.

Apart from the diversification of the export commodity base, there may also be a need to diversify export markets, so that there is less reliance on demands from a small number of countries. In this respect, the experience of GMS countries during the GFC does highlight the risks associated with significant dependence on extraregional demand for exports, especially the U.S. and EU markets. Although increasing the number of markets that GMS countries export to will reduce these risks, the GFC does nothing to invalidate the outward-looking, export-oriented growth strategies that these countries have been pursuing. This policy has delivered rapid and continuous economic growth and resulted in substantial improvements in living standards and significant reductions in poverty incidence. Thus, the subregion should maintain its vital trade links with the industrialized countries and the rest of the world.

At the same time, however, the transformation of East Asia from a relatively stagnant, low-income region to a dynamic, middle-income one, suggests that intra–East Asian trade offers the promise of a new source of demand and growth in future (Estrada et al. 2010). Strengthening intraregional trade will enable the region's economies to exploit potentially large but hitherto under-realized gains from trade (see ADB 2009*b*). Indeed, this is already happening for many of the GMS countries. From Figure 8.4, we can see this shift taking place. To a certain extent, the unexpectedly speedy and robust recovery currently taking place in the GMS countries reflects this shift in the geographical pattern of much of the region's exports. With the exception of Japan, East Asia is undergoing an almost V-shaped recovery reminiscent of the region's rebound from the Asian financial crisis. Given the relatively high share of intra–East Asian trade of most of the GMS countries, they are in a good position to ride this wave of recovery taking place around them.

Growth rebalancing literature suggests that a complementary strategy is for each country to shift the sources of growth from foreign towards domestic demand. There is certainly a case for the PRC to do this, as well as a number of other East Asian countries that continue to run large current account surpluses. As far as the GMS countries are concerned, however, almost all of them are net importers of capital, and run current account deficits (Table 8.10). Furthermore, the contribution of net exports to growth in most countries is either small or negative. These factors suggest that any policies designed to shift sources of demand from foreign to domestic would be misplaced as far as GMS countries are concerned.

TABLE 8.10
Product and Market Diversification

Indicators	Cambodia			Lao PDR			Myanmar			Thailand			Vietnam		
	1995–1999	2000–2004	2005–2008	1995–1999	2000–2004	2005–2008	1995–1999	2000–2004	2005–2008	1995–1999	2000–2004	2005–2008	1995–1999	2000–2004	2005–2008
No. of products exported	58.67	66.60	73	118.6	160.6	188	176	144.4	114	253.2	240.2	254	218.4	236.8	250
No. of products imported	229.2	178.8	240	227.4	227	238	248.8	245.8	246	254.6	249.6	257.5	247	252	256.5
Export product concentration index	35.04	40.32	35.47	29.27	33.10	32.72	27.18	29.58	43.52	10.03	9.69	9.10	20.81	22.53	22.53
Share of top 5 export markets of total goods exports	—	—	78.76	—	—	62.60	—	—	77.36	—	—	44.77	—	—	52.75
Export market destination concentration index	—	56.82	53.65	—	—	31.87	—	—	47.07	29.82	28.13	21.47	22.61	27.36	24.77

Source: World Bank World Trade Indicators 2009/10.

CONCLUSION

The GMS is one of the most successful stories of economic transition and integration among developing countries. Strong rates of economic growth since the early 1990s have been fuelled by increased trade and FDI in the subregion. This economic progress has translated into marked improvements in living standards and human development outcomes and dramatic reductions in poverty. Unilateral policy reforms and greater economic cooperation have led to positive trade growth in the GMS. These include participation in the GMS Programme, AFTA, WTO, and preferential trading agreements.

Despite these achievements, a number of critical challenges continue to limit the subregion's potential for reaping further gains from trade and investment. The trade policy reform agenda in particular remains incomplete. The biggest challenge facing the GMS countries in improving their trade performance relates to accelerating trade facilitation reforms and dealing with a wide range of non-tariff barriers that continue to interfere with trade flows. It is important that more traditional areas of trade reform are not neglected either, especially with regard to the rationalization of tariff structures following participation in AFTA and other PTAs. In this regard, the GMS members of AFTA should work towards multilateralizing their CEPT preferences in order to avoid trade diversion and deflection and remain globally connected. This should also be the objective for the various ASEAN+1 bilateral FTAs that they are participating in, as well as each country's bilateral FTAs. Retaining a multi-tier tariff system is unlikely to mitigate revenue loss, but could unnecessarily burden an already stretched bureaucracy, or create new avenues for rent-seeking behaviour. There is also an urgent need to address growing tariff escalation to remove the anti-export bias.

The GMS countries have also been subject to several external shocks, the latest being the GFC. In order to reduce vulnerability to external shocks, diversification of both export commodities and markets are being considered. Intrasectoral diversification of export commodities is likely to be more viable and less costly than intersectoral diversification. Trade expansion through intersectoral specialization is more likely to require factor transfer from export-oriented industries to import-competing industries, which would be difficult, whereas trade expansion through intrasectoral specialization may only require factor transfer within export-oriented industries. Growth rebalancing literature suggests that a complementary strategy is for each country to shift the sources of growth from foreign towards domestic demand. It is unlikely, however, that any such rebalancing of growth will be required in the GMS countries in order to increase resilience to external shocks. Most are capital importing countries, and the contribution of net exports to growth is either small or negative.

Notes

* We are grateful for comments from Prema-chandra Athukorala, Vo Trih Thanh, and participants at the Regional Conference on GMS: From Geographical Corridor to Economic Corridor at ISEAS, without implicating them in any way. The views expressed in this chapter are those of the authors and do not necessarily reflect the views and policies of the Asian Development Bank, or its board of governors or the governments they represent. Address comments or queries to: jmenon@ adb.org

1. The Greater Mekong Subregion Economic Programme was initiated by the Asian Development Bank (ADB) in 1992. The original members of the GMS programme were Cambodia, the Lao PDR, Myanmar, Thailand, Vietnam, and Yunnan Province of the People's Republic of China (PRC). In 2004, Guangxi Zhuang Autonomous Region of the PRC also joined the GMS. Due to the lack of provincial data for Yunnan and Guangxi, this chapter focuses on the five member countries of the GMS.
2. Myanmar has been a member of the WTO since 1995.
3. Products excluded from the CEPT Scheme are specified in the Highly Sensitive List (that is, rice) and the General Exception List.
4. Data for Thailand are unavailable.
5. To put this in comparative perspective, utilization rates of below 50 per cent are considered low in European preferential trading agreements (see, for instance, Augier et al. (2005).
6. Reported in "Diversity Holds Key to Success, Says PM", *Bangkok Post*, 11 October 2010, p. 1.

References

ADB. *Mekong Region Trade — Trends, Patterns and Policies*. Manila: ADB, 2006.
────. The GMS Cross-Border Transport Agreement. Manila: ADB, 2009*a*. Available at <http://www.adb.org/GMS/agreement.asp>.
────. *Asian Development Outlook 2009 Update: Broadening Openness for a Resilient Asia*. Manila: ADB, 2009*b*.
────. *Asian Development Outlook 2009: Rebalancing Asia's Growth*. Manila: ADB, 2009*c*.
ASEAN. *Statistics of Foreign Direct Investment in ASEAN*, Eighth Edition. Jakarta: ASEAN Secretariat, 2006.
────. *ASEAN Statistical Yearbook, 2008*. Jakarta: ASEAN Secretariat, 2008.

————. ASEAN Free Trade Area (AFTA Council). <http://www.aseansec.org/19585. htm> (accessed 15 October 2010).

————. "Protocol on the Special Arrangement for Sensitive and Highly Sensitive Products". Singapore: 30 September 1999.

Bangkok Post. "Diversity Holds Key to Success, Says PM". 11 October 2010, p. 1.

Calvo-Pardo, H., C. Freund, and E. Ornelas. "The ASEAN Free Trade Agreement: Impact on Trade Flows and External Trade Barriers". CEP Discussion Paper No. 930. London: Centre for Economic Performance, London School of Economics and Political Science, 2009.

Estrada, Gemma, Donghyun Park, Innwon, and Soonchan Park. "ASEAN's Free Trade Agreements with China, Japan and Korea: A Qualitative and Quantitative Analysis". Manila: ADB, 2010.

Feridhanusetyawan, Tubagus. "Preferential Trading Agreements in the Asia-Pacific Region". IMF Working Paper 149, Washington, DC: International Monetary Fund, 2005.

JETRO. *Current Status of AFTA and Corporate Responses*. Tokyo: JETRO, 2003.

Krueger, Anne O. "Free Trade Agreements versus Customs Unions". Working Paper No. 5084. Cambridge, MA: National Bureau of Economic Research, 1995.

Leung, Suiwah. "Integration and Transition — Vietnam, Cambodia and Lao PDR". Paper presented at the seminar "Accelerating Development in the Mekong Region — the Role of Economic Integration", Siem Reap, Cambodia, 26–27 June 2006.

Menon, Jayant. "Building Blocks or Stumbling Blocks? The GMS and AFTA in Asia". *ASEAN Economic Bulletin* 24 no. 2 (2007): 254–66.

Menon, Jayant, P. Athukorala, and S. Bhandari. *Mekong Region Foreign Direct Investment*. Manila: ADB, 2006.

Menon, Jayant and Peter B. Dixon. "Intra-industry versus Inter-industry Trade: Relevance for Adjustment Costs". *Weltwirtschaftliches Archiv* 133, no. 1 (1997): 164–69.

Syed, M. "Economic Development in the Mekong: An Overview of Trends, Prospects and Challenges". Paper presented at the seminar "Accelerating Development in the Mekong Region — the Role of Economic Integration". Siem Reap, Cambodia, 26–27 June 2006.

World Bank. *Global Economic Prospects 2005: Trade, Regionalism and Development*, Washington, DC: World Bank, 2005.

Online Statistical Databases Used

Asian Development Bank Statistical Database System (SDBS) <http://www.adb. org/statistics/sdbs.asp>.

ADB Asian Regional Integration Center (ARIC) Free Trade Agreement Database for Asia and Integration Indicators Database <http://aric.adb.org/>.

International Monetary Fund Direction of Trade Statistics, 2010 <http://www2.
    imfstatistics.org/DOT/>.
UN National Accounts Main Aggregates Database <http://unstats.un.org/unsd/
    snaama/selectionbasicFast.asp>.
UNCTAD COMTRADE Database <http://comtrade.un.org/>.
UNCTAD World Investment Report, 2010 <www.unctad.org/WIR>.
World Bank World Development Indicators 2010 <http://databank.worldbank.
    org/ddp/home.do?Step=12&id=4&CNO=2>.
World Bank World Trade Indicators, 2009/10 <http://go.worldbank.org/
    7F01C2NTP0>.

ANNEX A
List of PTAs Involving GMS Countries, as of July 2010

Cambodia
- ASEAN Free Trade Area (in effect)
- ASEAN-Australia and New Zealand Free Trade Agreement (in effect)
- ASEAN-EU Free Trade Agreement (under negotiation)
- ASEAN-India Comprehensive Economic Cooperation Agreement (in effect)
- ASEAN-Japan Comprehensive Economic Partnership (in effect)
- ASEAN-Korea Comprehensive Economic Cooperation Agreement (in effect)
- ASEAN-People's Republic of China Comprehensive Economic Cooperation Agreement (in effect)
- Comprehensive Economic Partnership for East Asia (CEPEA/ASEAN+6) (Proposed/Under consultation and study)
- East Asia Free Trade Area (ASEAN+3) (Proposed/under consultation and study)

Lao PDR
- ASEAN Free Trade Area (in effect)
- ASEAN-Australia and New Zealand Free Trade Agreement (in effect)
- ASEAN-EU Free Trade Agreement (under negotiation)
- ASEAN-India Comprehensive Economic Cooperation Agreement (in effect)
- ASEAN-Japan Comprehensive Economic Partnership (in effect)
- ASEAN-Korea Comprehensive Economic Cooperation Agreement (in effect)
- ASEAN-People's Republic of China Comprehensive Economic Cooperation Agreement (in effect)
- Asia-Pacific Trade Agreement (in effect)
- Comprehensive Economic Partnership for East Asia (CEPEA/ASEAN+6) (Proposed/under consultation and study)
- East Asia Free Trade Area (ASEAN+3) (Proposed/under consultation and study)
- Laos-Thailand Preferential Trading Arrangement (in effect)

Myanmar
- ASEAN Free Trade Area (in effect)
- ASEAN-Australia and New Zealand Free Trade Agreement (in effect)
- ASEAN-EU Free Trade Agreement (under negotiation)
- ASEAN-India Comprehensive Economic Cooperation Agreement (in effect)
- ASEAN-Japan Comprehensive Economic Partnership (in effect)
- ASEAN-Korea Comprehensive Economic Cooperation Agreement (in effect)
- ASEAN-People's Republic of China Comprehensive Economic Cooperation Agreement (in effect)

- Bay of Bengal Initiative for Multi-Sectoral Technical and Economic Cooperation (BIMSTEC) Free Trade Area ([FA] signed/FTA under negotiation)
- Comprehensive Economic Partnership for East Asia (CEPEA/ASEAN+6) (Proposed/under consultation and study)
- East Asia Free Trade Area (ASEAN+3) (Proposed/under consultation and study)

Thailand
- East Asia Free Trade Area (ASEAN+3) (Proposed/under consultation and study)
- ASEAN Free Trade Area (in effect)
- ASEAN-Australia and New Zealand Free Trade Agreement (in effect)
- ASEAN-EU Free Trade Agreement (under negotiation)
- ASEAN-India Comprehensive Economic Cooperation Agreement (in effect)
- ASEAN-Japan Comprehensive Economic Partnership (in effect)
- ASEAN-Korea Comprehensive Economic Cooperation Agreement (in effect)
- ASEAN-People's Republic of China Comprehensive Economic Cooperation Agreement (in effect)
- Bay of Bengal Initiative for Multi-Sectoral Technical and Economic Cooperation (BIMSTEC) Free Trade Area ([FA] signed/FTA under negotiation)
- Comprehensive Economic Partnership for East Asia (CEPEA/ASEAN+6) (Proposed/under consultation and study)
- East Asia Free Trade Area (ASEAN+3) (Proposed/under consultation and study)
- India-Thailand Free Trade Area ([FA] signed/FTA under Negotiation)
- Japan-Thailand Economic Partnership Agreement (in effect)
- Korea-Thailand Free Trade Agreement (Proposed/under consultation and study)
- Laos-Thailand Preferential Trading Arrangement (in effect)
- Pakistan-Thailand Free Trade Agreement (Proposed/under consultation and study)
- People's Republic of China-Thailand Free Trade Agreement (in effect)
- Thailand-Australia Free Trade Agreement (in effect)
- Thailand-Bahrain Free Trade Agreement ([FA] signed/FTA under negotiation)
- Thailand-Chile Free Trade Agreement (Proposed/under consultation and study)
- Thailand-European Free Trade Association Free Trade Agreement (under negotiation)
- Thailand-MERCOSUR Free Trade Agreement (Proposed/under consultation and study)
- Thailand-New Zealand Closer Economic Partnership Agreement (in effect)

- Thailand-Peru Free Trade Agreement ([FA] signed/FTA under negotiation)
- United States-Thailand Free Trade Agreement (under negotiation)

Vietnam
- ASEAN Free Trade Area (in effect)
- ASEAN-Australia and New Zealand Free Trade Agreement (in effect)
- ASEAN-EU Free Trade Agreement (under negotiation)
- ASEAN-India Comprehensive Economic Cooperation Agreement (in effect)
- ASEAN-Japan Comprehensive Economic Partnership (in effect)
- ASEAN-Korea Comprehensive Economic Cooperation Agreement (in effect)
- ASEAN-People's Republic of China Comprehensive Economic Cooperation Agreement (in effect)
- Chile-Vietnam Free Trade Agreement (under negotiation)
- Comprehensive Economic Partnership for East Asia (CEPEA/ASEAN+6) (Proposed/under consultation and study)
- East Asia Free Trade Area (ASEAN+3) (Proposed/under consultation and study)
- Japan-Vietnam Economic Partnership Agreement (in effect)
- Trans-Pacific Partnership (TPP) ([FA] signed/FTA under negotiation)
- Vietnam-European Free Trade Association Free Trade Agreement (Proposed/ under consultation and study)

Source: ADB Asian Regional Integration Center (ARIC) Free Trade Agreement Database for Asia.

9

ENHANCING FINANCIAL COOPERATION AMONG THE GMS COUNTRIES

Ulrich Volz

Financial market development is critical for economic development. This chapter explores the ways by which international financial cooperation — defined broadly to include cooperation in financial market infrastructure development, regulation, as well as the advancement of cross-border financial integration — can help the countries of the Greater Mekong Subregion (which comprises Cambodia, the Lao PDR, Myanmar, Thailand, Vietnam, and the Yunnan Province of the People's Republic of China) to foster the development of domestic and regional financial markets. The next section will briefly discuss why financial markets matter for overall economic development. The following section then discusses the benefits of regional financial cooperation for financial sector development in the GMS countries.

WHY FINANCIAL MARKET DEVELOPMENT MATTERS

The global financial crisis has forcefully shown the destructive potential of finance. Instead of being a lubricator of economic growth, the financial sector is now dragging down the real economy. Yet, as counter-intuitive as it might seem at first, one of the messages that policymakers in developing countries and emerging markets should take away from the current mess is that their economies need deeper financial markets, including capital markets, not less of them.

When examining the causes of the crisis, it is important to recognize that the crisis was first and foremost a consequence of inadequate supervision and regulation of financial firms (or in part even the complete lack of regulation, as in the shadow financial sector). The crisis is a long overdue reminder that perfect markets do not exist. It is astonishing how the efficient market hypothesis could rise to such prominence given the long and well-documented history of financial manias, panics, and crashes (for example, Kindleberger and Aliber 2005; Garber 2000). Irrational behaviour and phenomena such as speculative bubbles, collective mood swings, herd behaviour, bandwagon effects, panic trading, or trading by agents caught in liquidity shortage, have been long known in financial markets. A misguided belief in the self-regulating abilities of financial markets led to the devastating consequences that we are facing today.

What is to blame are not financial markets as such, but financial markets in which actors were driven by wrong incentive structures that had completely detached from the "real economy" — not least because regulators allowed excessive risk taking and a huge shadow financial sector to develop. Those countries whose financial regulators did not allow domestic banks and firms to invest in what Warren Buffet once famously dubbed weapons of financial mass destruction (and what is now commonly referred to as toxic assets) were proven right. Not long ago, Y.V. Reddy, the governor of the Reserve Bank of India until September 2008, had been blamed as a party pooper for not allowing Indian banks to play along in the glitzy game of international finance and invest in risky assets abroad. Today he is praised as a hero with foresight.

When demanding more financial market development in developing countries and emerging markets it is thus imperative to demand, at the same time, the development of public institutions in these countries taking charge of financial market regulation and supervision that are up to the task. Financial sector reform is a continuous process that needs to be in tune with macroeconomic realities and the state of maturity of institutions and markets. Innovative financial products, as great their potential benefits might be, should simply not be allowed if they are too complex for regulators to appraise their risk. If financial markets are sufficiently regulated and supervised, the risk of crisis can be minimized, while the gains of improved financial intermediation will be yielded.

The development of financial markets has long been recognized as a key determinant of economic development.[1] There is a firm consensus nowadays that a well-functioning financial sector is a precondition for the exploitation of an economy's growth potential. While there is still an ongoing debate on the exact transmission channels from finance to economic activity, and its quantitative impact in particular, a large and growing amount of empirical research has documented a robust correlation between finance and growth, and a causality running from financial development to economic growth.[2]

The economic literature highlights three main channels by which financial development can affect growth.[3] Firstly, a more efficient financial system reduces the cost of financial intermediation and hence raises the fraction of savings funnelled to investment. The more efficient the transformation of savings into investment, the lesser the loss of resources, and the more savings are channelled towards productive investment. Competition and increased efficiency should bring interest-rate margins down. The availability of credit to firms and households should correspondingly tend to increase.

Secondly, a well-functioning financial sector is a precondition for the efficient allocation of resources. Improvements in financial intermediation are expected to lead to a better allocation of resources across investment projects. A better trading, hedging, and pooling of risks allow the funding of highly profitable, but risky, investment projects that would be relinquished otherwise. The more advanced financial systems become, the better they should be able to deal with the problems of asymmetric information that are persistent in financial markets. This should further reduce the cost of financial intermediation. Moreover, a more sophisticated financial sector should be more capable of distinguishing between good and bad investment opportunities, thus increasing the social marginal productivity of capital.[4]

A third way by which financial development could affect economic growth is through influencing households' savings rates. While the effect in the two channels mentioned before is generally positive, it is ambiguous in this case. A higher efficiency of the financial system should yield more favourable return-risk combinations for savers. But it is not clear whether or not the prospects of higher returns or lower risk on savings would induce households to save more.

The developmental effects of a deepening of financial markets are high, particularly for those economies which face severe financing constraints for small and medium enterprises. Moreover, financial inclusion of households that hitherto had no access to the formal financial sector will improve the opportunities for those at the bottom of society in developing countries. The provision of basic banking services, including through innovative yet simple services such as mobile phone banking, should therefore be a priority for poorer societies. Yet there is also a strong case for the development of capital markets, bond markets in particular, in developing and emerging economies.

Developing domestic markets and reducing dependency on foreign financial markets will not only be more efficient and reduce the costs of domestic financing, but it will also reduce the risk associated with currency mismatches and of a sudden outflow of capital. This is not to say that international financial integration has no benefits to offer. But integrating into international financial markets at the expense of domestic financial market building is clearly not a good strategy. Further efforts to develop both the banking sectors and capital markets in developing and emerging economies are not only conducive to economic growth, but will also help to strengthen economic resilience. What developing countries certainly do not need are highly leveraged financial sectors that have lost touch with the real economy. But more solid banking — what Paul Krugman (2009) recently called "boring banking" — and bond markets which help the financing of private businesses and households is certainly needed.

Closely related to the development of financial markets is the topic of financial stability, and thus market supervision and regulation. The more financial markets develop, and the more complex they become, the greater the need for sophisticated supervision and regulation. While financial market development holds great benefits for the real economy, financial innovation also poses risks to financial stability. This is especially true for capital markets, where the systemic risk can be substantial due to huge leverage effects. As historical experience has shown over and over again, crises originating from the financial sector can have devastating impact on the real economy. History is full of examples where progress in economic development that had been made over many years was wiped out by a financial crisis within weeks or months. The global financial crisis that started in 2007 bears evidence of the destructive potential of financial markets. The Asian financial crisis of 1997–98 is yet another example.

Yet the Asian crisis also provides an example for the risk induced in financial systems if parts of the financial sector are not, or only poorly, developed: before the Asian crisis, the lack of well-functioning local-currency bond markets in most of East Asia had led to an over-reliance on bank lending. As a consequence, many long-term projects were financed with short-term bank loans which frequently had to be rolled over, causing maturity mismatches. In addition, the lack of funding in domestic currency caused local banks to refinance themselves internationally, which created currency mismatches. This double mismatch problem had fatal consequences when international investors started withdrawing money from the region and East Asian monetary authorities were forced to devalue their currencies against the U.S. dollar. As a lesson from the Asian and many other crises, the development of local-currency bond markets has been identified as a key policy challenge. This, as well as other fields of financial market development, should not only be addressed on a national level, but also through regional financial cooperation, as will be discussed in the next section.

THREE CASES FOR REGIONAL FINANCIAL COOPERATION AMONG THE GMS COUNTRIES

When looking at gross measures of financial market development of the GMS countries (leaving aside Yunnan Province), one can see that three of the five countries (Cambodia, Lao PDR, and Myanmar) have very weakly developed financial markets, with ratios of domestic credit to the private sector between 5 per cent and 23 per cent of GDP (Table 9.1), and ratios of domestic credit provided by the banking sector to GDP between about 10 and 25 per cent of GDP (Table 9.2), respectively. Thailand and Vietnam, in contrast, have

TABLE 9.1
Domestic Credit to Private Sector (% of GDP), 1990–2008

	Cambodia	Lao PDR	Myanmar	Thailand	Vietnam
1990		0.96	4.74	83.37	
1991		2.95	6.64	89.10	
1992		4.67	7.69	98.47	13.66
1993	2.37	6.93	6.40	111.36	16.53
1994	3.34	8.92	5.98	127.75	
1995	3.48	9.08	7.60	139.83	18.48
1996	4.72	9.02	9.51	147.19	18.67
1997	6.28	12.97	10.32	165.72	19.85
1998	5.59	12.62	9.68	155.90	20.12
1999	5.71	8.44	8.59	131.92	28.19
2000	6.38	8.91	10.44	108.26	35.26
2001	5.99	9.59	11.73	96.91	39.29
2002	6.31	8.18	10.82	102.54	43.14
2003	7.21	6.51	4.43	100.50	48.37
2004	9.02	6.34	4.72	101.96	58.72
2005	8.98	7.39		100.73	65.86
2006	11.99	5.76		95.14	71.22
2007	18.21	6.45		113.18	93.36
2008	23.45	9.51		113.11	90.63

Source: World Bank 2010 Development Indicators and Development Finance Database.

TABLE 9.2
Domestic Credit Provided by Banking Sector (% of GDP), 1990–2008

	Cambodia	Lao PDR	Myanmar	Thailand	Vietnam
1990		5.00	32.81	94.08	
1991		4.46	44.61	96.22	
1992		4.94	41.05	103.56	15.71
1993	5.03	5.94	34.45	116.03	22.46
1994	5.43	10.56	32.90	130.68	
1995	5.29	9.95	32.47	141.32	20.07
1996	6.17	7.63	33.61	146.36	20.12
1997	6.87	15.05	30.70	177.58	21.24
1998	7.16	15.40	28.18	176.75	21.97
1999	6.55	9.27	26.75	155.78	28.92
2000	6.42	9.00	32.10	138.27	35.15
2001	5.57	13.10	33.95	128.57	39.73
2002	5.63	9.95	28.68	127.78	44.79
2003	6.57	8.60	22.13	130.75	51.80
2004	7.98	8.16	24.84	124.53	61.93
2005	7.22	8.10		119.18	71.22
2006	8.86	6.29		108.88	75.38
2007	12.90	6.49		131.51	96.19
2008	16.22	10.48		130.57	94.99

Source: World Bank 2010 Development Indicators and Development Finance Database.

much further advanced banking sectors, even though they pale in comparison with advanced economies.

The need for further financial market development in the GMS countries, and Cambodia, Lao PDR, and Myanmar in particular, is evident. While the impetus for financial market reform and development certainly needs to come from the national authorities, and the basic preconditions for financial market development, such as macroeconomic stability, property rights, law enforcement, etc., have to be achieved primarily through domestic reform efforts, regional financial cooperation can offer several benefits.

First, countries don't need to reinvent the wheel every time anew when charting the course for financial market reform. An abundance of experience with successful as well as unsuccessful financial market reform exists that can be drawn upon. While much knowledge can be drawn from international financial organizations such as the World Bank or the Asian Development

Bank, for countries such as Cambodia, the Lao PDR, and Myanmar, it can be beneficial to learn in addition from the recent financial market reform experiences of their direct, more advanced neighbours, Thailand and Vietnam.[5] Moreover, a coordinated approach can create a momentum and peer pressure for joint reform efforts.

Second, with a view towards prospective regional financial integration, it makes sense for GMS countries (and ASEAN countries) to agree on certain norms and standards which will in the future facilitate regional cross-border activities of banks and other financial institutions. Regional financial integration, which can be defined as the process of opening up capital accounts among countries of geographical proximity, including a liberalization of cross-border activities of financial institutions within the integrating area, can provide important efficiency benefits resulting from economies of scale; stimuli for domestic financial reforms; increased competition and innovation; and expanded opportunities for risk diversification. Since all GMS countries (again with the exclusion of Yunnan Province) are ASEAN members, all of them have already signed up to various initiatives in ASEAN finance cooperation.[6] In particular, ASEAN countries have all agreed on the Roadmap for Monetary and Financial Integration of ASEAN, whose agenda includes financial services liberalization, capital account liberalization, and capital market development.[7] The road map is part of an effort to create an ASEAN Economic Community by 2015, which shall not only include a free flow of goods, services, and skilled labour, but also a free flow of capital, although the latter (and probably also the former) will not be achieved by 2015. Especially for the less-developed ASEAN countries — all of which happen to be GMS countries (that is, Cambodia, Lao PDR, and Myanmar)[8] — the sequencing of reforms will be critical. Given the state of their financial systems, these countries would be ill-advised to move ahead with capital account liberalization too quickly. In order to avoid disturbances caused by too swift financial liberalization and capital account opening, the nature and speed of reform will have to differ from the more-advanced ASEAN countries. A coordinated approach between this subgroup of ASEAN countries may hence be useful to orchestrate a multispeed process within the ASEAN road map, and make the voices of the GMS countries heard in the ASEAN group.

Third, as shown once more by the global financial crisis (as well as through the Asian financial crisis), financial market stability is an important public good. Since financial market instabilities can easily transmit from one country to another, financial market stability is also a regional public good. Contagion, that is, the cross-country transmission of shocks, makes it increasingly difficult, if not impossible, for open economies to isolate themselves from shocks to their trading partners or competitors. Research by Eichengreen, Rose, and Wyplosz (1996) and Glick and Rose (1999) has shown that financial and currency crises tend to spread along regional lines, and that trade linkages are an important transmission channel for crises. Glick and Rose's findings suggest that countries may be attacked because of the actions — or inaction — of their neighbours which tend to be trading partners merely because of geographical proximity. They conclude that "[c]ountries who trade and compete with the targets of speculative attacks are themselves likely to be attacked" (Glick and Rose 1999, p. 604). The risk of financial contagion provides a strong argument for regional financial and regulatory cooperation, that is, the presence of spillover effects or externalities justify intervention at the regional level and the need for regulation to limit cross-border contagion. Cooperation among the GMS countries could supplement the existing ASEAN and ASEAN+3 initiatives in the area of financial cooperation.[9]

While more financial cooperation among the GMS countries is desirable, this need not result in new institutions or a duplication of initiatives that are already taking place within the ASEAN and ASEAN+3 frameworks. Indeed, the GMS countries should make use of existing initiatives and institutions wherever possible. For instance, they could coordinate their activities with the Macroeconomic and Finance Surveillance Office (MFSO) at the ASEAN Secretariat and the ASEAN+3 Macroeconomic Research Office (AMRO), which was established under the Chiang Mai Initiative Multilateralization (CMIM) process in 2011. In addition, they could meet regularly at the sidelines of ASEAN or ASEAN+3 meetings to address issues that are of particular relevance to them, but less so for the advanced ASEAN countries, or the "plus three" countries, respectively.

CONCLUSIONS

This chapter made the case for financial cooperation among the GMS countries. After a brief review of why financial markets matter for economic development, the chapter outlines three reasons for financial cooperation among GMS countries: (i) an exchange of experiences in financial market reform and development can provide for mutual learning and peer pressure for progress in financial market reform; (ii) cooperation in setting common norms and standards will facilitate regional financial integration; and (iii) financial cooperation is crucial for securing regional financial market stability and enabling quick responses to fend off unintended cross-border spillovers.

Notes

1. The notion that financial development stimulates economic growth dates back to Adam Smith (1776, p. 394), who noted that once the first banks had been established in Scotland, "trade and industry ... increased very considerably" and "that banks have contributed a good deal to this increase, cannot be doubted". Walter Bagehot (1873) and Joseph Schumpeter (1912) similarly stressed a positive causal relationship between financial development and economic activity.
2. For surveys of the finance-growth nexus and a more detailed discussion, see Pagano (1993), Levine (1997, 2005), and Haber (2008).
3. See Pagano (1993) in particular.
4. Given the recent experience with the (dis)ability of leading financial institutions to distinguish between good and bad investment opportunities, the critical reader may have some reservations regarding this theoretical proposition.
5. The case of Vietnam's financial sector development, however, is a very special one, given the transformation of the Vietnamese financial sector from a mono-banking to a commercially oriented financial sector, which is nonetheless still state dominated.
6. Since 1998, ASEAN has installed a regional surveillance mechanism, namely the ASEAN Surveillance Process (ASP), through which regulatory issues in the financial sector are identified and discussed as part of the peer review process of finance ministers and their deputies. The informal peer review involves an exchange of views on key aspects of financial regulation and supervision, although outcomes are often cloudy and lack follow-up actions.
7. See ASEAN Secretariat (2010) for information on the Roadmap for Monetary and Financial Integration.
8. Cambodia, the Lao PDR, and Myanmar are classified by the World Bank as "low income" countries; Vietnam graduated only recently from this category and became a "lower middle income" country, like Thailand. See <http://data.worldbank.org/country>.
9. As a response to the Asian financial crisis, the ASEAN+3 countries (the ten ASEAN countries plus China, Japan, and Korea) have initiated various initiatives to foster regional cooperation, including an economic review and policy dialogue and the Chiang Mai Initiative for the provision of crisis financing. On the latter see, for example, McKay et al. (2011) and Kawai (2010).

References

ASEAN Secretariat. "Financial Integration in ASEAN", Factsheet. ASEAN Secretariat: Jakarta, 2010 <http://www.aseansec.org/Fact%20Sheet/AEC/AEC-04.pdf>.

Bagehot, W. *Lombard Street: A Description of the Money Market*. London: Henry S. King and Co., 1873.

Garber, P.M. *Famous First Bubbles: The Fundamentals of Early Manias*. Cambridge, MA: MIT Press, 2000.

Haber, S. "The Finance-Growth Nexus: Theory, Evidence and Implications for Africa". Paper prepared for the conference, "African Finance for the 21st Century" organized by the IMF Institute and the Joint Africa Institute, Tunis, 4–5 March 2008.

Kindleberger, C.P. and R.Z. Aliber. *Manias, Panics, and Crashes: A History of Financial Crises*. 5th ed. Hoboken, NJ: John Wiley, 2005.

Kawai, M. "East Asian Financial Co-operation and the Role of the ASEAN+3 Macroeconomic Research Office". In *Regional and Global Liquidity Arrangements*, edited by U. Volz and A. Caliari. Bonn: German Development Institute, 2010.

Krugman, P.R. "Making Banking Boring". *New York Times*, 9 April 2009 <http://www.nytimes.com/2009/04/10/opinion/10krugman.html>.

Levine, R. "Financial Development and Economic Growth: Views and Agenda". *Journal of Economic Literature* 35, no. 2 (1997): 688–726.

———. "Finance and Growth: Theory and Evidence". In *Handbook of Economic Growth*, edited by P. Aghion and S. Durlauf. Amsterdam: Elsevier, 2005.

McKay, J., U. Volz, and R. Wölfinger. "Regional Financing Arrangements and the Stability of the International Monetary System". *Journal of Globalization and Development* 2, no. 1 (2011).

Pagano, M. "Financial Markets and Growth: An Overview". *European Economic Review* 37, no. 2–3 (1993): 613–22.

Schumpeter, J.A. *Theorie der wirtschaftlichen Entwicklung*. Leipzig: Duncker & Humblot, 1912.

Smith, A. *An Inquiry into the Nature and Causes of the Wealth of Nations* (1997 edition). London: Penguin, 1776.

10

THE CHALLENGES OF GMS REGIONAL INTEGRATION
Case Study of Governance of the Logistics Industry in Thailand

Narong Pomlaktong, Chaiyasit Anuchitworawong, Rattana Jongwilaiwan, and Prakai Theerawattanakul

With the initiative and assistance of the Asian Development Bank, the Greater Mekong Subregion (GMS) economic cooperation programme was established in 1992 to promote closer economic cooperation among the GMS countries, which include Cambodia, the Lao People's Democratic Republic, Myanmar, Thailand, Yunnan province of China, and Vietnam. The GMS countries so far have a strong political will to foster closer cooperation through intergovernmental collaborations in such areas as agriculture, energy, telecommunications, tourism, transport infrastructure, and the like. However, different country backgrounds, objectives, and intentions among the GMS countries tend to create political impediments to cooperation and emerging innovative development.

In recent years, governance has emerged as a discipline for fostering development and cooperation because good governance theoretically and practically will deliver effective public service and create economic efficiency and equity for long-term and sustainable development of an economy. However, governance issues are likely to be much more complicated at an international level. To show that governance is an important element when discussing regional economic activities, this study therefore provides case studies in the logistics industry to demonstrate that governance is an important mechanism that should be promoted not only at a national level, but also at the regional level when dealing with development issues in the GMS.

The cross-border governance issues in the logistics industry become increasingly important as ASEAN moves towards the ASEAN Economic Community (AEC) in 2015 because the industry will be related to regional public goods provision which require effective national road infrastructure and coherent coordination of transport infrastructure policies across the GMS countries' borders. In tackling the problems that might occur, improved governance and a favourable policy and regulatory framework, along with capable institutions, will be the key factors for successful regional economic development and integration.

To investigate the governance issues in the logistics industry in Thailand and its importance at the regional level, this chapter explores the inefficient pricing framework, as well as weak regulatory and law enforcement in the Thai transport industry, and bottlenecks in cross-border transport in the GMS. Specifically, the chapter is divided into six sections. The next section gives an overview of governance in Thailand and other GMS countries. The section that follows discusses the challenges of the domestic transport market in Thailand. In this section, we attempt to show that weaknesses in pricing, regulatory and law enforcement, and corruption at the national level, are an output of bad governance of a weak institutional and regulatory framework, resulting in high transaction costs, poor quality of service provision, and reduced national competitiveness. The problem of national governance is a cornerstone for strengthening regional governance, which will certainly impinge on interstate transport and regional trade agreements. The next section provides an overview of the international road transport market in Thailand and further points out that weak governance caused by a poor institutional and regulatory framework will bring about an unfair allocation of costs and benefits, and high transactions costs of the cross-border transport market. Even worse, this will lead to poor public service provision and inefficiency in the market. Lastly, the concluding section provides some recommendations for policymakers and the GMS governments to help promote good governance practices in the provision of regional public goods and eventually help achieve the ultimate goals of sustainable development and regional integration.

OVERVIEW OF GOVERNANCE IN THAILAND AND OTHER GMS COUNTRIES

This section provides an overview of governance in Thailand and other GMS countries based on the World Bank's report of its Worldwide Governance Indicators (WGI) that identify six dimensions of governance indicators for 212 countries and territories (Kaufmann D., A. Kraay, and M. Mastruzzi 2009).

The six dimensions of governance indicators include:

1. *Voice and Accountability (VA)*: This measures the extent to which citizens are able to participate in selecting their government and to enjoy freedom of expression, freedom of association, and a free media.
2. *Political Stability and Absence of Violence (PV)*: This measures the perceptions of the likelihood that the government will be destabilized or overthrown by unconstitutional or violent means.
3. *Government Effectiveness (GE)*: This measures the quality of public and civil services, the degree of their independence from political pressures, the quality of policy formulation and implementation, and the credibility of the government's commitment to such policies.
4. *Regulatory Quality (RQ)*: This measures the ability of the government to formulate and implement sound policies and regulations that permit and promote private sector development.
5. *Rule of Law (RL)*: This measures the extent to which agents have confidence in, and abide by, the rules of society, including the quality of contract enforcement and property rights, the police, and the courts.
6. *Control of Corruption (CC)*: This measures the extent to which public power is exercised for private gain, including both petty and grand forms of corruption, and control of the state by the elite and private interest.

Overall, these indicators highlight the vital factors of failed governance in the GMS, while suggesting several approaches to promoting regional integration. Figure 10.1 presents percentile ranks for all governance indicators in the period 2004–8. For Thailand, the country has on average dropped in the ranking of almost all governance indicators, particularly in the area of government effectiveness, control of corruption, voice and accountability, and political stability. Over the period, political stability ranks the lowest, followed by voice and accountability. The deterioration in the ranking of the latter indicator may be due to persistent political conflicts in the country. This is likely to affect the progress of regional economic integration as the problem can drag

FIGURE 10.1

Governance Indicators of Thailand by Dimensions of Governance from 2004 to 2008

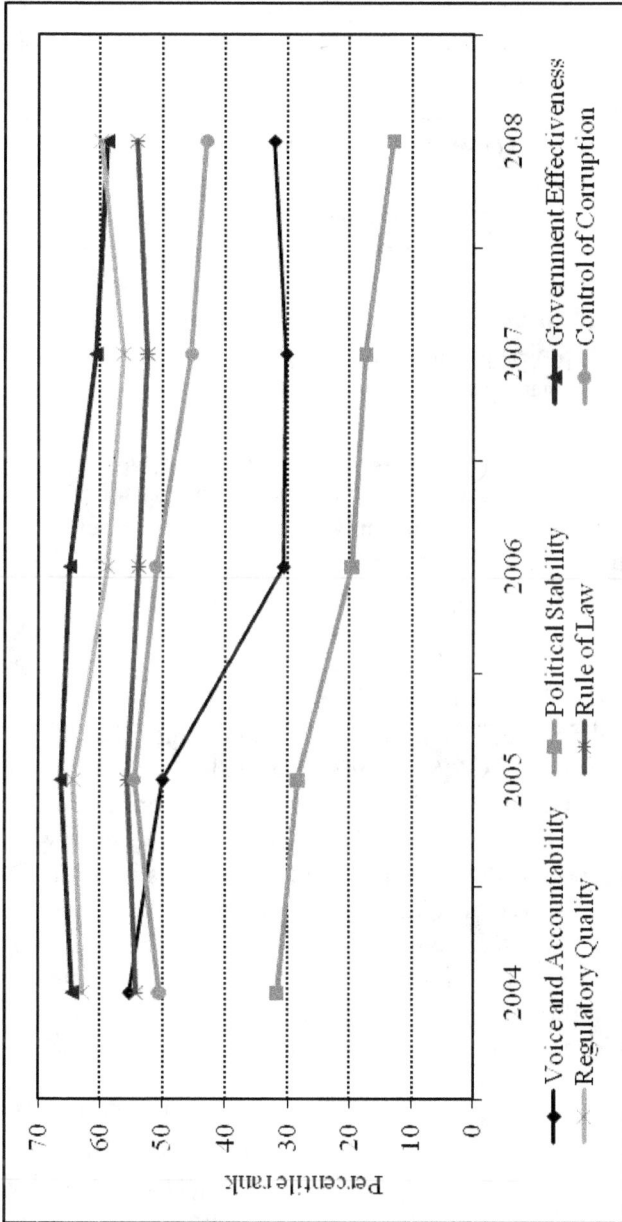

Source: Kaufmann D., A. Kraay, and M. Mastruzzi 2009.

down the national economy, affecting intraregional trade and causing a delay in the development of infrastructure projects that link Thailand with its neighbouring countries.

With regard to government effectiveness and control of corruption, the figure also shows that their ranking worsened to a certain degree, but not to the same extent as the two indicators mentioned above. The decline in government effectiveness score highlights the problem of lack of clarity about government policy. According to an interview with some Thai logistics providers, unclear government policies that make the private sector reluctant to make an investment are the most significant constraint for the GMS economic corridors development. Some notorious examples could be drawn from the case of the Southern Seaboard development project, or the energy development project in Surat Thani. To promote national logistics development and attract private sector investment, the government must come up with long-term credible investment policies and an appropriate legal framework. As importantly, all stakeholders' opinions and viewpoints must be taken into account and included as significant inputs in the logistics development plan, rather than have the plan rely only on the top-down approach in which the policies are formulated at the central government level only (TDRI 2009). As for the control of corruption, the case studies of road transport in Thailand to be described below further insist that institutional weakness, coupled with the lack of a regulatory framework and governance, would probably induce corruption at all levels in the sector.

In addition to governance in Thailand, this study also analyses the governance in other GMS countries. Generally, the literature on governance suggests that weakness and poor governance have considerable direct impacts on the economic growth and poverty reduction of a country. This therefore draws attention to the development of effective institutional and regulatory frameworks that complement regional economic cooperation frameworks such as the ASEAN Framework Agreement on Services and the ADB–Greater Mekong Subregion Economic Cooperation Program. Without good governance, the liberalization of the transport sector may create inefficiencies in the regional transport market and unfair practices that are detrimental to the interests of most countries in the region.

Comparing these indicators between Thailand and other GMS countries in 2008, we find that the governance of Thailand outperforms the other GMS countries in four areas, including regulatory quality, rule of law, control of corruption, voice and accountability, but is relatively weak in terms of political stability. With respect to government effectiveness, Thailand performs quite well compared with CLMV countries (Cambodia, Lao PDR, Myanmar, and

Vietnam); however, China ranked best among the GMS countries in this area (Figure 10.2). Strikingly, all the GMS countries do poorly under voice and accountability. This highlights the fact that in the countries where the people have no freedom to participate in selecting their governments, it may be hard to pressure public officials to be accountable to the public. As a result, it is not surprising that the score on control of corruption was quite low in all the GMS countries. Without public monitoring and pressure, the quality of

FIGURE 10.2
Governance Indicators of Thailand and Other GMS Countries by Dimensions of Governance in 2008

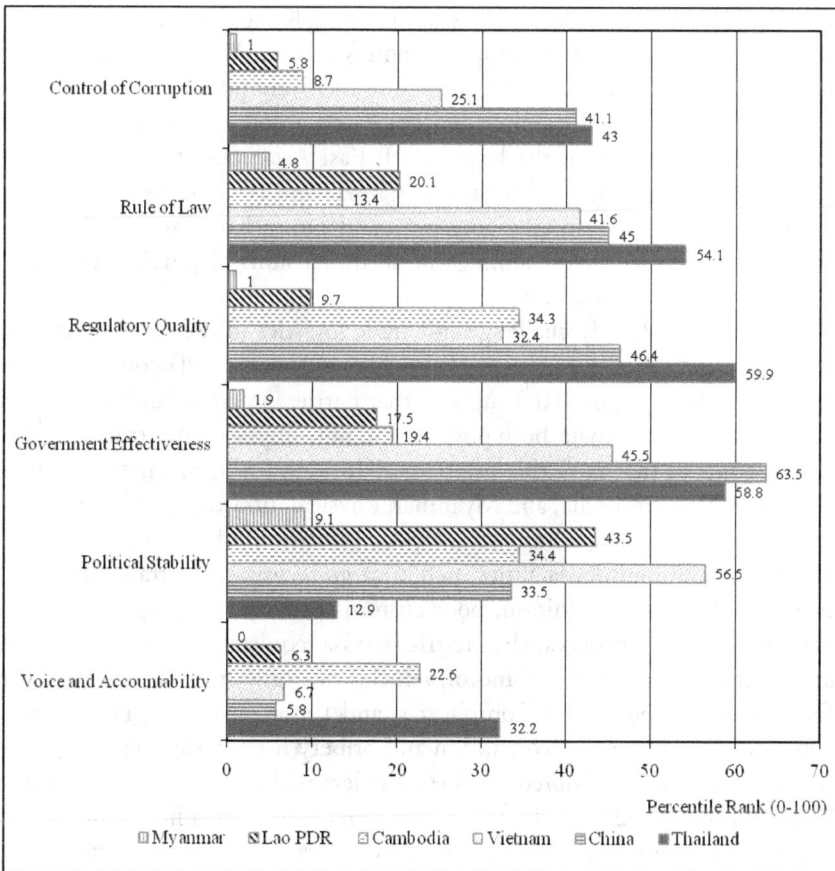

Source: Kaufmann D., A. Kraay, and M. Mastruzzi 2009.

civil service was therefore poor in those countries with a very poor score on the control of corruption and accountability.

In addition, some hindrance for logistics development in the region exists as the regulatory quality, policies, and regulations that permit and promote private sector development were rather limited in some countries such as the Lao PDR and Myanmar. Without active private-sector participation, the development and investment in infrastructure and logistics facilities would be a long process and would render the countries incapable of achieving effective transport linkages and an efficient logistics system in the region. Therefore, it is important for the GMS countries to enhance all aspects of good governance as a preliminary mechanism to creating trust and cooperation to achieve greater GMS integration.

Also reported in this study are the governance scores of several larger-GDP East Asian countries, including Singapore, Hong Kong, Taiwan, South Korea, Malaysia, Indonesia, the Philippines, and Vietnam. When compared with these countries, Thailand and China have relatively poor scores on control of corruption, political stability, and voice and accountability and were not comparable to several of the larger-GDP East Asian countries, particularly Taiwan, Singapore, South Korea, and China's special administrative region of Hong Kong. Interestingly, Singapore and Hong Kong are the only two that show strikingly high rankings in all dimensions of governance except for voice and accountability.

To further identify challenges for trade logistics in the GMS countries, this study examines the Logistics Performance Index[1] (LPI) constructed by the World Bank. Figure 10.3 suggests that barriers to cross-border trade can come in different formats, both physical and non-physical infrastructures. The three countries that have the lowest score in logistics infrastructure include the Lao PDR, Cambodia, and Myanmar. Physical infrastructure barriers may arise from insufficient infrastructure, poor conditions of road infrastructure, and the lack of logistics facilities such as cargo terminals for trans-shipment, or driver stations. In addition, poor customs performance might be due to software barriers. Barriers such as restrictive visa requirements for truck drivers and restrictions on entry of motor vehicles not only make border crossing formalities and procedures complicated and time consuming, but can also generate the channels for corruption and bribery for expediting cross-border transport operations. Moreover, these barriers will result in higher logistics costs and sometimes risk the loss of, or damage to, goods in transit. In this respect, the simplification of customs procedures by enhancing institutional quality and transparency can be an important method of improving customs performance which will result in trading cost reduction. The transparency

FIGURE 10.3
Logistics Performance Index of GMS Countries in 2010

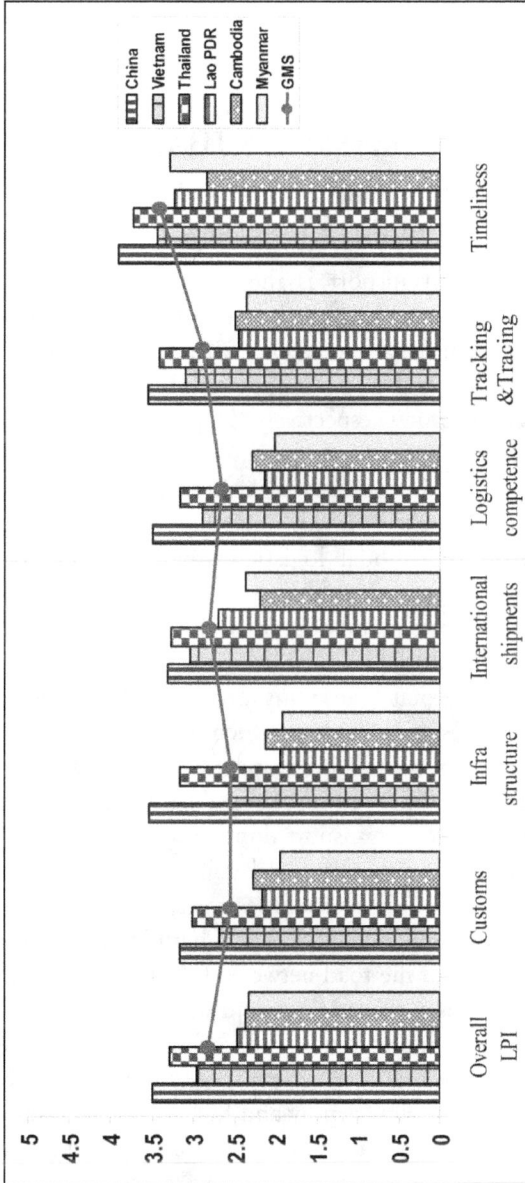

Source: World Bank 2010.

of import-export procedures and efficiency of regional international trade can be enhanced by IT modernization to create information linkages among central agencies, between central and border agencies, and between member countries, particularly import-export related agencies.

CHALLENGES OF THE DOMESTIC TRANSPORT MARKET IN THAILAND

Inefficient Road Pricing Framework: Price Distortion in Road Transport

In Thailand, road transport is the most important mode of transport, accounting for 63 per cent of total domestic passenger movement, and more than 80 per cent of freight transport, with 2 per cent of cargo moved by rail (424.5 million tonnes and 12.8 million tonnes out of the total freight quantity of 507.7 million tonnes respectively) in 2008 (Figures 10.4 and 10.5). The rest is split among inland waterway, coastal, and air transport. Nevertheless, Thailand's freight transport services exhibit some undue inefficiency caused by fleets of old trucks with low-load limits and low fuel efficiency, low penetration of multimodal logistics providers, limited capital for new investment by small firms, and limited use of Electronic Data Interchange for facilitating shipment and delivery and supply chain management (World Bank and NESDB, 2009).

Presently, the total land transport network in Thailand covers some 208,243 kilometres nationwide in which the road transport network takes up about 98 per cent and the rail transport network takes up 4,043 kilometres, accounting for only 2 per cent of the total land transport network (See Figure 10.6). The reason road transport dominates other modes of transportation in the movement of passengers and goods in Thailand is that the pricing method does not include externalities costs, such as infrastructure use, road damage, and environmental impacts. Such underpricing of road use therefore induces higher use of the road network. In other words, the longer length of the road network is a result of demand-driven policies and price distortion.

Without appropriate pricing, the road transport mode will still be widely used and it will be very difficult to promote a modal shift from road transport to more environmentally friendly and fuel efficient modes of transportation, such as rail and inland waterways. It is crucial for the government to have an appropriate pricing policy and vehicle taxation system for road and rail modes to reduce price distortion between the modes. Once the price is not distorted, rail transport prices can be lower than those for the road mode. This

FIGURE 10.4
The Modal Share in Passenger Transport in 2008
(Unit: thousand passengers)

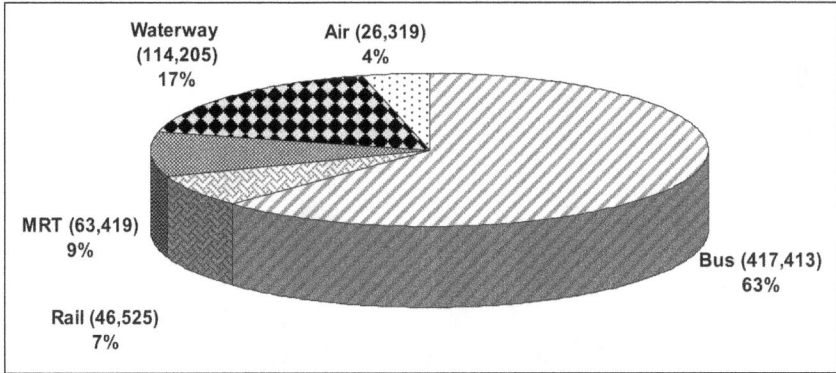

Waterway
(114,205)
17%

Air (26,319)
4%

MRT (63,419)
9%

Rail (46,525)
7%

Bus (417,413)
63%

Source: Ministry of Transport, Thailand.

FIGURE 10.5
The Modal Share in Freight Transport in 2008
(Unit: million tonnes per year)

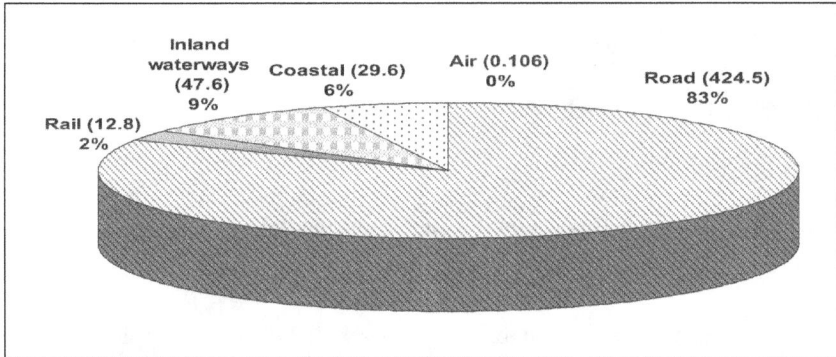

Inland
waterways
(47.6)
9%

Coastal (29.6)
6%

Air (0.106)
0%

Road (424.5)
83%

Rail (12.8)
2%

Source: Ministry of Transport, Thailand.

will rebalance the country's transport portfolio so that its railway network is expanded and benefits the transport and logistics sector, leading to a more efficient use of fuel and enhancing national competitiveness, particularly for long-distance freight shipment.

FIGURE 10.6
Road and Railway Networks in Thailand

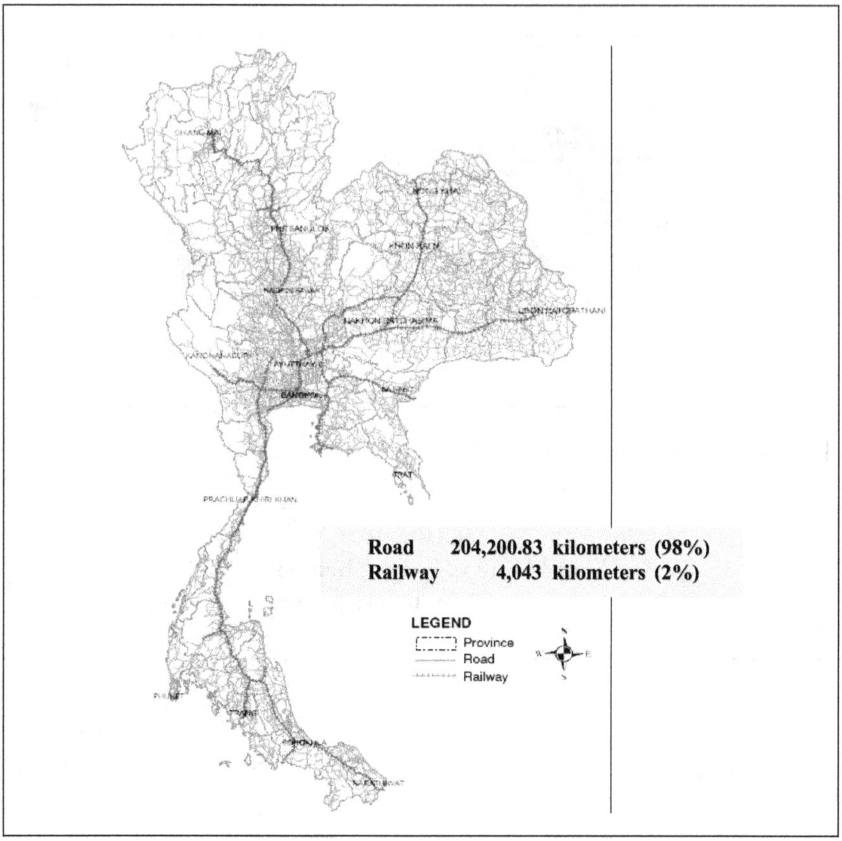

Road   204,200.83 kilometers (98%)
Railway   4,043 kilometers (2%)

LEGEND
- - - - Province
——— Road
- - - - - Railway

Source: State Railway of Thailand and Ministry of Transport (2009).

More importantly, road pricing issues will be more complicated after the liberalization of cross-border road transport. If the road pricing policy in Thailand remains as it is today, this means the country will allow foreign vehicles to use its national road infrastructure subsidized by national taxpayers. In the transport sector, since the ASEAN Framework Agreement on the Facilitation of Interstate Transport is a tool to further strengthen the transport facilitation and logistics environment, the country should take up the challenge to have an appropriate road pricing policy that also considers the cost of externalities involved in road transport.

To develop appropriate road pricing is one of the important governance issues in the provision of pubic goods because an appropriate pricing scheme will help promote proper cost and benefit sharing to ensure that the host country, which suffers from increased congestion, accidents, infrastructure damage, noise and air pollution, resulting from the use by neighbouring countries, will receive commensurate compensation. In other words, road prices need to be carefully regulated to ensure that regional public goods deliver the greatest benefit for society. Otherwise, simply building the physical transport infrastructure, without the introduction of efficient pricing and comprehensive information on actual costs from member countries, will not be sufficient to achieve the effective transportation linkages and efficient logistics of genuine economic corridors. Therefore, it requires the GMS institutional arrangement for appropriate road pricing method which charges users fairly so that the usage fee covers all relevant costs, including the cost of construction, maintenance, and externalities.

In order to strengthen our argument about the governance problem, we therefore provide two case studies associated with the poor governance problem in the following section to show that weakness in regulatory and enforcement agencies can cause high transaction costs and market inefficiency in Thailand's transport market.

Case Study 1: The Relationship Between Weakness of Regulatory and Enforcement Institutions, Diseconomy of Scale of Industry, and Market Inefficiency

Currently, the Department of Land Transport (DLT) under the Ministry of Transport, is the main regulator of land transport, responsible for administering vehicle registrations, taxation, vehicle inspections and regulations, and licensing, whereas the Traffic Police division under the Royal Thai Police is a traffic law enforcement agency (see Box 10.1). Technically, the traffic police division should work in collaboration with the DLT to ensure effective traffic law enforcement. For example, the two agencies have modernized law enforcement by having data linkages through the Police Information System, POLIS. This system reports on traffic law violations, with each case being sent to the DLT. A vehicle's owner must settle the police summons before paying the annual vehicle tax and have a driving licence renewal granted by the DLT. This measure is expected to encourage drivers to improve vehicle standards and safety practices, as well as reduce pollution and accidents. Nevertheless, the weakness of the regulatory framework set by the DLT causes diseconomy of scale for the industry and gives relevant agencies, such

---

BOX 10.1
Land Transport Regulatory and Law Enforcement Agencies

• **Department of Land Transport: A regulatory agency**
The Department of Land Transport was established on 11 September 1941. The DLT is responsible for the systematization and regulation of land transport by conducting monitoring and inspection to ensure the smooth running of, and conformity with, relevant land transport rules and regulations. Its duties also include administering vehicle registrations, taxation, vehicle inspections and regulations, driver training, testing and licensing, to prevent road accidents and promote national road safety. All these are handled by its respective offices at the head office in Bangkok and the provincial land transport offices in each province nationwide.

Public bus regulations
1) To supervise and control fixed-route buses to run on a fixed route and on the condition of picking up passengers at specific locations, according to a timetable, to collect bus fares at government regulated rates and to stop at regulated bus terminals;
2) To stipulate, improve, and revoke the bus route and to renew/withdraw bus operation licences;
3) To stipulate and improve the conditions of vehicle operations, and the number and category of vehicles;
4) To give information on fixing the fare rate to the Central Land Transport Control Board for approval;
5) To stipulate bus standards, to supervise the service quality of the transport operators in servicing passengers, to control bus safety (speed, duration of parking, and the age of a bus), and to control and examine the operation of the transport operators, crew and vehicles; and
6) To encourage and develop a system of mass transit by bus.

Freight transport regulations
All types of commercial fleets are regulated by DLT according to the provisions of the Land Transport Act, 1979, including truck for "hire and reward" to second parties and truck for own-account transport.

• **The Royal Thai Police: A traffic law enforcement agency**
The Royal Thai Police is a national law enforcement organization. Its main duties are crime prevention and suppression, and the promotion of the citizen's well-being, among which is the responsibility of traffic law enforcement. In the Bangkok metropolitan area, the Traffic Police Division and the nine metropolitan police divisions under the supervision of the Metropolitan Police Bureau are responsible for traffic surveillance activities. As for areas outside Bangkok, the Highway Police Division is responsible for traffic law enforcement on approximately 15,000 kilometre of national highways, out of a total of about 60,000 kilometre nationwide. The parts of highways not covered by the Highway Police are covered by the provincial police. They are responsible for traffic law enforcement such as speed and weight limits, pollutant emission levels of vehicles, checks, driving under laws, and so on.

as traffic police and private operators, some opportunity to be involved in corrupt dealings. This, in turn, creates high transaction costs and market inefficiency in the industry.

Weakness of Regulatory and Law Enforcement in the Bus Industry

At present, the public bus market in Thailand encounters several weaknesses, including high competition on overlapping routes, the presence of illegal vans and buses, unfair competition, as well as diseconomy of scale. The root causes of the problems are mainly due to the regulatory agency's inappropriate fare setting and licensing schemes, as well as weak enforceability.

First, the method for bus fare calculation, which is regulated by the DLT, is based on several assumptions that are very questionable, such as a maximum of seven years of vehicle use, and a 70–90 per cent load factor, varying with bus standards. In short, this cost-plus pricing[2] method does not take into account the addition to capacity and changes in load factor due to the issuing of new licences and actual passenger demand. Therefore, regulated bus operations generally have load factor levels and profit margins that are lower than the level that the DLT assumes. Consequently, bus operators have less incentive to make more investment and improve their quality of services. Not only does improper regulation affect service quality, but it also affects maintenance and replacement decisions. Nor can prices respond to demand shifts in the market: as the population increases, the gap between the quantity supplied and that demanded at the regulated price widens. This provides an incentive for the growth of an unregulated or "illegal" sector (TDRI 2010).

Second, although there is at present a policy of only "one licence per route", a firm granted such a licence usually will not operate the whole fleet itself, but will subcontract some of its operations to other private operators without competitive tendering. Thus, these operators have to compete with one another within the same route. Because of the poor licensing scheme and regulation by the DLT, the operators can subcontract the licence to small operators without competitive tendering, and illegal vans can operate in the market and only provide service on profit-making routes. The majority of bus operations are neither cost-effective nor cost-efficient. The bus operators, on average, face high costs per kilometre and lack economy of scale since there are many buses given the demand in the current market. The increase in the number of trips and trip distances will not create cost effectiveness, but rather lead to an oversupply of bus services in the market, thereby more loss-making operations as a consequence. Even worse, without strict enforcement by the regulator, many bus operators would use old vehicles, ignore maintenance and replacement requirements, and violate regulations. For example, bus operators in provincial areas would stop at places where they can pick up more passengers, but outside the designated stops that are allowed by the law. As the operators have been forced into using double standards, this gives rise to corruption and bribery to agencies (traffic police) to keep their operations going (see Box 10.2). Consequently it brings about negative social and environmental impacts to society as a whole, such as unsafe public bus service provision, high road accident rates, and environmental problems from the polluting vehicles.

In addition, the public bus provision is unable to meet the demand for bus services in suburban residential areas. The BMTA (Bangkok Mass Transit Authority) cannot provide adequate, convenient, and comfortable services for commuters who travel from suburbs to work in the city. Illegal vans can bridge the gap between the lack of public air-conditioned buses and the increasing demand of Bangkok-vicinity commuters. The DLT thus has a policy to legalize the operation of illegal vans. However, a large number of vans apparently continue to operate illegally, which will affect the number of passengers on a legal route, particularly air-conditioned bus routes, and the ability of the bus system to meet its service obligations. Illegal vans provide alternative services on the profit-making routes. The reason that illegal van operators have become more popular in recent years is that their services meet the people's need and changing lifestyle, that is, they are offering shorter and faster routes with guaranteed seats and also a door-to-door service.

Weakness of Regulatory and Law Enforcement in the Truck Industry

Similar to what has been experienced in domestic passenger transport, we can observe a weak regulatory environment in truck transport. Although the freight transport market in Thailand is considered a free competitive market as there is no price regulation by the regulatory agency, truck operators are required to satisfy stipulated vehicle standards through licensing conditions with very simple requirements.

However, without effective regulatory control and enforcement capabilities in the truck industry, there are too many "for hire and reward" truck operators in the market. Own-account trucks also compete with "for hire and reward" truck operators. Consequently the road freight transport market by truck is excessively competitive among small operators. Due to the excess supply of truck services in the market and without proper law enforcement, many truck operators often use predatory pricing to eliminate competitors for survival. To

BOX 10.2
Diseconomy of Scale of the Bus Industry and Poor Governance

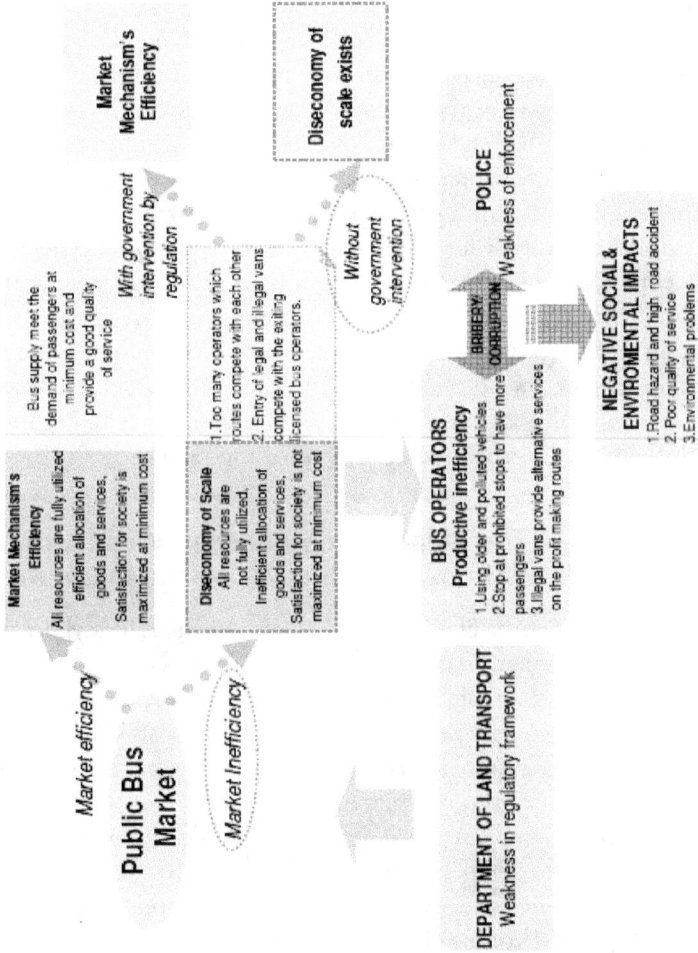

Public Bus Market

Market efficiency

Market Inefficiency

Market Mechanism's Efficiency
All resources are fully utilized, efficient allocation of goods and services. Satisfaction for society is maximized at minimum cost

Diseconomy of Scale
All resources are not fully utilized. Inefficient allocation of goods and services. Satisfaction for society is not maximized at minimum cost

Market Mechanism's Efficiency
Bus supply meet the demand of passengers at minimum cost and provide a good quality of service

With government intervention by regulation

1. Too many operators which routes compete with each other
2. Entry of legal and illegal vans compete with the exiting licensed bus operators.

Without government intervention

Diseconomy of scale exists

BUS OPERATORS
Productive inefficiency
1. Using older and polluted vehicles
2. Stop at prohibited stops to have more passengers
3. Illegal vans provide alternative services on the profit making routes

POLICE
Weakness of enforcement

BRIBERY, CORRUPTION

DEPARTMENT OF LAND TRANSPORT
Weakness in regulatory framework

NEGATIVE SOCIAL & ENVIROMENTAL IMPACTS
1. Road hazard and high road accident
2. Poor quality of service
3. Environmental problems

do this, they are forced to do anything (for instance, carry overweight loads and reduce the quality of service by using older and polluting truck fleets) to keep their operating costs at a minimum. But this comes at a cost to society because the operators would probably have to be involved in bribery and corruption to avoid paying fines for violating laws, thereby also indirectly causing road deterioration, unsafe traffic conditions, and environmental impacts (see Box 10.3).

According to the World Bank (2008), there should be a clearer regulatory framework and stronger enforcement mechanism to prevent overutilization of roads, as well as to enhance the efficiency of the freight transport industry. Specifically, the DLT and Traffic Police officers must enforce vehicle standards, licensing procedures, and traffic laws strictly, which will lead to an improvement in market efficiency and governance in the industry.

Another solution for the freight market is to have a general freight rate guideline for freight operators.[3] According to the guideline, the freight rate will be used as a reference price for operators so that they have a basis for pricing and can avoid predatory pricing practices and follow an appropriate pricing scheme that promotes quality competition. In an efficient market, the service quality of operators will be an important criterion for survival as inefficient operators will be driven out of the market.

Case Study 2: The Relationship between Weak Urban Town Planning, Regulations, and Impacts on the Domestic Market

During the past ten to fifteen years, changes in people's lifestyles, as well as their desire for convenience and assured quality, have been among several factors that have led to the rapid expansion of modern trade businesses in Thailand. These have grown in scale and number after the post-1997 financial crisis as foreign investors could gain substantial benefit from the sharp depreciation of the Thai baht during the period.

In general, the fast growing modern trade businesses tend to affect traditional trade retailers adversely (see Box 10.4). Although the Thai government agencies regulate the expansion of modern trade businesses in terms of size and zoning through town planning and building control laws under the Ministry of Interior, these laws are far from effective as they only regulate zoning and sizes of modern trade businesses away from the cities. With such a loophole, modern trade businesses can still expand their outlets by downsizing to the express stores form. At present the government still does not have any effective regulations to ensure fair competition between modern and traditional trade businesses and suppliers.

BOX 10.3
Diseconomy of Scale of Truck Industry and Poor Governance

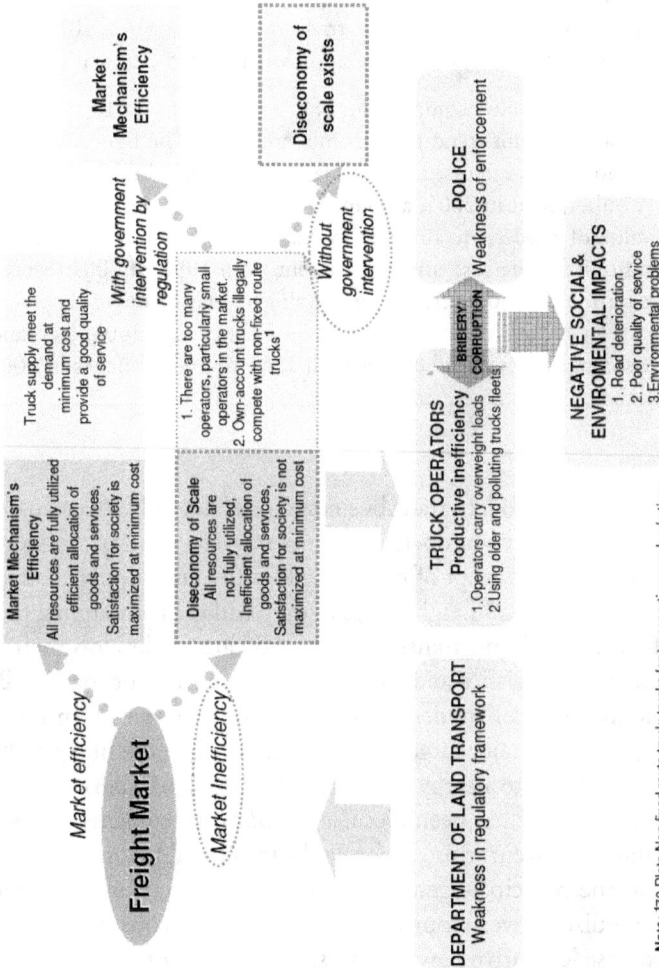

Freight Market

Market efficiency

Market Inefficiency

Market Mechanism's Efficiency
All resources are fully utilized efficient allocation of goods and services.
Satisfaction for society is maximized at minimum cost

Diseconomy of Scale
All resources are not fully utilized.
Inefficient allocation of goods and services,
Satisfaction for society is not maximized at minimum cost

Truck supply meet the demand at minimum cost and provide a good quality of service

With government intervention by regulation

1. There are too many operators, particularly small operators in the market.
2. Own-account trucks illegally compete with non-fixed route trucks[1]

Without government intervention

Market Mechanism's Efficiency

Diseconomy of scale exists

DEPARTMENT OF LAND TRANSPORT
Weakness in regulatory framework

TRUCK OPERATORS
Productive inefficiency
1. Operators carry overweight loads
2. Using older and polluting trucks fleets

BRIBERY CORRUPTION

POLICE Weakness of enforcement

NEGATIVE SOCIAL & ENVIROMENTAL IMPACTS
1. Road deterioration
2. Poor quality of service
3. Environmental problems

Note: [1]70 Plate Non fixed route truck: trucks for transporting goods of others.
80 and 90 Plate truck: private trucks transporting own goods (i.e. own account).
As of 2009, there are a total of 631,057 vehicles of private trucks (80/90 plate truck) and
154,298 vehicles of non-fixed route truck (70 plate-truck).

BOX 10.4
Impacts of Modern Trade Business on Traditional Trade Retailers

The expansion of multinational chains of hypermarkets has had an adverse impact on traditional stores since Thai firms lack the know-how and capital to compete with large foreign retailers. TDRI (2002) reported that within one kilometre around a hypermarket, traditional trade decreased by 17 per cent from April 2000 to July 2002, or approximately 8.5 per cent annually.

Comparing the value composition of the retail trade in 1998 and 2001, we can see a significant trend towards modern trade. The figures show that total retail trade value increased substantially from 660.8 billion baht in 1998 to 1,194 billion baht in 2001, accounting for an 80 per cent increase. Strikingly, the value of modern retail trade increased by 182 per cent while the value of traditional trade rose only 28 per cent from 1998 to 2001. Moreover, the contribution of modern trade in total value of retail trade rose apparently from only 34.1 per cent in 1998 to around 53.2 per cent in 2001. Its branches also increased rapidly from ninety-seven in 2001 to 166 branches in 2008.

The entry of modern trade businesses does not only affect small traditional retailers, but also freight operators as the modern retail businesses come with a more advanced concept of managing logistics and supply chains efficiently. This thus affects local freight firms as they will gain a marginal profit margin from focusing only on transportation and cannot develop their capacity to compete in the logistics and supply chain management market. Besides, the strategic locations of modern trade businesses are mostly in the inner areas of Bangkok and major large cities; therefore, they are likely to bring about traffic congestion to nearby areas (Figures 10.7 and 10.8).

To make what has been discussed about the problems in the retail trade sector more apparent, this section looks into the relationship between actors based on the principal-agent-client model. In the regulatory processes, one can distinguish between four actors: (i) the citizens/consumers/users; (ii) those who exercise legislative power, that is, politicians or the government; (iii) the regulatory agencies such as the Ministry of Interior or Ministry of Commerce; (iv) the regulated firm, namely modern trade businesses and traditional trade retailers (see Figure 10.9).

In principle, regulators should be able to regulate firms for the maximum welfare or benefit of citizens/consumers, as well as maintain fair competition among regulated firms. The problem, nevertheless, occurs when regulators

FIGURE 10.7

The Distribution of Hypermarkets in Thailand

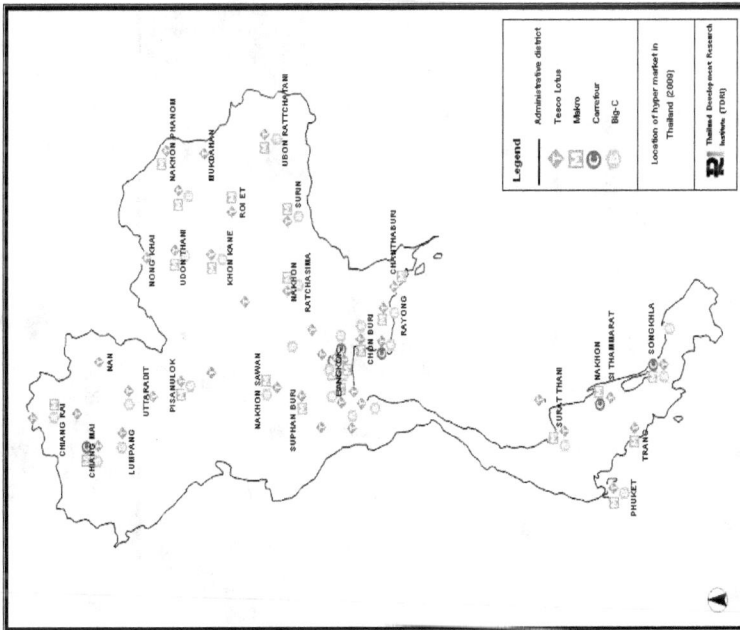

Hypermarkets	2001	2008	% change
Makro	20	30	33.33
Tesco-Lotus	33	67	50.75
Big C	30	47	36.17
Carrefour	14	22	36.36
Total	97	166	41.57

Source: Ministry of Transport 2008.

FIGURE 10.8
The Distribution of Hypermarkets in Bangkok

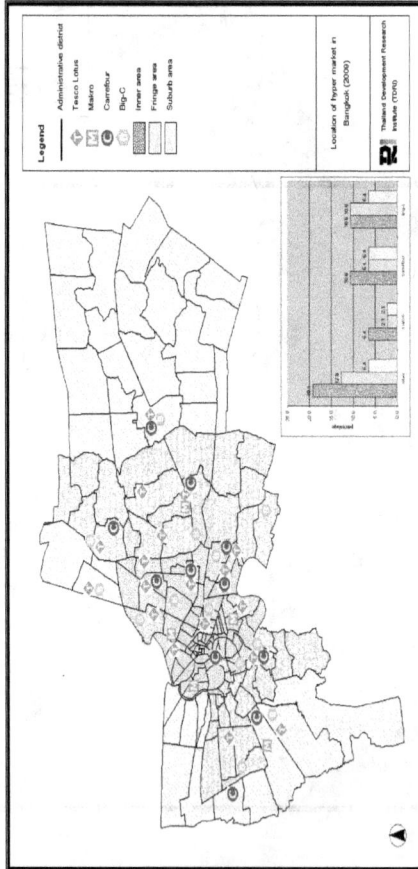

Bangkok	Total
Inner areas	22
Fringe areas	15
Suburbs	10
Total	47 (28.31% of the total number of hypermarkets in Thailand)

Source: Ministry of Transport 2008.

FIGURE 10.9
The Problems in Regulation of Retail Trade Sectors in Thailand

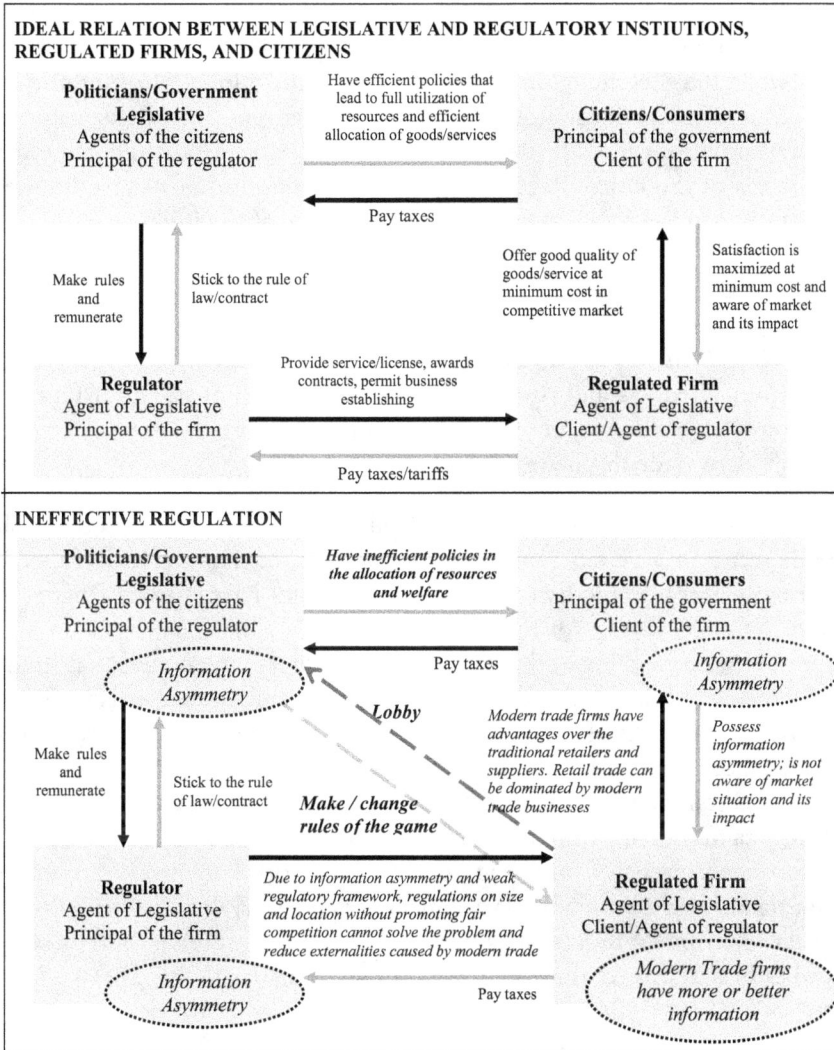

IDEAL RELATION BETWEEN LEGISLATIVE AND REGULATORY INSTIUTIONS, REGULATED FIRMS, AND CITIZENS

Politicians/Government
Legislative
Agents of the citizens
Principal of the regulator

Have efficient policies that lead to full utilization of resources and efficient allocation of goods/services

Citizens/Consumers
Principal of the government
Client of the firm

Pay taxes

Make rules and remunerate

Stick to the rule of law/contract

Offer good quality of goods/service at minimum cost in competitive market

Satisfaction is maximized at minimum cost and aware of market and its impact

Regulator
Agent of Legislative
Principal of the firm

Provide service/license, awards contracts, permit business establishing

Regulated Firm
Agent of Legislative
Client/Agent of regulator

Pay taxes/tariffs

INEFFECTIVE REGULATION

Politicians/Government
Legislative
Agents of the citizens
Principal of the regulator

Have inefficient policies in the allocation of resources and welfare

Citizens/Consumers
Principal of the government
Client of the firm

Information Asymmetry

Pay taxes

Information Asymmetry

Lobby

Modern trade firms have advantages over the traditional retailers and suppliers. Retail trade can be dominated by modern trade businesses

Possess information asymmetry; is not aware of market situation and its impact

Make rules and remunerate

Stick to the rule of law/contract

Make / change rules of the game

Regulator
Agent of Legislative
Principal of the firm

Due to information asymmetry and weak regulatory framework, regulations on size and location without promoting fair competition cannot solve the problem and reduce externalities caused by modern trade

Regulated Firm
Agent of Legislative
Client/Agent of regulator

Information Asymmetry

Pay taxes

Modern Trade firms have more or better information

Source: Adapted from Lambsdorff 2001 and Boethm 2007.

cannot take action because their legislative principles are very often influenced by lobbying.[4] This eventually causes failure in governance as there is no regulation and control over fair competition between modern trade and traditional trade businesses. However, the problem of unfair market competition also arises due to information asymmetries among regulatory institutions, consumers, and the firms.

- Only traditional trade businesses that gradually disappear from the market and suppliers that suffer from unfair trade practices desire the regulation, while the government may not see retail regulation as a high priority.
- Municipal administrators are not aware of adverse impacts or negative externalities caused by the presence of hypermarkets located in the inner areas of the cities. Regulators (municipal administrators) give licences to hypermarkets by considering only the size of the building and areas without taking into consideration all negative externalities such as traffic congestion, environmental impacts, and health problems caused to the residents.
- Consumers might not see the adverse impacts since hypermarkets offer cheap products and convenience. Thus, there is not sufficient pressure on the government to enact or amend the retail trade law to regulate modern trade businesses.

Overall, Thailand needs effective regulation of and enforcement in the retail trade sector to have fair competition between modern and traditional retail businesses because modern retail trade companies have many strengths in terms of scale, sources of funds, and know-how, while Thai firms do not. Due to the concern about the impact of modern retail trade, the Retail Trade Law has been drafted in order to limit the monopoly power of large firms, protect the interests of suppliers and traditional retailers, and protect market dominance by modern trade businesses in the long run.[5]

Based on the two case studies described above, we can easily understand that weaknesses in the governance mechanism, weak institutions, and enforcement agencies, and inappropriate regulatory frameworks are major constraints for the economic development of the country. It is the responsibility of the government to legislate and make policies to ensure market efficiency and public welfare, and to monitor and enforce laws strictly.

OVERVIEW OF THE INTERNATIONAL ROAD TRANSPORT MARKET IN THAILAND

International Transport under Bilateral Agreement

Apart from the development of the domestic road transport network, globalization has brought about a demand for goods and services that requires improved infrastructure and more efficient transport systems as a precondition for economic development. Thailand, which has paid attention to the intercity road transport linkages with neighbouring countries and subregional groups, recently signed several agreements to facilitate cooperation in the road transport sector.

Currently the international road transport service is not open to competition. Cross-border transport between Thailand and neighbouring countries is allowed only between border cities (that is, up to 7 kilometres from the borders). Cross-border transport must be operated under a bilateral agreement; for example, Thailand–Malaysia and Thailand–Lao PDR multilateral agreements such as the ASEAN Economic Cooperation Agreement and the Asian Development Bank (ADB)–Greater Mekong Subregion Economic Cooperation Programme (see below). The government regulates the international haulage by having an international haulage licence quota (except for the cross-border transport between Thailand–Lao PDR (see Box 10.5). The operators will be selected and approved by the DLT: under section 25 of the Land Transport Act, AD 1979, the operators provide transport under the bilateral and multilateral international road transport agreement between Thailand and its neighbouring countries.

BOX 10.5
Bilateral Agreements on Road Freight Transport Service

- *Thailand–Malaysia*: Memorandum of Understanding (MoU) between Thailand and Malaysia on the Movement in Transit of Perishable goods by road from Thailand through Malaysia to Singapore 1979. Under this bilateral agreement, cross-border transport is allowed only for perishable goods from Thailand to Singapore, travelling through Malaysia. It also has an annual quantitative limitation of goods as well as a specific transport route. The cross-border road transport service between Thailand and Malaysia is an oligopoly in which there are currently three transport operators under this agreement.

- *Thailand–Lao PDR*: Agreement Between the Government of the Kingdom of Thailand and the Government of the Lao People's Democratic Republic on Road Transport, 1999 and the Subsidiary Agreement Specifying Road Transport Arrangement between the Government of Thailand and the Government of the Lao PDR, 2001. This bilateral agreement is the first liberalization of international road transport services.

Source: Land Transport Promotion Center, Department of Land Transport 2010.

Multilateral Agreements

Multilateral agreements are also important for the structure of the road transport markets (TDRI 2010).

ASEAN Framework Agreement on Services

ASEAN started its services liberalization project with the ASEAN Framework Agreement on Services (AFAS). The liberalization of international road freight transport services is expected to be achieved by 2015. As for liberalization with respect to commercial presence, ASEAN nationals are allowed an equity participation of no less than 49 per cent by 2008, 51 per cent by 2010, and 70 per cent by 2013. AFAS also includes customs facilitation for transit goods that will be exempt from customs formalities. The transport facilitation will allow 500 vehicles in each member country to operate cross-border transport,[6] develop multimodal transport, and facilitate trade to allow the door-to-door delivery of goods, thus reducing the logistics, time and cost, and harmonizing road transport laws to facilitate movement across land borders, as well as supporting the regional supply-chain and logistics network.

ADB–Greater Mekong Subregion Economic Cooperation Programme

The Greater Mekong Subregion (GMS) regional economic cooperation framework was formulated in 1992 and funded by the ADB with the aim of facilitating efficient freight and passenger cross-border transport, which will improve intraregional market access for GMS products and trade competitiveness. The GMS programme covers nine sectors — agriculture, energy, environment, telecommunications, human resource development, investment, tourism, trade, and private sector development, with the priority being on the transport sector (JICA 2007).

Several flagship infrastructure projects were identified, and three "Economic Corridors" — the North–South Economic Corridor (NSEC, covering Southern China–Lao PDR–Myanmar–Thailand), the East–West Economic Corridor (EWEC, covering Myanmar–Thailand–Lao PDR–Vietnam), and the Southern Economic Corridor (SEC, covering Thailand–Cambodia–Vietnam) — were prioritized in the GMS transport sector development plan. Other corridors identified in the initial framework were: Western (Tamu–Mawlamyine); Eastern (Kunming–Ho Chi Minh City and Nanning–Bangkok/Laem

Chabang), Central (Kunming–Sihanoukville/Satthaip), and Southern Coastal (Bangkok–Namcan).

The performance of the economic corridors can be demonstrated by the reduction in time and cost of transport from Bangkok to Danang Port. Figure 10.10 shows that there has been a significant improvement in these performance indicators. The investment in infrastructure and facilities, particularly the second Mekong International Bridge and the cross-border formalities facilitation agreement has led to drastic reductions in logistics cost and time while increasing cross-border trade. The overall transport cost fell from approximately US$3,000 to US$2,070 and the transport time improved by almost 13 hours (from 40 hours 40 minutes in 2000 to 28 hours in 2007), although we could notice a slight increase in logistics costs in 2009 which was mainly due to a rise in fuel prices during the period. In addition, the bridge was likely to be an important factor that created a considerable impact on the increase in trade value between Thailand and the Lao PDR (see Box 10.6).

Overall the significant reduction in logistics time and costs in these economic corridors will benefit the transport of various types of goods to and from Thailand, particularly perishable goods where "time" is the essence for the traders' ability to ensure quality control. The GMS economic corridor development will enable Thailand to export fruit to China within three days and so leave it with more days to distribute fresher and higher quality fruit in China.

The GMS agreement also covers the removal of non-physical barriers to the cross-border movement of people, vehicles, and goods, such as facilitating border crossing formalities and the exchange of traffic rights through a GMS cross-border transport agreement (CBTA). There are seventeen annexes and three protocols which allow flexibility for ratification by countries: all member countries have ratified the annexes and protocols except for Thailand, which has not ratified Annexes 1, 4, 6, 7, 8, 9, 10, 14, and Protocol 3, and Myanmar, which has not ratified any of the annexes and protocols. In liberalizing international road transport, the agreement allows the admission of foreign vehicles registered in member countries for those that satisfy the technical requirements (for example, weight limit and vehicle length). Its implementation is divided into two phases. The first phase is committed to the reciprocal recognition of foreign vehicles by the quota limitation: the 500 permits that can be issued are subject to limits on frequency, capacity, and the number of transport operators. The second phase will open a free market system without any restrictions. The governments of the contracting parties are authorized to regulate the safety and weight limit of vehicles while

FIGURE 10.10

Time and Cost Improvement after the Bridge Opened, Bangkok-Danang Route

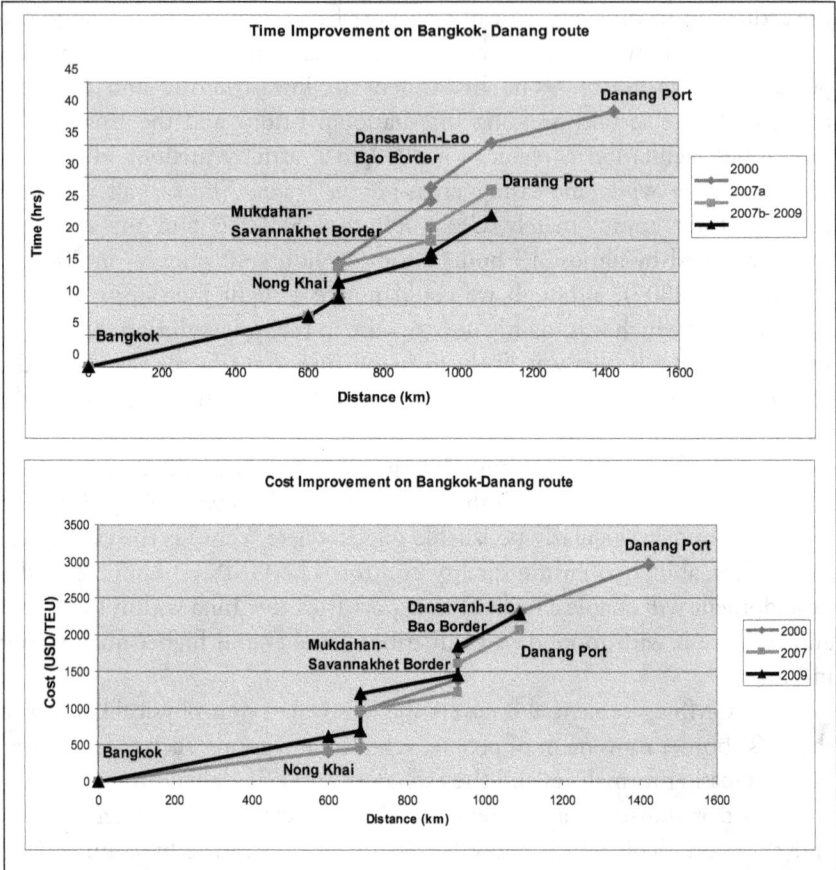

Source: TDRI 2010.

the pricing of cross-border transport will be determined by market forces. Each government is entitled to regulate the market domination under the supervision of the Joint Committee.

One of the major breakthroughs under the GMS is the trial of the Customs Transit System and Exchange of Traffic Rights in Thailand, Lao PDR, and Vietnam, which allows registered trucks in these countries to go through foreign territory on the R9 route from Mukdahan Province in Thailand to Savannakhet (Lao PDR), and then to Lao Bao, Dong Ha, and

---

BOX 10.6
Impacts from the GMS East-West Economic Corridor,
Mukdahan Checkpoint

The major consequence of an infrastructure development project, a second Mekong International Bridge, is the increase in trade value between Thailand and the Lao PDR. The total trade value between Thailand and the Lao PDR at the Mukdahan checkpoint has grown rapidly from THB4 billion in 2003 to THB24 billion in 2009. The export value has increased from THB3 billion in 2003 to THB9 billion in 2009 while the import value has significantly increased from THB665 million to THB15 billion. The average annual growth rate for the past seven years of import value is 68.1 per cent and of export value is 18.7 per cent.

Notably, the second Mekong International Bridge has resulted in a significant increase in the import of copper, wooden products, and metal from the Lao PDR. The bridge allowed the transport of heavy goods such as wood and metal products through the Mukdahan checkpoint since these could not be transported by ferry.

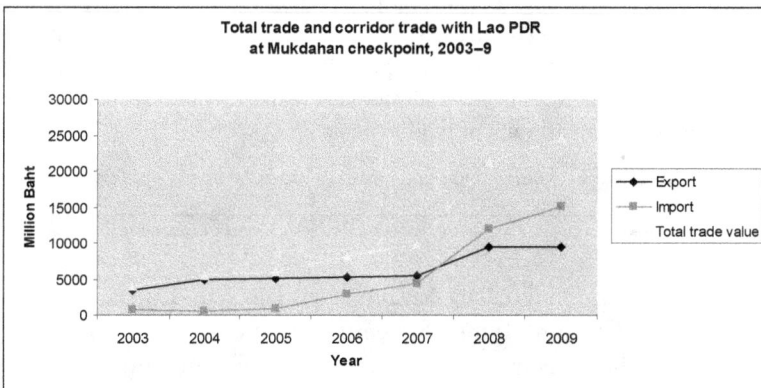

Total trade and corridor trade with Lao PDR at Mukdahan checkpoint, 2003–9

Source: TDRI (2010).

Danang Port in Vietnam. The trial of the "go-through" trucks was initiated on 11 June 2009, and 400 trucks of twelve Thai truck operators were issued GMS road transport permits by the Department of Land Transport (see Box 10.7). Despite this trial, there is no single transport operation using the allocated GMS permits for transport from Mukdahan to Vietnam on

---

BOX 10.7
The Initial Implementation of CBTA (IICBTA) among
Thailand, Lao PDR, and Vietnam

The first trial of CTS was undertaken on 11 June 2009. Thai trucks transported goods from Mukdahan checkpoint (origin) and passed through Savannakhet checkpoint arriving at Danang Port, Vietnam (destination) without any trans-shipment. So far, the Department of Land Transport has issued transport permits to twelve operators to operate 400 cross-border trucks, and Vietnam also allocated/issued another 400 permits to Vietnamese operators. The twelve Thai transport companies were selected by the Department of Land Transport based on the criteria of the companies' experiences. Each company was allocated the permit quota (400 permits in total) to operate cross-border transport. The operators must pay 2,500 baht per container for each operation to the Board of Trade of Thailand (BoT), which acts as a guarantee organization. Then, the BoT will issue CTS forms to the transport operators (each CTS form comprises of (1) GMS Transit and Inland Customs Clearance Document (TICCD), (2) Motor Vehicle Temporary Admission Document (MVTAD), (3) Container Temporary Admission Document (CTAD). The transport operators will present these forms at every border checkpoint and vehicles/containers will be allowed to pass through transit countries. These documents will be discharged after the trucks reach their destinations. It is expected that this initiative will significantly reduce logistics costs and time and prevent the risk of goods damage and loss en route from trans-shipment requirements.

Source: Mukdahan Customs House and Board of Trade of Thailand 2009.

---

designated routes[7] (Mukdahan–Savannakhet–Lao Bao–Dansavanh–Danang Port) since the Customs Transit System is not in effect yet.

Although the development of cross-border infrastructure seems to create positive economic impacts for a country, it can lead to a governance problem that may be a barrier to trade and economic growth in the region. In sum, while the logistics cost can be kept lower, the overall transaction cost may be higher. For instance, border officials (agents) act arbitrarily or unilaterally outside the law, and economic actors (such as transport operators) rely on bribery and corruption to facilitate their cross-border operations. Thinking based on the principal-agent perspectives, information asymmetry between central government (principal) and agency can cause higher transaction costs, resulting in the inefficiency of the cross-border transport market at the regional level as demonstrated by the following two case studies.

Case Study 3: The Relationship between the Exclusion of Key Stakeholder's Benefit and the Impact of Counter-productive Practice

A number of studies on GMS regional integration mainly prioritize the benefits of the free flow of goods and people, which is favourable to product owners, traders, or consumers. These studies may not address problems of key stakeholders who may lose benefits, such as logistics providers, border officials, people who live at the borders in some countries. For example, border officials may not follow the GMS CBTA as long as they lose benefits from such implementation.

The Mukdahan-Savannakhet border crossing point is a good example for explaining that counterproductive practices can occur if there is no proper sharing of the prevailing (formal and informal) benefits/costs among stakeholders. In the case of transit countries such as the Lao PDR, the facilitation of cross-border transport means that the benefit goes to other countries while leaving the costs of road maintenance, infrastructure investment, and social and environmental impact on the country. To counteract such circumstances, the Lao PDR might resort to the strategy of assembling traffic in its territory with little incentive to expedite customs, immigration and quarantine inspection processes. If this is the case, it will unfortunately be counterproductive. If more time is taken for customs formalities in the Lao PDR than in Thailand, the Lao PDR will obtain more than only road usage fees (see Figure 10.11).[8] The exclusion of some stakeholders, in turn, would hinder rather than facilitate trade flow across the countries. Simply put, the status quo or requirement of trans-shipment in the Lao PDR actually creates employment for the Laotian people from unloading/reloading activities, particularly those who are unskilled labourers. A NERI (National Economic Research Institute) (2010) study explains that the second Mekong Bridge changed the job composition of Laotians who live in the border city. Unskilled labourers have lost their jobs and there is only increasing demand for skilled labour to work in small shops, duty free shops, and casinos. So slower customs procedures in the Lao PDR actually benefit them.

The underinvestment of regional public goods can occur because of coordination failure. The uncertainty and risk of investing in a regional project are higher because the outcome of the project, and hence its benefit, depends on the performance of other countries. In the case of the transport facilitation framework, coordination failure occurs if a country fails to participate in the project due to perceived unequal benefits, or if other countries hesitate on the implementation of a joint project (Warr, Meonon, and Yusuf 2010).

FIGURE 10.11

The Problems of Possible Cross-border Truck Flow at Mukdahan–Savannakhet

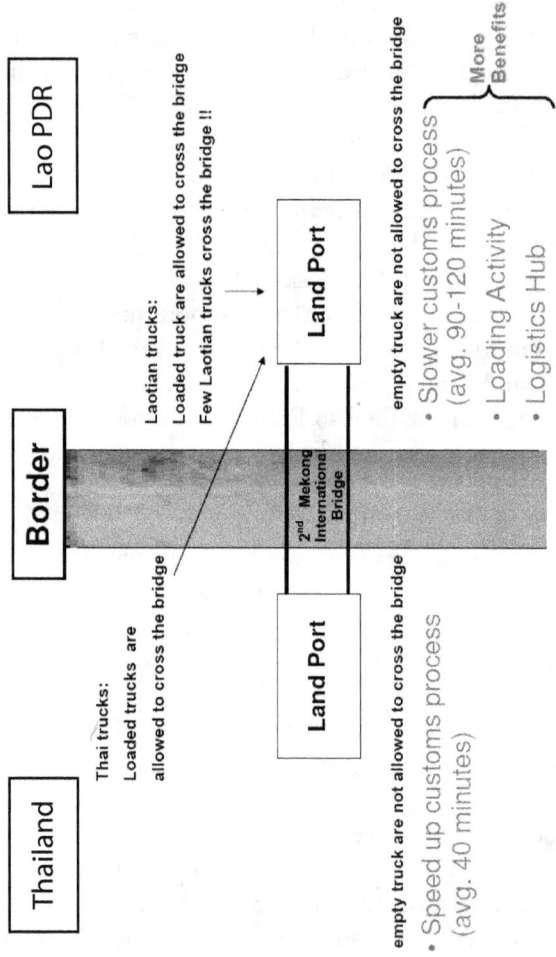

Source: TDRI 2010.

Therefore, GMS development must include compensation approaches for the country which has fewer, or loses, benefits. For example, neighbouring countries could also give financial aid to infrastructure investment and the maintenance cost of the Lao PDR by allowing transit fee collection to relieve the burdens of the transit country, establishing a road maintenance fund, or creating employment opportunities for Laotian people.

Case Study 4: The Relationship between Opportunism and High Transaction Costs of Cross-border Transport

The problem of bad governance on the GMS Economic Corridors hampers the efficient utilization of the transport infrastructure. Particularly, customs procedures, the lack of supporting policy frameworks, as well as human and institutional capacities, can cause very high transaction costs.

It is widely known that formality or protocol at national borders account for some of the most notorious bottlenecks in cross-border transport. On EWEC (Bangkok-Hanoi), for example, the operators have to pay unofficial fees to facilitate border procedures at every border checkpoint, which leads to paying US$447–US$549 in addition to transport costs by road. Furthermore, the unofficial payment for border crossing facilitation on NSEC costs about US$1,200 on top of transport costs (see Figure 10.12). However, transport operators perceive unofficial payment on NSEC as a commercially viable practice since most of the exported products to China are fresh fruit in which a shorter transport time opens up opportunities to transport them into inner-city areas.

Unofficial payment becomes a method for the business sector to circumvent complicated and lengthy customs procedures, resulting in an inefficient cross-border transport market in the GMS. Transport operators charge these transaction costs in the form of freight rates to the product's owners. Consequently consumers in the region pay more for goods and services. Corruption opportunities come up since regulation is inefficient, the customs official has jurisdiction, and transport operators wish to keep the operation going. The GMS governments need to focus reform on the removal of bottlenecks hampering transport flows which actually lie at national borders. Such reforms should take place at the national level and cross-border cooperation is also needed, for example, the harmonization of customs procedures, juxtaposed controls at border crossings (single-stop inspection), and coordinated facilitation measures along corridors, adequate and trained staff, as well as the provision of physical facilities and the modernization of import-export procedures.

FIGURE 10.12
Logistics Cost and Time from Bangkok–Kunming and Bangkok–Hanoi

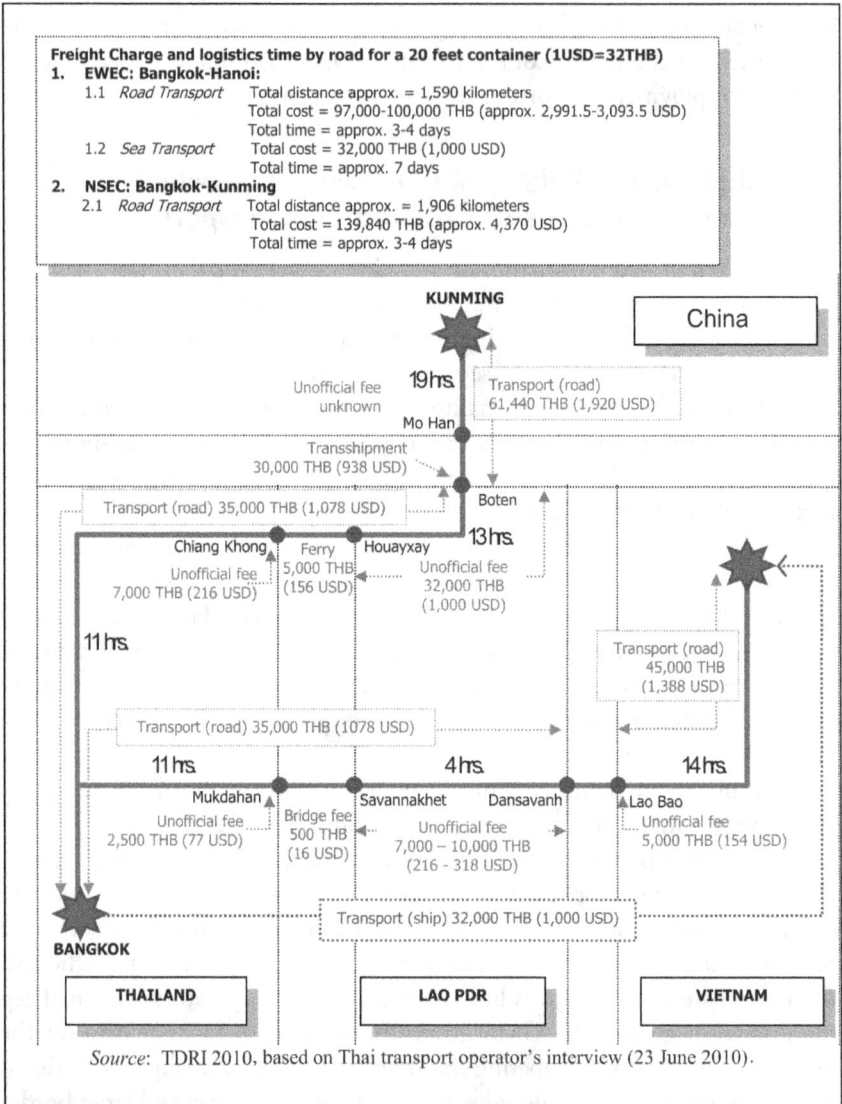

Freight Charge and logistics time by road for a 20 feet container (1USD=32THB)
1. **EWEC: Bangkok-Hanoi:**
   1.1 *Road Transport*   Total distance approx. = 1,590 kilometers
                          Total cost = 97,000-100,000 THB (approx. 2,991.5-3,093.5 USD)
                          Total time = approx. 3-4 days
   1.2 *Sea Transport*   Total cost = 32,000 THB (1,000 USD)
                          Total time = approx. 7 days
2. **NSEC: Bangkok-Kunming**
   2.1 *Road Transport*   Total distance approx. = 1,906 kilometers
                          Total cost = 139,840 THB (approx. 4,370 USD)
                          Total time = approx. 3-4 days

Source: TDRI 2010, based on Thai transport operator's interview (23 June 2010).

CONCLUSION AND POLICY RECOMMENDATIONS TO PROMOTE GOVERNANCE IN THE PROVISION OF REGIONAL PUBLIC GOODS

The case studies presented in this chapter highlight a number of topical and widespread governance issues in the logistics industry, both at the domestic and regional level. Regional integration can create both challenges and opportunities. Each GMS member state must be ready to be able to minimize the adverse effects and maximize the benefits of liberalization. Good governance of national institutional arrangements play a complementary role in the provision of international public goods. The drawback of national governance is the significant issue to be tackled for creating regional governance. Bad governance can weaken the domestic market's competitiveness (i.e., poor quality of service and predatory pricing) and cause negative social impacts. In this regard, when the market is liberalized, regional integration can cause more adverse effects on the domestic market and society in general. Therefore, each GMS member country must cope with its own institutional and regulation arrangements for strengthening its domestic market's competitiveness and readiness for the efficient delivery of regional public goods, so all can enjoy the benefits.

In the domestic market, for example, the state of bad governance in a weak institutional and regulatory environment creates market inefficiency. This forces operators to use non-conforming practices and be involved in corruption dealings between government agencies and firms. Not only high transactions costs, but the lack of good governance can also generate negative externalities, including economic and social impacts on society, and cause the country to lose its competitiveness. The country may hence be at a disadvantage once the transport market is liberalized.

Since the success of intergovernmental collaborations, including transport infrastructure projects and trade facilitation, rests considerably with good governance such as rules that apply and conform across borders, it is important for the GMS to target effective delivery of public service and welfare, fair and equitable costs, and benefit sharing by member countries and every stakeholder. The case studies of international transport point out that the lack of good governance is the critical barrier to trade and economic growth in the region. The exclusion of major formal/informal stakeholders' benefits can result in conflict and counterproductive practices against transport facilitation. Besides, transport costs in the GMS by road is noticeably high compared with sea transport due to the necessity of outlawed transaction costs. Border officials (agents) act arbitrarily or unilaterally outside the law and economic actors (such as transport operators) rely on bribery and corruption instead of the written GMS CBTA framework (such as the Customs Transit System and exchange of traffic rights) to facilitate their cross-border operations. Information asymmetry between the central government (a principal), which plays an important role in negotiating and signing the agreement, and agencies that actually implement and enforce the laws at the borders, is also the cause of high transaction costs leading to the inefficiency of the cross-border transport market. Moreover, the first and foremost among the governance problems in the GMS is the lack of a dedicated institution. The development of cross-border transport projects in the GMS involves not only economic considerations (such as a fair cost-and-benefit sharing mechanism), but also political issues that need to be addressed, negotiated, and agreed among member countries. Institutional capacity, therefore, is vital for setting the rules and regulatory framework so every member country can have fair and equitable gains from the cross-border projects.

To ensure the sustainable development of an economic corridor, good governance must be one of the development strategies for the GMS countries. Overall, there must be institutional reform, clear policies, and harmonized and modernized regulations to reduce overall transaction costs and create efficiencies, and appropriate cost-benefit sharing methods that will provide the right incentives to all member countries and stakeholders. All these will help reduce conflicts, barriers, and non-transparent and counterproductive practices, and thus lead to progress and achievement in regional economic integration, poverty mitigation, and enhancing the quality of life of the people in the GMS.

Policy Recommendations

A region's infrastructure network is a critical element created to enhance regional trade and economic development and growth. Infrastructure is seen as a quasi-regional public good that moves factors of production within and across countries, thus helping the region attain higher productivity and growth (ADBI 2010). International public goods include the rules that apply across borders, the institutions that supervise and enforce these rules, and the benefits that accrue without distinctions between countries. The recommendations in this chapter focus on the good governance of the provision of regional public goods, including institutional arrangements and the approaches for proper sharing of costs and benefits from infrastructure projects among member countries. The fair allocation of costs and benefits can reduce levels of conflicts and counterproductive practices that occur, since member countries tend to follow the rules that apply across borders.

Because of the differences in their levels of development, benefits and costs from the improvement of logistics tend to be allocated unevenly among member countries. The approach then requires compensation schemes for countries that are not in the position to enjoy a fair share of the benefits. For example, relatively less-developed countries such as Cambodia and the Lao PDR might just become transit countries. Allowing foreign vehicles from neighbouring countries to pass through, using their national infrastructures, will leave the cost of this to them. Therefore, until they can also enjoy a fair share of the benefits, these countries will not be so enthusiastic about implementing the CBTA. It is the premise of this chapter that if all member countries obtain the compensation for costs, while sharing some benefits from logistics improvement, regional integration will progress more quickly. Therefore, it is important to find an approach to make the utilization of the transport corridors more efficient and cost-effective, as well as ensure proper cost and benefit sharing among the GMS countries.

Inclusion of All Stakeholders and Providing the Right Incentives

The exclusion benefits to any key stakeholder, such as border officials, local politicians, local authorities, all private sector agents (logistics providers, customs agents, transport operators) could lead to their having the incentive to maintain the status quos and oppose the initiatives that they might not gain from, or gain less of, thereby resulting in a poor governance problem. Good governance can be achieved through cost-benefit sharing methods and providing the right incentives to all member countries and stakeholders. This is also one approach for reducing conflict and non-transparent and counterproductive practices.

For example, Thailand solved the corruption problem of customs officials by regulating the fee charged for customs services (THB 200/declaration form). This amount of money is divided among the customs officials. However, such a fee does not completely solve the problem due to the "cake cutting problem" (the higher ranking officials get a bigger share than the lower ones).

Appropriate Institutional Arrangement

Since the GMS infrastructure is an international public good in which not all benefits accrue nationally, any decision on it should not be limited to any particular institution, agency, or single state. Instead, each member country and stakeholder at all levels should be involved. Successful regional infrastructure development requires appropriate institutional arrangements. The GMS regional institution and national mechanism, namely the National Transport Facilitation Committee Joint Committee (NTFC) is currently an "ad hoc" rather than "standing" committee. This leads to a lack of continuity and creates counterproductive practices of member countries since the uneven allocation of benefits and costs, challenges and opportunities have not been addressed by member countries. An effective and sustainable institutional mechanism must put GMS development as a top-level issue. This means that the GMS summit needs to be organized more regularly instead of once every three year. This institution must commit to GMS development and major issues for logistics improvement, such as compensation for the Lao PDR, a road maintenance fund (from toll collection to a contribution fund from member countries), completion of missing link infrastructure, accelerating GMS CBTA, and updating the regulatory framework to be in line with real commercial needs.

Moreover, GMS transport sector cooperation must be handled by a pool of government agencies instead of a single organization. Therefore, it is not only the responsibility of the Ministry of Transport or customs, but also that of more extensive agencies such as finance, commerce, education, health, cultural development, to negotiate and work on the GMS multilateral agreement covering various issues. Establishing a GMS infrastructure fund that mobilizes a GMS and international fund is also suggested. This requires the setting up of formal institutional arrangements to manage the fund to mobilize international funds (public and private) and help prioritize, prepare, and finance regional infrastructure projects. A regional infrastructure fund should have the goal of increasing sustainable development by supporting projects that lead to "eco-friendly transport" such as shifting from road to rail transport; the Marco Polo Program in the European Union is a good example.

In addition, GMS development plans also need greater involvement and input from the private sector. They require more public-private dialogues to plan the further improvement of the corridors, such as the PPP (public-private partnership) approach to financing and operational management. Thus, it is recommended that governments and agencies should hold regular consultations with private stakeholders. The GMS-Business Forum, with its regional network through the GMS countries' national chambers of commerce and industry, needs supportive policy, that is, setting up a working committee on transport and logistics development, and organizing more regular meetings. The inputs from the GMS-Business Forum must be integrated into the GMS development process to ensure linkages with, and inclusiveness of, the private sector.

Sharing Infrastructure Cost

It is important in the provision of international public goods to address the issue of fair sharing of costs and benefits. Road improvements in some countries, especially for mere transit countries, such as the Lao PDR, enable neighbouring countries to enjoy the benefits while possibly causing externality costs to the host country. Transit pricing is one approach for cost sharing with the country which benefits from using the regional infrastructure network. Therefore, it needs the political agreement of the GMS task force committee to work on a fair and acceptable transit fee for users and providers. The transit fee charge for cross-border traffic has been commonly agreed in principle among member countries (see Box 10.8). However, such charges have not been agreed in detail and are not in effect yet.

BOX 10.8
Permissible Charges According to GMS CBTA

According to the GMS CBTA, Protocol 2: Charges concerning transit traffic, in Article 6 and Article 8, the permissible charges which could be levied, are the following:

1) Tolls: direct charges for the use of road sections, bridges, tunnels, and ferries;
2) Charges of excess weight, where permissible under the national law and/or regulations of the host country;
3) Charges for administrative expenses;
4) Charges for the use of other facilities or services;
5) Taxes on fuel purchases in the host country; and
6) Road maintenance charges (to the extent not included in the charges mentioned above). Road maintenance fees levied shall be commensurate with the road maintenance fees levied on domestic vehicles.
   Road maintenance fee may be based on the ratio of the length of their scheduled stay in its territory to the period covered by the road maintenance fee charged on its domestic vehicles.

All charges are levied on a legal basis only.

Source: Greater Mekong Subregion Cross Border Transport Agreement (Department of Land Transport, Thailand 2008).

The GMS working committee on transit charge and maintenance fund has to work on a fair charging method that covers the construction, maintenance, and external costs in each country. At the outset, the national country must internalize externalities. Taxation imposed on domestic trucks must include an externality cost, which can then be applied to the charge on foreign vehicles when the regional agreement is implemented. The toll fee for heavy vehicles must be higher.

Nevertheless, it will be unfair if the collected fee cannot cover 100 per cent of the road maintenance cost and the Lao PDR must borrow the balance from neighbouring countries.[9] However, the maintenance fund cannot only come from tolls, because the tolls will be very high, which would result in high logistics costs. Expensive goods and services would not promote intraregional trade. Therefore to prevent the toll from being too high, GMS countries need to agree on the road maintenance fund by considering every route that each country can benefit from.

The contribution from GMS member countries to the fund is a major challenge since it is not only an economic but also a political issue as different benefits accrue from each road project. Therefore, this requires some economic and financial analyses to find the contribution formula. For the road network, the "weighted sum aggregation technology" could be used, whereby the contribution depends on each country's specific benefit. A large weight means that any country which uses the road or enjoys the benefit must pay higher charges or contribute more to the supply.

Capacity Building

GMS member countries must be aware of the fact that the status quo on the economic corridor actually creates employment for Lao people from unloading/reloading activities. Therefore, GMS development should also include a compensation approach or the right incentives by providing job opportunities for Laotians. This can be done through establishing a special economic zone (SEZ), and FDI by neighbouring countries such as Thailand, which can help the Lao PDR to increase its productivity, promote its production base, or tourism. The Lao people can benefit from the skills and technologies from more-developed countries that are transferred to the Lao people. Furthermore, Thailand also gains benefits through FDI since the country can increase its productivity from the cheaper labour and abundant land in the Lao PDR.

Official development assistance can be granted for use in building vocational and agricultural schools. Human capacity development is a way to enable the Lao people to obtain greater benefit. For example, Thai and Vietnamese firms can contribute to the development of skills, technology, and innovation of the Lao people in the area of logistic service provision.

Financing Infrastructure Investment through PPP

Since public budget alone might not be sufficient to create physical connectivity in the region, a public private partnership (PPP) could be the approach which allows the achievement of efficiency improvements, while easing the pressure on public budgets. The finance for the infrastructure improvement project can use the PPP, implemented on a concession basis, such as the build-operate-transfer (BOT) or build-own-operate-transfer (BOOT). However, the success of PPP requires "good governance", which in PPP denotes strengthening institutions and the supportive regulatory framework and procedures which will be used to achieve better service delivery outcomes at lower costs. In strengthening good governance in PPP, the following issues must be considered:

- *Cooperative risk sharing*: PPP must be a risk/benefit allocation between government and private sectors. The risk guarantee of "the return to private sector" is a key of PPP. To encourage private-sector investment requires government intervention to guarantee against major risks such as operation, financial, political risks, and ensure financial return. Since private sectors also have debt burdens, governments must guarantee investment return through methods such as contract timing and well-structured tariffs. Governments may also subsidize a PPP through loan guarantees or by contributing to the total cost of the project.
- *Accountability to the public*: Governments should also have effective regulatory frameworks that protect public interests. In this respect, governments should regulate management on items such as "fare" or "PPP contract".
- *Supportive legal framework*: A national legal and institutional framework is always complicated (see Box 10.9). Particularly for cross-border transport, it is more difficult for a PPP to have a single whole system when building new infrastructure to connect with the old one. For example, in the case of Cambodia, the ADB has provided a loan to the country to build a linking railway from Phnom Penh to the Thai border. Under the conditions of the project, the service provider will be the private sector, but the State Railway of Thailand, run by the state, has no clear policy on whether to give permission to private-sector operated railways from neighbouring countries to arrive at Laem Chabang Port.

This creates constraints in linking the Thai railway with the railways of neighbouring countries.

• *Capacity building of governments in PPP operation*: Once engaged in the PPP approach, the capacity building of the regulator is important, for example, on contract design, bidding, and monitoring.

Facilitation of Customs Clearance Formalities

As mentioned above, institutional weaknesses are significant barriers and create higher transaction costs. Government institutions such as customs and other export-import related agencies must practise good governance that will help reduce trade and transaction costs. Currently, export-import procedures in the GMS countries are still paper-based, which create opportunities for corruption. This problem can be lessened through deploying information and communication technology (ICT) to prevent corruption. The National Single Window (NSW) or paperless customs which reduces face-to-face contact between officials and economic actors thereby reduces corruption or bribery opportunities. NSW will integrate electronic data of import/export related agencies but have IT platform at their central government.[10] NSW, with modernized technology, will control and regulate transaction costs and create efficiency through a simplified and quick documenting process.

However, differences in the countries' levels of technology and development may be a hindrance. Take the example of Thailand and the Lao PDR. Thailand has already initiated e-customs (paperless) while the Lao PDR customs still uses paper-based documentation. Without modernization on customs formalities from both sides, cross-border transport activities will not run smoothly and effectively. To solve such a problem, Thailand should provide some sort of official development assistance or technical assistance to help the Lao PDR develop equivalent technical capacity regarding customs procedures. Thailand can provide technical assistance on customs reform and IT to the Lao PDR in various areas such as SWI (Single Window Inspection), SSI (Single Stop Inspection), and NSW. In sum, the GMS countries should begin to work on their NSW and develop to integrate with neighbouring countries to move towards creating an ASEAN single window, which is expected by 2015.

Notes

1. The Logistics Performance Index is based on a survey of operators worldwide (global freight forwarders and express carriers), providing feedback on the logistics

friendliness of the countries in which they operate and those with which they trade.

2. The public bus fare is regulated by the Land Transport Committee, the Land Transport Policy Committee, the Central Land Transport Control Board, and the Provincial Land Transport Control Board (prices are based on a cost-plus formula, including a target rate of return and an allowance for an expected load factor. The fare measured in baht per kilometre is adjusted according to a change in the diesel price, with twenty-five steps ranging between THB10.07 and THB40.57: for example, if the diesel price increases from THB28/litre to THB30/litre, the seventeenth fare rate (THB0.56/km) will be applied and used to multiply the actual operating vehicle kilometres to provide a new fare for travelling on that section.

3. The freight rate should include infrastructure and externality costs to reflect actual cost. An appropriate pricing policy for truck transport, which reflects externality costs, will be even more significant once the cross-border transport market has been liberalized. This requires further in-depth study on pricing policy and the vehicle taxation system before the liberalization is fully effective.

4. A retail business law has been submitted twice, but was rejected. A retail business law is now under screening by the Council of State (*Retail Digest*, 2008).

5. Currently, the retail business law is under screening by the Council of State <www.lrc.go.th>.

6. In January 2009 the Thai Parliament approved the ASEAN Framework Agreement on Facilitation of Interstate Transport (Office of Transport and Traffic Policy and Planning).

7. The customs official at Mukdahan checkpoint confirmed that GMS road transport permits have not been used by any transport operators (telephone interview on 5 July 2010).

8. Based on the MOU IICBTA between the Lao PDR and Thailand: Time Release Study (2007), the Customs import procedure is 40 minutes in Mukdahan and 120 minutes in Savannakhet; and the export procedure is 46 minutes in Mukdahan and 90 minutes in Savannakhet.

9. Based on the National Economic Research Institute, although ADB has some kind of road maintenance fee for the Lao PDR, it only covers 60 per cent of road maintenance costs and the Lao PDR must borrow from neighbouring countries for the rest of it (*Sharing the Benefits from Transportation Linkages and Logistics Improvements in the GMS: A Study of the East-West and North-South Corridor*". PowerPoint presentation, Bangkok, Thailand, 20–21 July 2010.)

10. In Thailand, the Customs Department, a chief agency, has signed an MoU with thirty-five other agencies to link e-data with the Customs Department so that data and information can be used to speed up customs release and clearance under the NSW system.

References

ADB–ASEAN: Regional Road Safety Program. *Thailand Road Safety Action Plan 2004–2008*. ADB-ASEAN Regional Road Safety Program: Country Report, 2005.

ADBI. "Governance, Institutions, and Regional Infrastructure in Asia". ADBI. Working Paper Series no. 183, January 2010.

Boethm, F. "Regulatory Capture Revisited — Lessons from Economics of Corruption". Internet Centre for Corruption Research (ICGG) Working Paper no. 22 <http://www.icgg.org/corruption.research_contributions.html>.

JICA. "The Research on the Cross-border Transportation Infrastructure: Phase 2, Final Report". Japan International Cooperation Agency (JICA), December 2007.

Kaufmann D., A. Kraay, and M. Mastruzzi. *Governance Matters VIII: Governance Indicators for 1996–2008*. Washington, DC: World Bank, 2009.

Lambsdorff, G. J. "How Corruption in Government Affects Public Welfare — A Review of Theories". Center for Globalization and Europeanization of the Economy. Discussion Paper 9. January 2001.

NERI. "Sharing the Benefits from Transportation Linkages and Logistics Improvements in the GMS: A Study of the East-West and North-South Corridor". National Economic Research Institute. PowerPoint presentation, Bangkok, Thailand, 20–21 July 2010.

Retail Digest. "Thailand's Battle between Modern and Traditional Trade Food Retailers". 2008.

TDRI (Thailand Development Research Institute). *The Retail Business in Thailand: Impact of the Large Scale Multinational Corporation Retailers*. Bangkok (in Thai), 2002.

————. "Sharing the Benefits from Transportation Linkages and Logistics Improvements in the GMS: A Study of the East-West and North-South Corridors". Focus group meeting, 7 August 2009.

————. "Road Transport in Thailand". In *The Impacts and Benefits of Structural Reforms in Transport, Energy and Telecommunications Sectors*. Report written for the Policy Support Unit of the APEC Secretariat in Singapore and the University of Adelaide, 2010.

Tokrisna, R. *Thailand Changing Retail Food Sector: Consequences for Consumers, Producers, and Trade*. Kasetsart University, Thailand, 2005.

UNESCAP. "Public Private Partnership in Thailand: Past Experiences and Future Prospects". Presentation given by Chalongphob Susangarn, Ministry of Finance, Thailand, to the Asia-Pacific Ministerial Conference on "PPPs in Infrastructure", 5 October 2007, Seoul, South Korea. United Nations Economic and Social Commission for Asia and the Pacific (UNESCAP), 2007.

Warr, P., J. Menon, and A. Yusuf. "Regional Economic Impacts of Large Projects: A General Equilibrium Application to Cross-Border Infrastructure". *Asian Development Review* 27, no. 1 (2010): 103–34. Asian Development Bank.

World Bank. *Thailand Infrastructure Annual Report.* 2008.

World Bank and NESDB. *Thailand: Making Transport more Energy Efficient.* 2009.

———. *Connecting to Compete: Trade Logistics in the Global Economy — The Logistics Performance Index and Its Indicators.* Washington, DC, 2010.

Websites

World Bank <http://www.worldbank.org/wbi/governance>.

Ministry of Transport <http://vigportal.mot.go.th/portal/site/PortalMOT/>.

Law Reform Commission <http://www.lrc.go.th>.

Land Transport Promotion Center, Department of Land Transport <http://www.ltpcenter.com>.

Office of Transport and Traffic Policy and Planning <http://www.otp.go.th>.

Mukdahan Customs House <http://www.danmuk.org>.

Board of Trade of Thailand <http://www.thaiechamber.com>.

11

ENERGY SECTOR INTEGRATION FOR LOW-CARBON DEVELOPMENT IN GMS
Towards a Model of South-South Cooperation

Yongping Zhai and Anthony J. Jude

The Greater Mekong Subregion (GMS) comprises Cambodia, the People's Republic of China (PRC), Lao People's Democratic Republic (Lao PDR), Myanmar, Thailand, and Vietnam. In 1992, with the Asian Development Bank (ADB)'s assistance, the six countries entered into a programme of subregional economic cooperation designed to enhance economic relations among the countries. The establishment of an integrated subregional electric power market is a major component of the economic cooperation of the GMS countries.

When the idea of the subregional power market was first conceived in the early 1990s, the main concern was to ensure an adequate energy supply at the least cost to meet the requirements of economic development in the subregion, which is one of the fastest growing areas in the world. As the subregional power sector integration gradually takes shape amid growing international concerns on climate change, the GMS countries have come to realize that cooperation in the energy sector is also an effective way to achieve low carbon development in the subregion. To this end, the GMS countries decided to expand their cooperation in the energy sector to include energy efficiency, renewable energy, and clean fuels.

On the basis of an overview of the current status of the energy sector integration, particularly in the power sector of the GMS countries, this chapter analyses the potential for carbon emissions reduction in the GMS countries through subregional cooperation. In particular, the GMS cooperation model in the energy sector is proposed as one of the means of addressing global climate change.

CURRENT STATUS OF POWER INTERCONNECTION AND ENERGY SECTOR COOPERATION IN THE GMS

The GMS has diverse energy resources that are unevenly distributed among its member countries. Although the subregion is well endowed with hydropower and fossil fuel resources, most of the exploitable resources are concentrated locally. Hydropower resources are abundant in the Lao PDR, Myanmar, and Yunnan, PRC, and are expected to exceed their own demands for the foreseeable future. Most of the fossil fuel resources (oil and gas) are in Yunnan, PRC, and Myanmar, and, to a lesser extent, in Vietnam. Thailand has limited domestic gas and oil reserves, and the country is expected to rely on imports for its future energy needs. Cambodia currently also relies on imported energy (petroleum products and electricity) though its resources (hydropower, oil and gas) have been largely untapped. Therefore, the region's uneven energy endowment and geographic proximity of member countries makes the GMS an ideal region for power interconnection and energy sector cooperation.

The quality of the power transmission infrastructure in the GMS is also very uneven. On the one hand, the PRC, Thailand, and Vietnam have well-developed power grid systems, with 500 kV integrated backbone transmission grids. On the other hand, Cambodia, the Lao PDR, and Myanmar have only low and medium voltage power systems of limited extent, quality, and reliability. Electricity consumption in the GMS in 1990 and 2008 grew slightly faster than the growth rate of electricity production (9.5 per cent per annum). The average per capita consumption of electricity in the GMS was 1,045 kilowatt-hours in 2008, with Thailand posting the highest consumption of 2,105 kilowatt-hours, and Cambodia, the lowest, at 124 kilowatt-hours.

Power Trade and Interconnection

To enable reliable exchanges of power and develop opportunities for power trading, without negatively affecting reliability of their own systems, the GMS countries must connect and synchronize the operations of their national grids. To achieve subregional power interconnections fully, the GMS countries prepared a road map with phased development in stages and involving both infrastructure development and institutional building activities.

Phased Development in Four Stages:

In 2005, through a memorandum of understanding (MOU-1) which was reconfirmed and strengthened by another MOU (MOU-2) in 2008, the GMS countries committed to embarking on a road map for the phased development of subregional power interconnection in four stages as follows:

Stage 1: This corresponds to the regional power transactions that are possible currently and in the near future, with development of the first cross-border connections. In this stage, transactions will only be possible between two neighbouring countries. Stage 1 is oriented to take advantage of surplus capacity of cross-border transmission facilities that are developed and linked to specific power purchase agreements (PPAs).

Stage 2: This corresponds to the moment when trading will be possible between any pair of GMS countries, eventually using the transmission facilities of a third regional country. However, in this stage the available cross-border transmission capacity is limited and based on surplus capacity of transmission lines linked to PPAs. The switch from Stage 1 to Stage 2 will occur once enough cross-border transmission capacity is operative, thus allowing power transactions amongst all (or most) of the GMS countries.

Stage 3: This will be linked to the development of transmission links specifically dedicated to cross-border trading. During this stage some GMS countries may have completed the transition to competitive markets, where multiple buyers-sellers are allowed to enter into cross-border transactions. The regulatory framework will allow the simultaneous existence of countries with multiple sellers-buyers alongside others with integrated utilities. The switch from stage 2 to stage 3 will occur when lines specifically dedicated to cross-border trading are commissioned.

Stage 4: This corresponds to the situation when most of the GMS countries have moved to a multiple sellers-buyers regulatory framework, so a regional, wholly competitive market can be implemented. The switch from stage 3 to stage 4 will occur when most GMS countries have moved to a power-sector regulatory framework that allows multiple sellers-buyers to participate in cross-border trading.

Infrastructure Development:
Power trade in the GMS originated in 1971 when the Lao PDR and Thailand entered into a power purchase agreement for the export of power from the Nam Ngum 1 (30 MW, extended to 150 MW) Hydropower Plant in the Lao PDR to northeast Thailand. From 1990 onward bilateral power trade arrangements have intensified as memoranda of understanding were signed between various governments in the subregion. Thailand and Cambodia are net importers of electricity, while the Lao PDR is a net exporter. Regional power interconnections in the GMS are mainly via medium-voltage transmission lines. At present the only high-voltage cross-border transmission line within the GMS is the line from the newly commissioned Nam Theun 2 Hydropower Plant in the Lao PDR to Thailand. Work on the first high-voltage transmission line between Cambodia, the Lao PDR, China, Myanmar, and Vietnam, and several other cross-border initiatives are ongoing. At this stage, power flows are mostly one-way through power purchase agreements.

As of June 2010, the existing and planned major power trade flows (excluding minor border power exchanges) are shown below:

(1) From the Lao PDR to Thailand
- Theun-Hinboun Hydropower (210 MW), 230 kV transmission line (86 km from Theun-Hinboun Power Station to Thakhek on the Thai border), commissioned in April 1998. An expansion of Theun-Hinboun is ongoing, in which an additional 220 MW will be available for export to Thailand and an additional 60 MW for domestic consumption in 2013;
- Houayho Hydropower (150 MW), 230 kV, 230 km, commissioned in 1999;
- Nam Leuk Hydropower (60MW), 115 kV transmission lines (85 km from Nam Leuk to Pakxan and 11 km from Pakxan to Bungkan near the Thai border), commissioned in March 2000;
- Nam Theun 2 Hydropower (1,070 MW), 500 kV transmission line (130 km to the Thai grid), commissioned in March 2010;
- Hongsa Thermal Power Plant (1,878 MW) to be commissioned in 2015, 550 kV transmission line from Hongsa in Xayabury Province, Lao PDR, to Mae Moh in Thailand (55 km);
- Nabong to Udon Thani, 500 kV transmission line (27 km) commissioned in March 2010.

(2) From China to Vietnam
- Xinqiao, Yunan-Lai Cai, 250–300 MW, 56 km in China, commissioned in 2006;
- Maguan, Yunan-Ha Giang, 200 MW, 220 kV, 51 km commissioned in 2007.

(3) From Vietnam to Cambodia
- 230 kV, Chao Doc-Phnom Penh (110 km), commissioned in 2009;
- 230 kV, Tay Ninh-Kg Cham (75 km), under construction, to be commissioned in 2012.

(4) From Thailand to Cambodia
- Bantey Meanchey–Siem Reap–Battambong, 115 kV, 203 km, commissioned in 2007.

(5) From Myanmar to China
- Shweli 1 Hydropower-Dehong, Yunan, 600 MW, 220 kV, 188 km, commissioned in 2008;
- Tasang- Yunnan (2000 MW), via 500 kV.

(6) From Lao PDR to Cambodia
- Ban Hat-Stung Treng-Kratie-K Cham, 230 kV transmission line (220 km);
- Ban Sok-Stung Treng-Tay Ninh, 500 kV transmission line (200 km) under planning.

(7) From Myanmar to Thailand
- Tasang Hydropower Project, Lop Buri, Bangkok (5,000 MW), via double circuit 500 kV, under construction with phased commissioning beginning in 2017;
- Upper Hutgyi (1,200 MW) to Mae Sot, Ang Thon, Thailand, via 500 kV transmission lines.

Going forward, the GMS power systems aims to achieve Stage 4 of the road map by 2025, that is, a fully interconnected market.

Institutional Build-up:
The institutional set-up of the GMS energy programme has evolved over the past eighteen years. At the first GMS summit held in 2002, the leaders of the six countries signed the Inter-Governmental Agreement on Regional Power Trade (IGA). The Energy Power Forum set up initially in 1995 has also evolved into two separate institutional structures, the Energy Sector Forum and the Regional Power Trade Coordinating Committee (RPTCC). The latter consists of two subgroups — a focal group and a planning working group — and is developing the framework for regional trade in

power. The RPTCC group meets once every year, chaired by a GMS country on a rotating basis, and co-chaired by the ADB, to review and discuss the progress of the power sector integration. It is noted that among the functions of the RPTCC defined by the IGA (Article 4.3 — Role of the RPTCC), the RPTCC shall provide to the parties a recommendation for the overall policy and day-to-day management of regional power trade, including the necessary bodies for coordination.

Following progress on the infrastructure front with increasing bilateral power trade, the GMS countries started to consider undertaking further institutional strengthening to facilitate power trade in real interconnected power systems. As shown by the experience of other regions (Europe, Southern Africa, etc.), such institutional set-up is essential to help remove barriers to power trade, that is (i) removing provisions within existing laws or regulations which might hinder the move to a more competitive regional market; (ii) consistency in the content and implementation of rules governing access to the transmission network; (iii) development of a standardized protocol governing the operation of a regional transmission network (the absence of which might undermine system reliability). Through these institutional developments, the GMS countries will commit to the transparency of costs for generation and, in particular, for transmission (for which wheeling tariffs have to be separated out).

In its eighth meeting held in November 2009 in the Lao PDR, the RPTCC deliberated options for further institutional strengthening by the creation of a formal and permanent power trade body. Tentatively, this proposed body may be named the GMS Power Trade Coordination and Information Centre, and in its first phase this GMS power trade organization will promote operational coordination between transmission owning/operating members through actual day-to-day information sharing/exchange among the GMS countries. Other functions of the proposed GMS Power Trade Coordination and Information Centre will include (i) collecting, analysing, and disseminating information needed to gauge the evolution of an interconnected electricity generation and transmission system in the subregion; (ii) facilitating the development of common operational norms and standards for data acquisition and processing and performance control; and (iii) monitoring the development of the GMS regional power grid.

Ultimately, this body will be responsible for coordinating, planning, monitoring, and, possibly, regulating the operation and development of the regional power system with the mandate to (i) operate the regional electric power system and organize the corresponding bulk power market and (ii) establish and implement the necessary rules, standards, guidelines, procedures, and corresponding practices to develop regional electricity cooperation and integration.

The ADB, in coordination with other development partners, is considering providing needed financial and technical support for the establishment of the proposed GMS Power Trade Coordination and Information Centre.

Expanded Cooperation in the Energy Sector

The GMS energy sector initiatives have centred around the power sector, with a focus on cross-border electricity trading and the interconnection of transmission networks to link stronger energy-demand growth centres to rich indigenous energy-resource centres. The GMS countries recognize that access to energy is critical to economic development and that there are potential benefits to be gained from expanding cooperation in energy beyond the power sector. Each country has its own energy needs that are derived from different resources. Integrated regional planning and coordination will allow for the identification of the most cost-effective energy projects as some individual national markets are too small to justify the large investments needed for economy of scale. Therefore, cross-border energy supply not only allows for the diversification of energy sources, but also enhances supply security.

Moreover, the need to respond to climate change impacts in the GMS is real and imminent, as the region is expected to suffer from detrimental impacts from sea level rise, changing precipitation patterns, and more intense tropical storms. Coupled with recurring food, oil, and financial crises, climate change will have very serious implications for the region's economic development and the livelihoods of its population. Mitigation measures to address climate change needs public policy actions, not only at the national level, but also at the regional level. Regional cooperation and integration have the potential to enhance the efficiency of the entire regional energy system by exploiting subregional resources in an optimal manner with the least environmental impact. Moreover, regional cooperation will also enable the propagation of best practices in developing energy efficiency, renewable energy, and clean energy technologies.

In June 2009, the fifteenth GMS Ministerial Meeting adopted a road map for expanded cooperation in the energy sector of the GMS, taking into account the need for improved energy security in the subregion, better utilization of energy resources, and mutually beneficial energy trade, to meet national and regional energy needs in a sustainable manner. The road map specifies (i) the goal and strategic objectives for expanded GMS energy cooperation, to provide overall guidance to the GMS countries' energy cooperation; (ii) a desired policy framework that includes the measures and actions that should be given priority in expanding GMS energy cooperation; and (iii) a concrete, practical, and implementable short- to medium-term (2010–15) work plan that details the specific activities and general timetable for realizing the road map's objectives.

Harmonizing Policy Framework:
The goal of GMS expanded cooperation is to deliver sustainable, secure, competitive, and low carbon energy in the subregion through a cooperative and integrated approach. Specifically, the road map for expanded GMS energy cooperation will focus on the following four major strategic objectives: (i) enhance access to energy for all sectors and communities, particularly the poor in the GMS, through the promotion of best energy practices in the subregion; (ii) develop and utilize more efficiently indigenous, low-carbon, and renewable resources, while reducing the subregion's dependence on imported fossil fuels; (iii) improve energy supply security through cross-border trade while optimizing the use of subregional energy resources; (iv) promote public-private partnership and private sector participation, particularly through small- and medium-sized enterprises for subregional energy development. In each of the above four strategic objectives, the GMS countries are committed to undertaking a series of policy measures and actions.

In order to enhance access to energy for all sectors and communities in the GMS, the following policy measures and actions will be undertaken by each GMS country:

- Making regional cooperation a pillar of national energy strategy, with the establishment of interconnection arrangements that will harness the energy complementarities existing in the subregion, such as in natural gas, in addition to current efforts in GMS power trade development.
- Promotion of innovative, cost-effective, rural electrification schemes for poverty reduction, taking advantage of regional grid infrastructure development.
- Promotion of best regional practices of off-grid/decentralized energy systems for integration and the accelerated development of isolated areas, using in particular, renewable energy resources.
- Coordination with other GMS countries in transport, trade, agriculture, and tourism to maximize synergies.

In order to develop and utilize indigenous, low carbon, renewable resources more efficiently, the following policy measures and actions will be undertaken by each GMS country:

- Sharing national experience in energy efficiency, renewable and clean coal technologies, and establishing subregional best practices and technical standards.
- Supporting the formulation of renewable and energy efficiency laws and a regulatory framework.
- Promoting the use of renewable energy resources, including biomass, biofuels, solar (photo-voltaic), wind, micro-hydro, and other locally available energy sources by up-scaling best practices and pilot projects in the GMS.
- Promoting the development of subregional engineering and manufacturing capacity for renewable energy such as mini-hydro, wind, and solar power.
- Enhancing energy efficiency and conservation on both the demand and supply side, improving their availability and affordability, by scaling up best practices and pilot projects in the GMS.
- Ensuring benefit sharing and risk monitoring from energy projects in one GMS country that impact other GMS countries.
- Developing technologies and promoting best practices to improve the efficiency of thermal power plants, particularly for locally available gas and coal.
- Developing institutional capacity to develop renewable energy projects, particularly mini-hydropower using the clean development mechanism (CDM).
- Monitoring technology development of carbon capture and storage (CCS) and studying the feasibility of such technology to control greenhouse gas emissions.

In order to improve subregional energy supply security, the following policy measures and actions will be undertaken by each GMS country:

- Strengthening information exchange and collaboration among national and regional institutions in energy policy and planning, and supply security through the establishment of a community of practice (COP) for subregional energy development.
- Enhancing institutional and technical capacity in developing cross-border trade and energy integration beyond the power sector.
- Improving the transport modal mix to sustain growth in the transport sector.

In order to promote public-private sector partnership and private sector participation, particularly through small- and medium-sized enterprises, in subregional energy development, the following policy measures and actions will be undertaken by each GMS country:

- Enhancing an institutional and regulatory environment that is conducive to private sector investment.
- Sharing and coordination of best practices in terms of the incentive package provided to private project sponsors.
- Promoting networking and exchange of knowledge on and experiences in state-of-the-art energy efficiency and renewable and clean energy technologies adapted to the needs of the subregion.

A Joint Medium-Term Cooperation Work Plan (2010–15):
To realize the goal of expanded energy cooperation, a joint GMS Work Plan (2010–15) was developed to implement the priority regional initiatives: (i) promoting environmentally sustainable regional power trade planning, coordination, and development in the GMS, with a view to establishing a joint programme for the comprehensive promotion of a strategic environmental assessment (SEA) and other environmental management tools to ensure that environmental and social aspects, including cumulative and indirect impacts, are considered at an earlier stage in the power sector plans in the GMS; (ii) improving energy efficiency (EE) through demand-side management (DSM) and energy conservation (EC) in the GMS, with a view to establishing a joint programme to ensure the rapid development and adoption of DSM and EC programmes, and reduce energy consumption per unit of GDP generated; and (iii) promoting the development of renewable energy (RE) and clean fuels (CF) in the GMS, with a view to establishing a joint programme to promote and propagate best practices and realize a more optimal energy mix that reduces greenhouse gas emissions in the subregion.

Promoting energy efficiency (EE) and the use of renewable energy (RE) and clean fuel (CF) resources (biomass, biofuels, solar, wind, and micro/mini-hydropower) will be critical in meeting the subregion's energy objectives. RE and EE promotion will increase the utilization of indigenous, low-carbon resources and move energy consumption away from imported fuels. In the process this will help enhance access to modern energy (thereby reducing poverty), contribute to mitigating climate change, improve energy supply security, and enhance public-private sector partnerships in GMS energy development. In particular, promoting the development of RE/CF/EE in the GMS will support (a) the promotion of cost-effective, environment-friendly decentralized systems in rural communities (e.g., mini-hydro, solar); (b) the utilization of local RE/CF resources (e.g., biomass); (c) the propagation of appropriate EE measures; (d) the improvement of energy security by reducing reliance on imported fuels; and (e) the promotion of private sector participation in RE/CF/EE development.

Through the implementation of the joint work plan, the GMS countries will establish the regional database of best practices and technologies on RE/CF/EE, to be linked with existing databases such as those of the United Nations Framework Convention for Climate Change (UNFCC) and Regional Power Trade and Coordination Committee (RPTCC). Regional performance targets in RE/CF/EE development and compliance mechanisms will be developed. Such performance targets will help identify GMS-appropriate practices and technical standards in (i) RE/CF/EE enabling policy frameworks, incentive schemes, technology promotion; (ii) development of off-grid/decentralized energy systems using RE/CF; and (iii) specific EE measures such as efficient lighting, heating and cooling, power station retrofits, and system loss reduction from power transmission/distribution upgrades.

Within the framework of the expanded GMS cooperation in the energy sector, the ADB is considering financing at least five feasibility studies/project proposals for (i) small-scale, community-based, isolated RE/CF energy systems (mini-, micro-hydro, biomass, solar, wind); (ii) thermal generation efficiency improvements in existing power plants and/or power transmission system upgrades for reduced system losses; and (iii) efficient lighting, heating or cooling programmes in households (individual and combined) and/or the commercial sector for financing by the ADB and other financing agencies, including the application of the clean development mechanism (CDM).

POTENTIAL OF CARBON EMISSION REDUCTIONS IN GMS THROUGH ENERGY SECTOR COOPERATION

The subregional cooperation in the GMS was initially based on economic benefits. The disparity between energy demand and resource endowment in the GMS means that there is significant potential to reduce overall energy costs for the region and for individual countries through exploring energy supply options beyond national borders. Therefore, a least-cost approach to meeting GMS energy needs may involve cooperation and substantial energy trade between GMS countries. For example, both Thailand and Vietnam are currently importing electricity from the Lao PDR. As the GMS economies grow, and their energy demands increase, satisfying that demand at least-cost through trade and cooperation will offer increasingly greater benefits than satisfying demand through local energy production.

The ADB commissioned a study in 2009 undertaken by Integrated Resource Management (IRM). IRM developed a model of energy production, consumption, and trade within the GMS to predict optimal energy production, consumption, and trade within the GMS under different scenarios. With the growing awareness of the threat of global climate change, the GMS countries have now found another strong justification to promote cooperation in the energy sector as regional environmental benefits may also accrue from more efficient use of energy resources, reducing the overall need for energy production and thereby potentially reducing carbon emissions and land-use impact from energy-related activities. During the course of the IRM study, many scenarios were constructed to assess the implications of the various policy issues facing the GMS, using MESSAGE (Model of Energy Supply Systems Alternatives and their General Environmental Impacts). From these scenarios, three relevant ones are presented here, viz. the High Growth Scenario, the GMS Integrated Scenario, and the Low Carbon Scenario.

High-Growth Scenario vs GMS Integrated Scenario

The high growth scenario is based on higher-level demand forecasts, which assume that overall GMS energy growth will be 7.1 per cent compared with that in all other cases. Due to limits in the availability of natural resources and the environment's ability to absorb the harmful impacts of increased exploitation of natural resources, the results of this scenario provide quantitative information on the multiple impacts of significantly higher energy demand and the risks associated with it. These risks include impacts on the local and global environment, a very high level of energy import dependence, and a high level of use of coal. In spite of the global financial crisis, all indications suggest that the GMS countries' growth rate would remain robust. Therefore, this high-growth scenario can be considered the business-as-usual scenario.

The GMS integrated scenario assumes that the entire GMS is a single energy-economy system. This means that resources are shared in the sense that only their costs are considered and not their prices. It assumes that the economic cost of energy supply is equal to the production and delivery cost of energy rather than the world market price. Energy trade — especially in electricity and gas — requires infrastructure development; the cost of such investments are included as total systems costs.

The results from various runs of MESSAGE using different scenarios indicate that, under the high growth scenario, overall energy consumption is greater by 38 per cent (and as much as 51 per cent for coal and 40 per cent for crude oil) compared with the GMS integrated scenario. The model suggests that 319 GW of new generation capacity from 2005–25 will have to be added under the high growth scenario, while the capacity addition will be

238 GW under the GMS integrated scenario. In particular, the requirement of coal-based generation capacity will be 126 GW under the high growth scenario compared with only 72 GW under the GMS integrated scenario.

Regional cooperation reduces overall energy costs (investment and operational costs). In fact, the overall discounted cost under the high growth scenario is US$1,268 billion for the period 2005–25, while that under the GMS integrated scenario amounts to US$1,123 billion, that is, a saving of US$145 billion, or 11 per cent lower. These benefits are significant when compared with the current GDP of the GMS economies, which ranges from US$6 billion for the Lao PDR to US$264 billion for Thailand.

As shown in Table 11.1, in terms of CO_2 emissions, there are significant differences between the high growth scenario (with an increase of 1,815 Mt of CO_2 equivalent) and the GMS integrated scenario (with an increase of 1,141 Mt of CO_2 equivalent) from 2005–25.

GMS Integrated Scenario vs Low-Carbon Scenario

The low-carbon scenario is constructed to assess the impacts of internalizing the external environmental and social costs of energy choices.

Though the overall discounted cost of the low-carbon scenario (US$1,145 billion) is somewhat higher than for the GMS integrated scenario (US$1,123 billion), the discounted environmental costs are much lower for the low-carbon case. When the environmental costs of emissions are internalized, the capacity mix is different for these two cases although the overall capacity

TABLE 11.1

High Growth Scenario vs. GMS Integrated Scenario (2005–25)

	High Growth Scenario	GMS Integrated Scenario
Discounted Costs ($ billion)	1,268	1,123
New capacity (GW)	319	238
Coal-based (GW)	126	72
Hydropower (GW)	85	83
Nuclear (GW)	17	10
Gas (GW)	45	40
Others (GW)	47	35
Increase in CO_2 Emissions (Mt Equivalent)	1,815	1,141

levels are similar. Under the low-carbon scenario, coal-based power generation is only half the level the GMS integrated scenario recommends. Against a capacity of 72 GW, the low-carbon scenario requires only 37 GW of coal-based power capacity. Hydropower capacity is higher by 11 GW, and gas-based capacity is higher by about 13 GW. The overall capacity for renewable energy sources and other off-grid solutions is higher by 11 GW under the low-carbon scenario. Finally, the low-carbon scenario envisages nearly double the level of investment in decentralized photovoltaic technology compared with other scenarios. Even for hydropower plants, it has chosen smaller sizes for generating capacity.

As shown in Table 11.2, in terms of CO_2 emissions, the low-carbon scenario will lead to an increase of 785 Mt CO_2 equivalent from 2005 to 2025, compared with 1,141 Mt CO_2 equivalent under the GMS integrated scenario, a net reduction of emissions by over 30 per cent.

Moreover, an enhanced share of renewable energy scenario was modelled using specific national targets for renewable energy, announced in various policy statements over the last few years by the GMS countries. Two of the results from running this scenario are interesting to note in terms of their policy implications. First, introducing such national targets implies additional costs. In particular, overall discounted costs were higher by 2.5 per cent than in the case where targets were not introduced. Second, when specific targets are introduced for a segment of the energy system, overall cost rises, but emission levels do not necessarily fall. For example, when wind power targets led to a higher level of wind-based electricity production, the overall

TABLE 11.2

High Growth Scenario vs. Low Carbon Scenario (2005–25)

	High Growth Scenario	GMS Integrated Scenario
Discounted Costs ($ billion)	1,268	1,437
New capacity (GW)	319	239
Coal-based (GW)	126	37
Hydropower (GW)	85	94
Nuclear (GW)	17	10
Gas (GW)	45	53
Others (GW)	47	46
Increase in CO_2 Emissions (Mt Equivalent)	1,815	785

share of solar and other environment-friendly technologies was much lower under this scenario than in the low-carbon case.

In comparison, by internalizing environmental costs, the overall final energy use was 5 per cent lower, implying that the model chooses more efficient energy technologies. The relevant policy implication is that taxation (carbon taxes) and pricing are much better instruments for curtailing emissions and rationalizing overall energy choices than specific renewable technology targets.

CONCLUSIONS: TOWARDS A MODEL OF REGIONAL ENERGY SECTOR COOPERATION FOR LOW-CARBON DEVELOPMENT

The GMS is one of the most dynamic parts of the developing world, with a high growth rate. The subregion is characterized by uneven energy resources, different levels of economic development, diversified cultures, and distinct government systems. However, the common challenge to all countries of the subregion is to sustain their economic growth while limiting or arresting environmental damage.

The perspectives of global climate change will affect the GMS countries significantly. In this context, the GMS countries are facing a challenge to make significant efforts to mitigate greenhouse gas (GHG) emissions, particularly CO_2 emissions. Under the business-as-usual scenario, CO_2 emissions will continue to grow at a high pace as a result of the significant additions of coal-based electricity generation capacity.

In some parts of the developing world, economic growth and intended poverty reduction are perceived as fundamental rights which cannot be compromised even under the threat of global climate change. Developing countries are calling on developed countries to take more responsibility in cutting their CO_2 emissions significantly given their accumulated emissions during their industrialization process. Developing countries are also pushing for more funding from developed countries to meet the incremental cost of low-carbon technologies. During the last few years, clean technology development mechanisms (CDM) and some other initiatives have had limited effects in curbing GHG emissions, and the fund has essentially been giving out to a just a handful of developing countries. Many developing countries are in dire need, but have not been able to avail themselves of adequate funding or the technologies. Moreover, the prevailing intellectual property rights regime has made technology transfer from developed countries to developing countries very difficult. Without access to the right technologies, the developing countries' shift to the low-carbon development path is unlikely and, in any case, unsustainable.

Given these conflicting positions, international negotiations on a new regime of international responses to climate change have been deadlocked in Copenhagen and future discussions do not suggest a major breakthrough anytime soon. In this context, it is highly relevant to design and propose a new model of regional cooperation in the energy sector that will provide a fresh perspective for ongoing international negotiations.

Such a regional cooperation model should be built based on the following principles:

1) Continued focus on inclusive economic growth and poverty reduction;
2) The economic growth should be on a low-carbon and sustainable path;
3) Low-carbon development is mainly achieved though a regional cooperation framework consistent with national policies;
4) The incremental cost of low-carbon solutions will be covered (at least partly) through the benefits of regional cooperation;
5) Both poverty reduction and emission targets should be monitorable, reportable, and verifiable.

In terms of its implementation modalities, the regional cooperation model should include the following arrangements and conditions:

1) Joint commitments of participating countries to comply with the above stated principles through a framework agreement;
2) Set national performance standards and development objectives for low-carbon solutions (including energy efficiency, solar, biomass, wind, biofuels, clean coal, etc.) based on inventory of available options;
3) Within the participating countries, establish the best policy and institutional and fiscal practices that are aimed at achieving the targets of low carbon solutions;
4) Set up joint research and development programmes for manufacturing tailor-made, low-cost, and low-carbon technologies and equipment to meet energy demands;
5) Zero-trade barriers for the transfer of low-carbon technologies within the participating countries;
6) Set up a joint expert group for advising participating governments on climate change-related international negotiations.

Through regional effort on power interconnection and expanded cooperation in the energy sector, the GMS countries have actually moved ahead consistently with the above principles and implementation mechanism. As such the GMS may be an embryo of an RCM which, as demonstrated in preceding sections, will (i) achieve least cost in energy investment through resource optimization and (ii) mitigate CO_2 emissions with the increasing use of renewable energy within the context of sustainable economic growth. The GMS Regional Power Trade Coordination Committee and the GMS Energy Forum will be instrumental in further developing a successful RCM for the benefit of the GMS, but also for developing countries and the world at large.

The RCM is a realistic and feasible option for developing countries and strengthens their negotiating position in international climate change negotiations. Just as the European Union Emission Trading System is a model of North-North cooperation, the GMS will set a model for regional cooperation that will add a new dimension to the existing cooperation through a renewed Clean Development Mechanism.

References

Asian Development Bank (ADB). *The Economics of Climate Change in Southeast Asia: A Regional Review*. April 2009.

———. *Building Sustainable Energy Future: The Greater Mekong Subregion*. 2009.

———. "Energy Policy". Policy Paper, June 2009.

———. *Energy Outlook for Asia and the Pacific*. October 2009.

Prins, Gwyn et al. "The Hartwell Paper: A New Direction for Climate Policy after the Crash of 2009". International report by Institute for Science, Innovation and Society. Oxford University; London School of Economics, May 2010.

Regional Technical Assistance (RETA) No. 6440. "Facilitating Regional Power Trading and Environmentally Sustainable Development of Electricity Infrastructure in the Greater Mekong Subregion". Interim Report, December 2009.

World Resources Institute. "A Roadmap for a Secure, Low-Carbon Energy Economy — Balancing Energy Security and Climate Change". January 2009.

12

LINKING THE SOCIAL TO THE ECONOMIC
Broadened Ambitions and Multiple Mitigations in New Mekong Corridors

Chris Lyttleton

Rapid social change, in and of itself, is not new to the region as it has been marked historically by imperialism, wars, and multiple migrations. The Upper Mekong, a previously remote area, has often been the subject of ambitious visions of infrastructure development, but, until recently, seldom the site of their realization. In the nineteenth century, British and French colonial authorities sent numerous missions to the region in search of land-based trade routes that might link mainland Southeast Asia to China. The French built a railway from Haiphong to Kunming via the Red River, while the British considered doing the same from northern Thailand. Later in 1937 the Chinese, seeking trade links with India, extended a road from Kunming as far as the Myanmar frontier. Subsequently, World War II, the Communist Revolution in China, and minority rebellions in northeast Myanmar halted further development of cross-border transport and trade connections. Likewise, the Cold War and regional geopolitics further hampered subsequent linkage projects.

But since the 1990s, economic reforms have given renewed impetus to streamlining trading arrangements in the border regions of Thailand, Laos, Vietnam, Cambodia, Myanmar, and southern China. By the turn of the millennium, visions of an integrated economic entity finally began to take shape when the Asian Development Bank launched the Greater Mekong Subregion Program. The initiative aims to build corridors that link the Mekong countries and provide the ability for trade goods, trucks, travellers, and tourists to move rapidly between and through previously remote and hinterland areas of neighbouring states. In a mid-term review of the regional programme, the ADB notes:

> The GMS (Greater Mekong Subregion) Program has made very good progress in the "hardware" aspects of cooperation involving the first strategic thrust of the GMS–SF, but less so in the "software" components of cooperation involving the four other thrusts of the GMS–SF, especially in the measures necessary to enhance competitiveness and in activities addressing social and environmental issues in the GMS. This is not surprising, as the initial phases of the GMS Program had placed substantial emphasis on the need to remove the physical barriers to subregional economic cooperation. (ADB 2007, p. viii)

The first strategic thrust referred to in the ADB review is "Strengthening Infrastructure Linkages", with a transport component which includes three (nearly) completed economic corridors linking countries of the Mekong Subregion and various other thoroughfares under construction. These new roads have now greatly improved physical connectivity, allowing increased mobility and cross-border trade while at the same time, bringing economic opportunities to previously remote areas. In so doing, national polities are physically stitched together with a new architecture that is transforming local livelihoods and diverse aspects of everyday life. Nowadays, as other chapters in this volume discuss, economic integration is indeed becoming concrete throughout the GMS as increased traffic and commerce offer clear indicators of progress. New corridors are thereby a cornerstone of a globalizing marketplace and expanding neoliberalism which, as Harvey (2005, p. 2) describes, is "in the first instance a theory of political economic practices that proposes that human well-being can best be advanced by liberating individual entrepreneurial freedoms and skills within an institutional framework characterized by strong property rights, free markets and free trade". While it can be debated to what extent states and individuals in the region either create, or have the leeway to act as fully fledged neoliberal subjects, there is no doubt premises underlying

FIGURE 12.1
The Northern Economic Corridor

the construction of the new economic corridors support ongoing privatization and market expansion.

As such, roads and infrastructure development are about more than just the increased movement of people and growth in trade and commerce. They also envisage other types of mobility: the movement of ideas, changing lifestyles, and above all, evolving entrepreneurialism — that is to say, the "software" components indicated in the above-mentioned ADB review. At heart, the notion of regional integration via these corridors relies on people interacting with people. Roads are magnets as well as thoroughfares. Despite being about movement, they are also about openings, connections, opportunities, and new forms of economic and social engagement. For thousands — perhaps millions — they represent new choices due to the conduits and passage they provide. And people connect in any number of social and trade-related interactions, from the clinical handshake over a cultivation contract, through to a sexually intimate sojourn in a local village, all in the name of economic integration. This chapter thus argues that understanding the impact of new economic corridors requires an analysis of social factors and, in particular, how one addresses "negative externalities" that emerge as a consequence of rapid economic growth. In what follows I focus primarily on the newly completed Northern Economic Corridor linking Yunnan with North Thailand, and bypassing two of the poorest provinces in North Lao PDR (where it is simply called Route 3). In early 2008, the upgraded R3 (see Figure 12.1) was officially opened and one can now drive from Thailand to China, passing through 226 kilometres of the Lao PDR in roughly three hours. Thailand, the economic hub of mainland Southeast Asia, is now stitched via efficient and serviceable tarmac to the economic powerhouse of Southern China.

A ROAD'S SOCIAL FOOTPRINTS

I will begin with three vignettes from along the R3 to foreshadow that, in addition to concrete and economic variables, we also need to think closely about forms of human and social capital that provide the raw constituents of economic growth in the first place. For it is here that we find intricate modalities of both entrepreneurship and exploitation.

Scene 1: In 2003, Boten was a small non-descript border crossing. Several years later, a large entertainment/hotel complex with a casino is a booming focal point of a small Chinese town constellating around it: Golden Boten City, emerging amidst the forested hills flanking the Lao-China border. Far more grandiose constructions are under way, including more hotels, entertainment venues, and a planned conference centre. The casino and associated services have employed thousands of Chinese workers. Many more come on fleeting visits to gamble, shop and "visit" the Lao PDR. It is Lao land, but has Chinese occupancy — a Hong Kong company owns a lease for thirty years, extendable twice more, on five kilometres of land running alongside the R3. A second casino, Golden Kapok Flower, was completed in 2009, near the other end of Route 3 — on land flanking the Mekong in the Lao district of Ton Perng, just across from Thailand. Here large tracts of leased land are also being used for multiple purposes, including for housing tourist attractions such as local ethnic villages, and zones of agricultural production to support the growing Chinese population. Chinese clientele can access this megacomplex from the R3 or large tourist boats that navigate the heavy waters of the Mekong River down from Jinhong, the capital of Xishuangbanna. In both instances foreign leaseholds for these casinos were established on the premise of ushering economic growth and trade to undeveloped parts of the Lao PDR, although it remains to be seen how sustainable and beneficial these long-term ambitions will be (Lyttleton and Nyiri 2010).[1]

Scene 2: Between these geographic bookends of capitalist hedonism, Lao agriculture is changing dramatically. Here too aspirations are fired by speculation, in this instance, villagers gamble with their land in long-term contractual commitments. The new road is not solely responsible for this — but it does make it easier for various forms of investment to move capital and material assistance south of the Chinese border and allow produce to move north (cf. Sturgeon 2010). Throughout Northern Lao PDR, in particular in areas close to the border, Chinese financed contract farms are creating a steady source of sugar, cassava, watermelons, and capsicums back into Chinese markets. Rubber is the new crop in town. Since 2004 its cultivation has expanded dramatically (Alton et al. 2005). Heady visions of indefinite profits based around China's booming automobile industry have brought numerous players to believe in plantation futures. Chinese companies and many small-scale entrepreneurs bring money, knowledge, rubber seedlings, and ad hoc contracts for the lease of local land, ranging from large military holdings through to smallholder village entitlements. Who will provide the labour once these trees begin producing latex is an open and complicated question. Currently ethnic Akha from both sides of the border forge informal arrangements to pursue dreams of growth in ways that draw together interpersonal and sometimes intimate relationships alongside economic agreements (Lyttleton and Sayanouso 2011).

Scene 3: The road comes first, and then come small shops servicing road construction labourers, and after that traders and travellers. In a previous study of the impact of the road we showed that the number of small stores increased dramatically after construction as these sites offer the first and most readily accessible means for villagers to enter a petty commodity market (Lyttleton 2009). The commodity sold most in these stores is alcohol — beer and whiskey — as the first step in a very particular economic trajectory with specific social and health implications. Some stores diversify their market and become places where men stop and drink for more than fleeting sessions because the company of young village women entices them to stay and consume further. Female attention is not in short supply, as more young women are recruited from villages further afield. Makeshift teams of itinerant young women move throughout the Lao PDR, working in "hospitality venues" as serving staff. As numbers expand, so too do venues — or vice versa. Women working this seam of income stay in one spot a few months and then move to a new venue, usually unglamorous, small drink shops (like those along the R3) or the smattering of nightclubs in the towns. They move following a type of in-built redundancy, in search of better money and a suitable place to live. Money comes from the sociable company they provide to the thirsty traveller or the local lad alike. In some sites they provide sex. As a result resilient networks are growing that bring large numbers of women from specific ethnic minorities, particularly the Khmu, into these expanding market relations and that place women in a subordinate position where they are ill-equipped to negotiate personal and physical safety (Lyttleton and Vorabouth 2011).

IMPACT ASSESSMENT

There is no doubt that improved access to markets, goods, and services helps reduce poverty. One case study from the Lao PDR found that about one fourth of the reduction in poverty incidence in the Lao PDR's rural population, from 42.5 per cent in 1997–98 to 37.6 per cent in 2002–3, "can be directly attributed to the conversion of roads that are accessible only in the dry season into roads that are accessible in all seasons" (Menon 2005). Along the R3 data are still unclear as to specific and generalizable economic improvements (Sathavandit 2011), and while villagers enjoy many aspects of improved transport and less dust from the new tarmac, there is also an awareness that economic growth is not automatically achieved by all sectors of the population, no matter which economic corridor we consider. Thus, the ADB review stresses that there should be more emphasis on programmes that can assist the poor, in particular, vulnerable groups such as ethnic minorities in remote areas, to take advantage of the new infrastructure developments, noting "Further measures are required to minimize and mitigate the adverse impact of subregional economic integration" (ADB 2007, p. 12). Typically negative externalities along new roads are framed in three main areas: HIV/AIDS, environmental damage, and illegal migration, including people trafficking.

This combination of hope for economic growth and concern over negative consequences reflect the crucial but increasingly contentious role of impact assessment and its basis for subsequent mitigation activities. Recognition that development and rapid social change do not improve everyone's lives at an even pace, and furthermore, that there is potential for "damage", drives the need for impact assessments. However, while most Western donors acknowledge their importance (cf. World Bank 1998), impact assessments are not without problems both in conception and implementation (Burdge 2003). If we accept that the breadth of impact assessment should include "processes of analysing, monitoring and managing the intended and unintended social consequences both positive and negative of planned interventions and any social change processes invoked by those interventions" (Vanclay 2003, p. 2), then it is safe to say that its role in improving outcomes will never be an easy task. Any instrument that seeks to evaluate comprehensively ways in which "people and communities interact with their socio-cultural, economic and biophysical surroundings" (Vanclay, p. 2) will be fraught with methodological and conceptual challenges. Frequently such difficulties lead to a preference for a streamlined package of more readily measurable impacts, such as demographic movements, health indicators, or shifting employment statistics. In an attempt to clarify and fine-tune approaches, Vanclay (2002) makes an important distinction between social impacts and social change processes that are set in place by project activities or policies.

Social change processes are the basis of all development activities that seek to alter people's lives: they in turn lead to specific impacts that "are experienced or felt in corporeal or perceptual terms" (Vanclay 2002, p. 200). In order to bring the vast range of social change processes into a more meaningful calculus, Vanclay recommends specific constellations of social transformation — demographic, economic, geographical, institutional and legal, emancipatory, and sociocultural — and proceeds to delineate numerous potential outcomes implicit to each grouping. The important point for our purposes is that, despite a dizzying array of variables, to understand impacts we need to understand processes. This in turn allows us to discuss what it means when roads become socio-economic corridors and thereby transform the lives of those living near, or benefiting more peripherally from, these roads.

MITIGATION MODELS

For over a decade, Michael Cernea, a sociologist with the World Bank sought to derive models that both explain and remedy negative effects of targeted interventions, in particular processes that lead not to economic growth, but rather to its opposite: impoverishment. He championed the idea of mitigation as a means to safeguard against foreseeable problems based on a simple logic. Development is important, necessary, and inevitable. Alongside positive consequences, negative outcomes, so experience tells us, are also seemingly inevitable for some populations or subsectors of affected communities. Pre-emptive problem solving is thus the basis of successful mitigation. It relies on being able to predict problems and implement strategies that prevent their emergence.

Focusing on impoverishment caused by a downwardly spiralling quality of life, Cernea (1996; 2000) devised an influential solution called Impoverishment Risks and Reconstruction Model (IRR). Like Vanclay's call for more attention to social change processes, Cernea's model is simple in structure, but complex in its implications. It talks about risks that could potentially make life worse for individuals or groups adversely affected by large-scale infrastructure development. This model has been adopted widely in mitigation programmes of most Western and multilateral donors. The idea is that if we can categorize and quantify risks, we can mitigate their impact. The IRR model cites diagnostic categories responsible for impoverishment:

1. **Landlessness** removes the main source of people's wealth and is therefore the main cause of impoverishment
2. **Joblessness** is high in urban and rural wage-labour settings, as it is hard to create new jobs artificially
3. **Homelessness** tends to be temporary, but in a broader cultural sense, loss of a group's territorial space results in alienation and loss of social status.
4. **Marginalization** occurs when there is a loss of economic power and downward mobility as one's status and occupation are not maintained after relocation. Economic marginalization is often accompanied by social and psychological marginalization.
5. **Food insecurity** is the increased vulnerability to undernourishment — makes normal growth or work impossible.
6. **Increased morbidity or mortality**; health vulnerability often accompanies rapid change that includes stress. Unsafe water increases infectious diseases; economic need can increase STDs (sexually transmitted diseases) through engagement in commercial sex.
7. **Loss of access to common property** reduces income dramatically — it is particularly relevant to communities that have used shared resources as a basis of livelihood.
8. **Social disarticulation** happens when resettlement rips apart social fabric, when the sense of local community is dissipated, when social capital is destroyed.

The IRR model rests on a key assumption — with the right planning the impoverishment processes can be corrected. Thus one can posit a series of corrective measures to be utilized for each of the above-listed concerns, for example, resettlement for those who are made landless. Cernea's focus was on a broad problematically termed "development-induced displacement" that was largely linked to dams. But even as not all variables have equal urgency, road construction programmes fit the same generic problem-solving paradigm and mitigation programmes have been central in the planning of new economic corridors. Social action plans (SAPs) along new roads throughout the GMS now target many of Cernea's problem areas through health, income generation, and land compensation activities.

But if we take seriously the notion that socio-economic corridors also set in place diverse and vibrant chains of entrepreneurialism, then we must also consider that social changes processes move beyond readily identifiable threats. According to their critics, current mitigation strategies focus only on measurable forms of "loss" and thereby cannot take into account the larger issues of social marginalization that occur over time, in particular, in areas with high levels of ethnic diversity. As Dwivedi notes, "While some losses can be computed, others cannot; assets and livelihood losses can be valued, but identities and networks cannot. Only those losses that can be computed can be prevented" (2002, p. 718). In other words, if we follow a compensatory logic, the only problems leading to impoverishment that can be effectively mitigated are those that can be measured. Compounding the difficulties facing targeted mitigation activities, the model highlights interlinkages between each of the designated categories. Changed economic opportunities create new forms of workplace and livelihood engagement. New livelihood strategies create new forms of wage-labour relations. These can, in turn, create new forms of social hierarchy if the social and economic competencies of those entering these new relations are not equal. In short, when people from many different backgrounds increasingly interact as a product of increased mobility, exploitative relations can and do take place as one group is better positioned to take advantage of another in both economic and social contexts. This leads directly to marginalization, both within and between communities; it also leads to social disarticulation. In circular fashion, social disadvantage can lead directly to physical and material consequences: marginalization can lead to health vulnerability, livelihood insecurity, and, potentially, to homelessness and joblessness. In other words, the categories Cernea itemizes are linked in multidirectional ways with no specific causal primacy. It means we have to think of the social costs of development as every bit as important as the physical transformations they produce. Thus mitigation is, of necessity, about more than material or economic compensation. Just as spreading neoliberalism underpins attempts to improve conditions of generic well-being across the board, so too mitigation should be about ensuring the sustainability of this well-being in a broad sense of the word.

The extent to which Cernea's advice to the large donors has been taken seriously is shown quite clearly in the extent to which social action plans (SAPs) have been enacted in the construction phases of new economic corridors. These plans include social safeguard activities to cover vulnerable populations in accordance with ADB's Social Safeguard Policies. Other initiatives aim to prevent familiar problems (for example HIV/AIDS and trafficking), but, at the same time, pre-empt growing problems that will likely take place in the wake of economic development. In the GMS, the ADB has taken seriously the notion that mitigation processes should have long-term horizons. For example, in each of the new economic corridors, post-construction HIV programmes are funded by ADB precisely because it is aware social change processes continue to lead to negative impacts.

But the problem remains. If we anticipate negative social consequences, then how do we measure the social change processes underpinning these problems to ensure our compensatory initiatives are adequate? This is not an issue of financial equitability. Conceptualizing potential social dilemmas that do not so much have immediate and concrete manifestations as a series of related consequences, is not straightforward, and not usually adequately incorporated within social action plans (Beesey 2010). As various commentators have indicated, one of the key problems facing rapid infrastructure development taking place under the guise of development and modernization is precisely forms of emergent inequality that are born of hierarchical social relations. This in turn has led to what some call a "capabilities" approach (Sen 1999). Alternative approaches suggest that a fundamental premise of rights-based development should not just be to ensure that damage is mitigated in a technical sense. Instead it should engage a vision of development that effectively empowers as its goal, rather than minimizes damage.

Many donors are aware of this "first do no harm" premise, which is precisely why social impact assessments are undertaken in the first place, although it must also be noted that not all major donors support the need for mitigating social impacts of economic growth. Clearly outcomes are multiple and cannot be pigeonholed as exclusively positive or negative. ADB's GMS mid-term evaluation notes bluntly that the positive outcomes far outweigh the negative, and that economic growth is occurring widely and overall poverty is declining. Financial security is empowering individuals and communities through increased options, a significant outcome that should be strongly emphasized. But the review also notes that the "soft" aspects are of increasing concern — environmental damage, illegal migration, and infectious disease need more emphasis "to be contained and mitigated" (ADB 2007, p. 34) and that "It will be important to continue to find ways of integrating the poor into the mainstream of economic development and prevent them from being 'crowded out' in this process" (ADB 2007, p. 12).

NEOLIBERAL ENGAGEMENTS

The cool hills that flank the contiguous border areas of the Greater Mekong Subregion (GMS) are home to roughly twenty-one million people from ethnic minority groups. As state-based land management strategies seek to eliminate traditional swidden lifestyles and promote modernization through agricultural and demographic transition, for many of these ethnic groups economic diversification is central to a changing livelihood. In the Lao PDR, over 90 per cent of the population in the roadside villages through which the R3 passes is from ethnic minority groups. Likewise in Vietnam and Yunnan, the new corridors pass through areas highly populated by minority groups. Processes of social marginalization exacerbate the poor health, limited educational opportunities, and insecure livelihoods that characterize minority or indigenous people's lives in the region. As Formoso (2010, p. 314) notes, the lack of progress has its roots in commonplace perceptions: "According to a still dominant, but misleading, imagery, 'backward' hill tribes live entrenched in remote places, hemmed in by immemorial traditions. They are believed not to be amenable to change and progress, to be reluctant to adopt 'stateness', or to be the passive recipients of policies that escape their common understanding." Thus, it is not just social exclusion in the sense of being ignored or crowded out that is at stake. Rather, given this divergence in cultural understanding, it is also the means by which the (ethnic) poor are integrated into changing economic structures that becomes crucially important.

It is widely commented that spreading neoliberalism is a central part of global trade and mobility structures worldwide and it operates first and foremost through an encouragement of individualized entrepreneurialism and self-interest (Lazarotti 2006; Feher 2010). Of course, there are various ways in which this takes place and others have argued that in Asia the state still maintains variable degrees of control over growing individualized desires (Ong 2007; Sigley 2006). As the opening vignettes of this chapter indicated, expanded corridors are bringing new opportunities for populations along their carriage ways and entrepreneurialism is encouraged in diverse forms. The growing importance of capital in people's lives is increasingly evident along these thoroughfares, even as "the social forces it engenders militate against a smooth separation of the social world into independent constituent parts staffed by citizen consumers under the formal rationality of the market". (Taylor 2010, p. 573). A further vignette highlights how entrepreneurialism is never just a simple product of market rationality, but inevitably brings into intimate engagement other forms of social and human capital. R, an ethnic women of twenty-three, whom we met in her village near the R3, encapsulates these dimensions.

Scene 4: R grew up in a remote Lao village some hours' walk from the main road. At the age of sixteen she was almost raped by a truck driver from whom she had requested a ride down to a nearby border town. During another visit to this town not long afterwards, she decided to take her chances at finding work in Thailand and crossed the border to Chiang Khong during a festival. There she met a Japanese man with whom she lived for a month or so and she subsequently returned to the Lao PDR with money to renovate her parent's house (she had enough for a corrugated iron roof). She returned to Thailand, but this time went to Bangkok to work in a restaurant, and became close friends with other Lao women working in bars. She married a Thai man and bore his child (three years old at the time we met her). After a year, she went back to her home village again to organize a marriage there as well, so her parents might know what had happened to her. At this point, the local village headman, under pressure to detain anyone working illegally in Thailand, reported her to the district authorities. She was fined $90 which she raised by selling her necklace and bracelets, and was prohibited from returning to Thailand. Accepting that she could not return, within a year she married again — this time a local man, an ex-teacher from a village near the lignite mine on the R3. She now has a second child who was one year old when we met.

When we talked with her she had opened a small shop in her house as a means to make a modest income. She had recently persuaded her two nieces, aged thirteen and fourteen, to join her from their more remote village. Her rationale is that on most evenings, truck drivers from the nearby lignite mine wander into the village looking for somewhere to pass a few hours. She figures that the men will be far more likely to hang out at her house drinking if she can provide them with company. The two young nieces had only been there a week when we met R. They work in the fields during the day, but in the evening they provide the drawcard for customers. She is annoyed that they have not yet fully understood the logic of this enterprise. They are frightened when the men sit too close and run away when the men try to hug them. She tells them the men mean no harm. R might well be thinking that further relationships will take place when the girls get more comfortable. She is hoping to be able to start a small food shop/restaurant if she can save enough money. She says she will be able to do this if the girls stay because she will easily make money then. This, she feels, will cement her place in the village as the one most actively looking for a niche to make money from the proximity to the lignite mine.

Trajectories of petty commercialism in areas of infrastructure development often have close links to the growth of commercial sex and, in many places, it is more than coincidence that they are overwhelmingly staffed by ethnic minority women (Lyttleton and Vorabouth 2011). In this case, as part of the trajectory from small-scale shops to one also selling sex, it is easy to see moral difficulties in the strategy R has chosen. But, at the same time, we should also recognize that she is maximizing self-interest in ways that are seemingly supported by free market models. Just as the "rise of human capital as a dominant subjective form" has been described as central to neoliberalism (Feher 2010, p. 24), we might describe R as replicating this important transformation and becoming "an entrepreneur of oneself, maximising himself or herself as 'human capital'" (Lazarotti 2009, p. 111).

In other words, R is using what skills she has, in this instance, her knowledge of service provision in Thailand, and family connections, to create a market niche. She builds on existing social norms — the accepted presence of young women accompanying men while drinking beer in many Lao social settings — and utilizes kin-based relations to develop a mode of primitive capital accumulation. There are of course all sorts of difficulties with looking on this process as value-free. It would be easy to imagine R as a perfect target for the calibrated mitigation programmes accompanying the R3's construction. Anti-trafficking projects might have been concerned that she had recruited her two young nieces, both under eighteen, with the prospect, at least, to have them subsequently engage in sexual relations. HIV prevention activities would also have sought her as a ready recipient of warning messages. But both these discourses move in the opposite direction to the thrust of many other messages she has received about the positive impact of the new thoroughfare. The optimism that economic growth is available to all has been a mantra cited from the early days of road construction at both the state and local level. The appeal of livelihood improvement and modernity premised on material growth has so far vastly overshadowed any cautionary or legalistic lectures R might have received. It is not surprising that she utilizes what human and social capital resources she has at her disposal and ignores any conflicting advice (even if she had ever received it).

There are many other examples of evolving forms of sexual interaction as part of an entry into neoliberal expansion and increased mobility afforded by new corridors. Despite a predominant focus on material growth in analyses of the impact of infrastructure development, when we look closely at the lives of people caught up in the rapid slipstream of these new thoroughfares, it is impossible to ignore the interpersonal and subjective elements of their experiences. For example, in another border zone with improved transport facilities near the China/Myanmar border, many ethnic Dai women now leave their home villages to work in South Thailand in massage parlours (Lyttleton, Deng, and Zhang 2011). Previously this migration was channeled through agents and often women were victims of trafficking. More recently, building on established networks of kin and community and the newly authorized freedom to travel legally across borders, they go voluntarily due, in part, to a growing economic sensibility within China that encourages entrepreneurialism and proliferating desires to be modern (Rofel 2007). Many of these women are married; their husbands remain at home tending to their children as wives seek new partners as a means to capital accumulation. These relationships are made evident within an intense localized competition to demonstrate acquired wealth and modern status through the construction of new homes. Hence, aspirations take very specific forms in this part of China and, insofar as the women remain married, are quite different from networks into commercial sex typical in rural areas of other parts of Southeast Asia. Demonstrating what Ong (2006) describes as "promiscuous" capitalism's ability to find new forms, Dai women are able to utilize social (gender independence and transnational connections) and cultural (Chinese language) capital to find material support through relations with Chinese-Malaysian men at the Thai-Malaysian border.

ASPIRATIONS IN PRACTICE

An important World Bank–sponsored volume discusses the importance of considering culture in approaches to reduce poverty wherein Appadurai (2004) describes the "capacity to aspire" as a generative framework anticipating an improved future usually born of diversified market opportunities. Fostering the achievement of aspirations is also implicit in the global expansion of trade and mobility within increasingly borderless markets. Promoting one's capacity to aspire is central to donor and state modernization programmes in regions where economic corridors open up new worlds and proliferating ambitions fuel individual choices. Turning to the vignettes with which I started the chapter, we see that the capacity to aspire takes on multiple dimensions as it underpins the investment of human, social, and material capital. Focusing only on intimate relations implicit in these scenarios, we see that in the casinos near the borders with China and Thailand, men come to play for money; while doing so many also wish to partake in sex with local women. Local ethnic sex services are dramatically altered by the presence of these facilities. Likewise the many local and imported staff running these gambling halls are mostly young and single, and they too find themselves in a social environment characterized by the dearth of family or social sanctions. Unsurprisingly sex and drugs are common. People take chances with these relationships and health dilemmas are ever-present. Visiting men want to experience local female sexuality as part of their cross-border experience: safe sex is often seen to undermine this "tourist" engagement. Young male and female staff have numerous fleeting relationships as they too respond to the particularly detached nature of these zones. Abortions in local clinics are frequent. In both these instances, cultural assumptions and sexual opportunities are refracted through the movement of large amounts of money, all packaged in the guise of national and regional development.

Amongst Akha communities in Northern Lao PDR, abiding optimism that rubber will mean a highly prosperous future is fuelling a headlong and competitive rush to acquire or convert as much land as possible into rubber plantations. Numerous small- and large-scale Chinese investment initiatives are fuelling this growth. The previous history of contract farming in Lao districts bordering China has shown that many young ethnic women, particularly Akha and Kwii, have become sexually integrated into the social and material exchanges linked to agricultural investment. In these instances, market gardeners utilizing ethnic go-betweens try to exploit cultural familiarity with local practices and social networks to gain sexual access to young women. There is a gradual and insidious move to incorporate financial exchange and/or nationalist appeal to facilitate relationships. Cross-border affiliations are both strategic and intimate for men and women from both sides of the border. Chinese men represent potential husbands and thereby access to Chinese modernity. Local women become the doorway into kin-based access to Lao land. The expansion of rubber within ethnic areas in North Lao PDR underpins the increased monetization of sexual exchange and increased "intimization" of land deals. Here too people take chances that certain relationships will be beneficial in a material sense.

Heading to another border zone on the, as yet, uncompleted East-West Economic Corridor we also see that migrants are impacted in development zones that are structured not by rampant hedonism as in the casinos, but instead by conflict and civil strife and those able to capitalize on it. Tens of thousands of young men and women from Myanmar seek work in factories in the Thai border district of Mae Sot. In this district, HIV is noticeably higher amongst the Burmese population. This occurs for a number of reasons, central to which is the insecurity and fragility of everyday life for displaced peoples. In environments where exploitation is rife, the need for emotional connection becomes paramount. Relationships between young migrant workers are often fleeting as the exigencies of transient labour and highly controlled work environments create little opportunity for long-term relationships. Romance is a key means of coping with a difficult work life; the ways in which it takes shape are strongly linked to specific development policies governing the industrial zones in this district. In other words, the intimate lives of factory workers are heavily structured by the particularities of the cross-border environment. Likewise the capacity to be safe from infectious disease is compromised by forces that dictate the way relationships can take place.

One could readily list other ways in which individuals make choices that entail more than the simple investment of physical labour throughout the region where new roads are changing social landscapes. As Feher notes, a characteristic of neoliberal expansion is a broadening of utilizable personal resources: "The various things I do in any existential domain (dietary, erotic, religious, etc.) all contribute to either appreciating or depreciating the human capital that is me, no less than does my diligence as a worker or my ability to trade my professional skills" (Feher 2010, p. 30). In other words, people are encouraged to invest whatever they see as having value in marketplace engagement. People don't just utilize their labour as a market tool, they commodify their land, their bodies, their nieces, their emotional companionship. Thus invariably intimate economies blend with material economies as neoliberal changes in the economic realm have corollaries in the subjective realm of identity and experience. And these are the precise processes of social change that mitigation finds so hard to grapple with, in particular when entrepreneurialism oftentimes evokes exploitation as individuals or groups have differential degrees of social and economic competencies. In each of the above examples, one group is poised to utilize the relative marginalization of another group and, in the process, increases, rather than improves, that marginalization.

Beyond sexual risk, in each of the scenarios I described, elements of social hierarchy allow individuals and groups to jockey for advantage. For example, rubber contracts are signed without adequate protection for the signees; young women are recruited into bars, duped into thinking it is their only choice to gain an adequate income to become "modern" citizens; sexual companionship is sold to overseas Malaysian men as a preferable strategy to avoid prejudice back home in China; Thai border factory owners breach international workplace standards due to the presence of a voiceless migrant workforce. None of these choices is institutionally favoured, but they take place in the complex intersection of individual desires and loosening social and political constraints to allow what Ong (2006) has termed "experimentations with freedoms". Individuals and larger coalitions actively make choices to use human and social capital to gain an economic foothold. However, as the story of R demonstrated, these choices are not always made with adequate oversight of dangers and indignities implicit in these choices, not to mention potential child rights violations.

CONCLUSION

Consequences of the development of socio-economic corridors are multidimensional. Numerous positive outcomes are evident, ranging from physical improvements in people and traffic mobility through to efficiency in coordination and implementation of trade. However, there are difficulties in adequately appreciating negative consequences as they relate to changing social conditions when they are constitutively bound to the very processes being encouraged. Social transition, every bit as much as economic growth, is core to the vision of a better future provided by the GMS programme. In addition to trade, communication, and commerce, new economic corridors are also direct conduits of new forms of social relationships born of what has been termed "a neoliberal subjectivity". People are called upon to imagine a different future and encouraged to invest whatever aspects of themselves they can to become entrepreneurs and to broaden the engagement in market economies. The respective nation states still have a crucial role in governing the parameters of these changes, but this is sometimes contingent and variable (Sigley 2006). And one must recognize that there are multiple levels at which self-interest is served, as competition is the heart of a free market economy.

But if there is to be any oversight of negative externalities, and if, in fact, the concept of mitigation is to have any meaning in the process of infrastructure development, then one also has to consider the parameters defining one's approach to negative outcomes. Donors usually accept that certain social consequences are undesirable. The process by which they occur is harder either to examine or curtail. As Rao and Walton have argued, understanding social and cultural dimensions to change must "confront difficult questions in terms of *what* is valued in terms of well-being, *who* does the valuing, and *why* economic and social factors interact with culture to unequally allocate access to a good life" (2004, p. 2). Obviously no one wants HIV/AIDS to escalate as a product of aid assistance, and many programmes address this. But as I indicated earlier, when social change processes and "risk" also incur forms of impoverishment, including marginalization, then this is hard both to conceptualize in empirical forms, and mitigate. The contentious issue facing development policies then is whether to ignore its potential completely, on the assumption that the positive outweighs all negatives, or if not, how one should ensure "the poor are not crowded out".

I have discussed elsewhere the health implications of these differing situations. Here my intention has been to expand our consideration of the role of self-enterprise as a key underpinning of proliferating social impacts. It is a crucial piece in the transition from geographic to socio-economic corridors. For even as neoliberalism champions forms of individual enterprise in a globalizing marketplace — and the new economic corridors provide numerous opportunities — it would be wrong to think of these changes as premised on purely rational economic logic, which we can target with instrumental mitigation programmes to address any unforeseen consequences. As Bogard reminds us, "all forms of rational action operate within a dynamic framework of unacknowledged conditions and unanticipated consequences" (1988, p. 149). Nowadays it is more in keeping with contemporary free market sensibilities to note that, at heart, aspirations are speculative (Feher 2010). People take chances with their futures in attempts to appreciate (in the sense of increase) their worth. And as people do indeed enter new forms of social and economic relationships based on expanded opportunities, then the question for state and development planners becomes: to what extent should they — the state or donors — be responsible for outcomes predicated on speculation, and the implicit impossibility of anticipating speculative (in Cernea's self-defeating sense) outcomes.

There is no simple solution to this issue. But if we accept that utilizing personal and individualized resources has become the key mode by which newly neoliberal subjects (and communities) are encouraged to engage opportunities along new economic corridors, then this needs to be the level of focus. If we assume a laissez-faire market will determine what elements of human capital are the most conducive to self-enterprise, then as the above examples demonstrated, negative consequences are inevitable. People are not always equipped to make choices that are in their own long-term best interests in a rapidly changing socio-economic context, putting instead their bodies or those of their relatives to various forms of physical and social risk. Others have argued comprehensively for the need to think of capabilities as essential to equitable outcomes of development (Nussbaum 2004), but I will not reproduce their persuasive prescriptions here. If human capital is in fact the commodity at the coalface of the new socio-economic corridors, then more proactive, broad-based, and practical education opportunities would be one means by which to prepare and condition people, in particular, groups already marginalized by ethnicity, class, religion, or gender, to be able to engage more productively with the new economic opportunities. Successful mobilization would require not just the coordination of economic corridors, but also regional, state, and donor cooperation on how best to prepare a citizenry and its human capital for diverse forms of economic growth.

Note

1. Golden Boten City was closed in 2011 following pressure from the Chinese Government but the owners intend to reopen the zone in the near future avowing to place less emphasis on gambling as the key drawcard.

References

ADB. Mid-term review of the Greater Mekong Subregion Strategic Framework 2002–12. Manila: ADB, 2007.

Alton, C. et al. Para Rubber Study. Lao PDR. Vientiane: GTZ, 2005.

Appadurai, A. "The Capacity to Aspire". In *Culture and Public Action*, edited by V. Rao and M. Walton. Stanford: Stanford University Press, 2004.

Beesey, A. "Along the Road of Vulnerability and Risk: A Comparative Analysis of Risk Settings in Infrastructure Projects". Draft report. Manila: ADB, 2010.

Burdge, R. "The Practice of Social Impact Assessment — Background". *Impact Assessment and Project Appraisal* 21, no. 2 (2003): 84–88.

Cernea, M. *Impoverishment Risks and Livelihood Reconstruction: A Model for Resettling Displaced Populations*. Washington: World Bank, 1996.

———. "Introduction". In *Risks and Reconstruction: Experiences of Resettlers and Refugees*, edited by M. Cernea and C. McDowell. Washington: World Bank, 2000.

Dwivedi, R. "Models and Methods in Development-Induced Displacement". *Development and Change* 33, no. 4 (2002).

Feher, M. "Self-Appreciation; or, the Aspirations of Human Capital". *Public Culture* 213 (2009): 21–41.

Formoso, B. "Zomian or Zombies: What Future Exists for the People's of the Southeast Asian Massif?" *Journal of Global History* 5, no. 2 (2010): 313–32.

Harvey, D. *A Brief History of Neo-liberalism*. Oxford: Oxford University Press, 2005.

Lazzarato, M. "Neoliberalism in Action: Inequality, Insecurity and the Reconstitution of the Social". *Theory, Culture and Society* 26, no. 6 (2009): 109–33.

Lyttleton, C. *Build It and They Will Come*. Manila: ADB, 2009.

Lyttleton, C., R. Deng, and N. Zhang. "Promiscuous Capitalism Meets 'Exotic' Ethnicity: Intimate Aspirations Amongst Cross-border Chinese Dai". *Australian Journal of Anthropology* 22, no. 3 (2011): 314–31.

Lyttleton, C. and Nyiri, P. "Dams, Casinos and Concessions: Chinese Megaprojects in Laos and Cambodia". In *Engineering Earth*, edited by S. Brunn. Springer Press, 2011.

Lyttleton, C. and Sayanouso, D. "Cultural Reproduction and 'Minority' Sexuality in the Upper Mekong". *Asian Studies Review* 35, no. 2 (2011): 169–88.

Lyttleton, C., S. Vorabouth. "Trade Circles: Aspirations and Ethnicity in Commercial Sex in Laos". *Culture Health and Sexuality* 13, no. 2 (2011): 5263–77.

Menon, J. *The Mekong Region: Economic and Social Impact of Projects*. Manila: ADB, 2005.

Nussbaum, M. "Beyond the Social Contract: Capabilities and Global Justice". *Oxford Development Studies* 32, no. 1 (2004): 3–18.

Ong, A. "Experiments with Freedom". *American Literary History* 18 (2006): 229–44.

————. "Boundary Crossings: Neoliberalism as a Mobile Technology". *Transactions of the Institute of British Geographers (Trans. Inst. Br. Geogr.)* 32 (2007): 3–8.

Rao, V. and M. Walton. "Introduction". In *Culture and Public Action*, edited by V. Rao and M. Walton. Stanford: Stanford University Press, 2004.

Rofel, L. *Desiring China: Experiments in Neoliberalism, Sexuality and Public Culture*. Duke University Press, 2007.

Sathavandit. S. "The Socioeconomic Impacts of the Northern Economic Corridor Project on Local Livelihoods". Presented at ANR Transiter/Southeast Asia Regional Workshop, Vientiane, Lao PDR, 14–17 December 2010.

Sen, A. *Development as Freedom*. Oxford: Oxford University Press, 1999.

Sigley, G. "Chinese Governmentalities: Government, Governance and the Socialist Market Economy". *Economy and Society* 35, no. 4 (2006): 487–508.

Sturgeon, J. "Governing Minorities and Development in Xishuangbanna, China: Akha and Dai Rubber Farmers as Entrepreneurs". *Geoforum* 41, no. 2 (2010): 318–28.

Taylor, M. "Conscripts of Competitiveness: Culture, Institutions and Capital in Contemporary Development". *Third World Quarterly* 31, no. 4 (2010): 561–79.

Vanclay, F. "Conceptualising Social Impacts". *Environmental Impact Assessment Review* 22 (2002): 183–211.

————. "Social Impact Assessment: International Principles". IAIA Special Publication Series no. 2, 2003.

World Bank. *Assessing Aid: What Works, What Doesn't and Why*. Washington DC: World Bank, 1998.

Acknowledgements

This chapter was prepared building on research supported by AusAID, ADB and Macquarie University. I wish to offer my thanks to the many individuals in the different field sites who generously shared their time and knowledge with me.

INDEX

A

access to finance, 41, 43
accountability to public, 211
ADB. *See* Asian Development Bank (ADB)
ADB–GMS Economic Cooperation Programme, 176, 196
AEC. *See* ASEAN Economic Community (AEC)
AFTA. *See* ASEAN Free Trade Agreement (AFTA); ASEAN Free Trade Area (AFTA)
agreements, trade, 125–30
agribusiness, 41, 45
agricultural income, 86
agricultural sector
    and gross domestic product (GDP), 6
    of Myanmar, 51, 56, 58, 59
    population working in, 45
agro-industry products, 41
aid in Yunnan and GMS, 107–8
AMRO. *See* ASEAN+3 Macroeconomic Research Office (AMRO)
annual vehicle tax, 183
anti-trafficking project, 245
ASEAN. *See* Association of South East Asian Nations (ASEAN)
ASEAN+3, 18, 22, 29

ASEAN Charter, 25–26, 29
ASEAN-China investment fund, 107–8
ASEAN Connectivity, 96
    Master Plans for, 100
ASEAN Countries
    human development index of, 89
    development gaps, 88
ASEAN Economic Community (AEC), 3, 83, 100, 173
ASEAN finance cooperation, 168, 170n6
ASEAN Framework Agreement on Facilitation of Interstate Transport, 182
ASEAN Framework Agreement on Services (AFAS), 176, 196
ASEAN Free Trade Agreement (AFTA), 14, 129, 143, 145, 147, 155
    regionalism through, 146
ASEAN Free Trade Area (AFTA), 32
ASEAN integration, 85, 95, 99
ASEAN+3 Macroeconomic Research Office (AMRO), 15, 169
ASEAN-plus integration, 85, 95
ASEAN Vision, 86
Asian Development Bank (ADB), 32, 76, 78, 84, 104, 125, 156n2, 172, 216, 226, 234, 242

RETAs (Regional Technical
Assistance), 94
review, 234–35, 238
Asian economic crisis, 51
Asian financial crisis, 165, 168,
170n9
Asia-Pacific Economic Cooperation
(APEC), 74
Association of Southeast Asian Nations
(ASEAN), 3, 32, 74, 84
"bridging the development gap" in,
25–26
China's trade with, 105
exports, 113
investors, 137
membership in, 127–30, 146
trade between Yunnan and, 105

B
Bangkok, 184
hypermarkets distribution in, 192
Bangkok–Danang route, 198
Bangkok–Hanoi, logistics cost and
time from, 203–4
Bangkok–Kunming, logistics cost and
time from, 204
Bangkok Mass Transit Authority
(BMTA), 186
banking sector, 165
domestic credit provided by, 166,
167
Berlin Wall, fall of, 76
bilateral agreement, 194–95
Board of Trade of Thailand (BoT),
200
bond markets, 165
border officials, 201, 205–6
Bridgehead Strategy, 14
of China, 109
concept of, 109–10
framework of, 111
regional economic integration, 110
Yunnan's role in, 111–12

budget deficit in Myanmar, 56, 57, 68
Buffet, Warren, 163
build-operate-transfer (BOT), 211
build-own-operate-transfer (BOOT),
211
Burmese population, 247
Burmese Way of Socialism, 48
bus fare calculation, method for, 185
bus industry
diseconomy of scale of, 187
weak regulatory and law
enforcement in, 185–86
business environment, 39–41, 43

C
CAFTA. *See* China-ASEAN Free Trade
Agreement (CAFTA)
Cambodia, 16, 104
Annamite Mountains of, 85
Asian future of, 29–30
China's aid to, 107
communication development in, 7
conflict in, 20
2008–9 crisis in, 22–25
and development paradigm, 21–22
economy of, 23
foreign investment regime in, 124
future scenario for, 26–28
GDP growth rate of, 2–3, 88, 120
global financial crisis in 2008, 13
and GMS, 18, 27
imperatives for, 25
independence for, 75
logistics infrastructure in, 178
low income level in, 85
manufactured products in, 140
poverty rates in, 120
primary commodities in, 136
trade and investment policy in,
123–24
trade in, 130
Cambodia, Lao People's Democratic
Republic, Myanmar, and

Vietnam (CLMV), 75, 87, 88, 119, 123, 127, 129
government effectiveness in, 176–77
independence for, 75
MFN and preferential tariffs in, 143, 145
Cambodian economy, 21
Cambodian People's Party (CPP), 20
Cambodia-Thailand border, 12
"capabilities" approach, 242
carbon capture and storage (CCS), 224
carbon emission reduction, potential of, 226–27
CC. *See* control of corruption (CC)
Central Bank of Burma (CBM), 57
Central Land Transport Control Board, 184
CEPT. *See* common effective preferential tariff (CEPT)
Cernea, Michael, 239
Chiang Mai Initiative Multilateralization (CMIM), 15, 169
child mortality rate, 62, 67
China, 75, 76, 104
  communist revolution in, 233
  in cross-border cooperation, 111–12
  domestic construction of high-speed railways, 118n23
  economic growth, 112
  economies of, 1–2
  energy cooperation with GMS, 106
  financial crisis, 3–4
  foreign aid, 107
  in GMS, 76
  governance scores of, 178
  hydropower plants in, 78
  investment in GMS, 114
  national development strategy in, 110–11, 117n10, 117n16

oil imports, 111
oil pipeline from Bay of Bengal, 107
trade with ASEAN, 105
trade with GMS, 90, 109
CHINA–ASEAN EXPO in 2004, 108, 117n16
China-ASEAN Free Trade Agreement (CAFTA), 104, 108, 111
China-ASEAN Investment Agreement, 116
China-ASEAN trade, 113
China-GMS economic relations, 107
China-Myanmar crude oil and gas pipeline, 106
China National Petroleum Corp (CNPC), 106
China's Indian Ocean Strategy, 110
China's Ministry of Environmental Protection, 116
China's "Peaceful Development" strategy, 110
Chinese population, 236
clean development mechanism (CDM), 224, 226, 230
clean fuels (CF), 225
climate change impacts in GMS, 222
CLMV. *See* Cambodia, Lao People's Democratic Republic, Myanmar, and Vietnam (CLMV)
CMIM. *See* Chiang Mai Initiative Multilateralization
CO_2 emissions, 229, 230
Cold War, 19, 20, 76, 104, 233
colonial authorities, 233
colonial period in Thailand, 75
commodity market, 237
common effective preferential tariff (CEPT), 129, 143, 145
communication development, 7
community of practice (COP), 224
Comprehensive Asia Development Plan (CADP), 94, 96

consumer price index, growth rates of, 53, 54
consumers, 194
Container Temporary Admission Document (CTAD), 200
control of corruption (CC), 174, 176, 178
corporate social responsibility (CSR), 115
corruption, 41, 43
cost-benefit sharing method, 206
cost-plus pricing method, 185
counterproductive practice, benefit and impact of, 201–3
CPP. *See* Cambodian People's Party (CPP)
crisis in Cambodia (2008–9), 22–25
cross-border financial integration, 15
cross-border governance issues, 173
cross-border issues in Thailand, 79
cross-border trade, 2
cross-border traffic, transit fee charge for, 209
cross-border transmission capacity, 218
cross-border transport, 173, 182, 195, 206
   Lao PDR, 201, 202
   opportunism and high transaction costs of, 203–4
cross-border transport agreement (CBTA), 25, 126, 197
   implementation of, 200, 207
   permissible charges according to, 209
CSR. *See* corporate social responsibility (CSR)
currency crises, 165, 169
currency, Myanmar, 68, 71
customs and transit systems (CTS), 44, 198, 200
customs clearance formalities, facilitation of, 212
customs performance, 178

customs procedures, harmonization of, 203
Cyclone Nargis, 48

D
dam-building projects, 114
Danang Port in Vietnam, 199, 200
DCI. *See* Domestic capital investment (DCI)
decentralization and deconcentration, 21
demand-side management (DSM), 225
democratic development, strengthening of, 27
Deng Xiao Ping, 78
Department of Land Transport (DLT), 183, 184, 185, 188, 199
development gap, 88, 96
   GMS economies, 87
diversification
   of export, 149–54
   product and market, 154
DLT. *See* Department of Land Transport
Doing Business Ranking, 41, 42
Domestic capital investment (DCI), 38–39
domestic divergences, 114
Domestic energy supply, 45
domestic markets, 205
   developing, 162, 165
   impacts on, 188–94
domestic transport market in Thailand, 180–83
drinking water in Myanmar, 67
Dwivedi, R., 241

E
Early Harvest Programme in ASEAN-China FTA, 26, 29
East Asian countries, 95
   inflation rate in, 53, 55

East Asian economies, 84
East Asian integration,
    institutionalized process for, 99
East Asia, transformation of, 153
East–West Economic Corridor
    (EWEC), 44, 45, 196, 203
    impacts from GMS, 199
eco-friendly transport, 208
economic cooperation, 86, 87, 172,
    216
    membership in, 125–30
    Yunnan–GMS, *See* Yunnan–GMS
        economic cooperation
economic corridors, 94, 126, 196
    development of, 32, 44
    impact of, 236
    performance of, 197
economic development, 230
    in Lao PDR, 32–34
    level, 112
    in Myanmar, 50–62
economic diversification, 243
    in Cambodia, 26
economic downturn in Cambodia, 22
economic growth, 11
    in Cambodia, 23, 24
    in GMS, 2, 14
    in Myanmar, 51, 65
    rates of, 120, 155
    and restructuring in GMS
        countries, 122
economic indicators in Yunnan, 104
economic integration, 85, 234, 236
economic level, Thailand, 75–76
economic literature and financial
    development, 164
economic performance of Lao PDR,
    35–36
economic reforms, 84, 234
economic region, 95
economic relations of Yunnan, 104
Economic Research Institute for
    ASEAN (ERIA), 94

economic structure of Myanmar,
    57–58
economic growth, 35
education in Lao PDR, 33–34
education sector in Myanmar, 68–69
elections in Cambodia, 20, 21
electricity, 219, 222, 226, 227
    in Greater Mekong Subregion, 217
    in Lao PDR, 34, 45
Electronic Data Interchange, 180
employment
    in Lao PDR, 39
    in Myanmar, 56, 70
energy conservation (EC), 225
energy efficiency (EE), 224, 225
energy efficiency laws, 224
energy in China and GMS, 106
Energy Power Forum, 220
energy projects in GMS, 78
energy resources, 86, 217
energy sector, 226–27
    expanded cooperation in, 222–23
energy supply, sources of, 81
energy trade, 227
entrepreneurialism, 243
environmental damage, 238, 242
environmental protection measures,
    12
ESCAP. *See* United Nations Economic
    and Social Commission for Asia
    and the Pacific (ESCAP)
ethnic groups in Thailand, 75
ethnic minority groups in Yunnan,
    103
European Union Emission Trading
    System, 232
European Union, Marco Polo Program
    in, 208
EWEC. *See* East–West Economic
    Corridor (EWEC)
Exchange of Traffic Rights, 198
export-oriented sectors, strengthening
    of, 24, 26

export products
  in Cambodia, 137
  demand for, 136
exports
  changing structure of, 130, 136–37
  costs and documentary
    requirements, 127
  diversification of, 149–54
  GMS, 138
  in Lao PDR, 37–38
  of Myanmar, 58, 60, 61, 62
  from Thailand to GMS, 80
  Yunnan's exports to GMS countries,
    105

F
FDI. *See* Foreign direct investment
  (FDI)
Feher, M., 248
FIMC. *See* Foreign Investment
  Management Committee (FIMC)
financial cooperation in GMS
  countries, 166–69
financial crisis, 3–4, 162–63, 165, 168
financial institution, liberalization of,
  168
financial market development, 15,
  162–66
  in developing countries, 163
  and economic growth, 164
  in GMS countries, 167
financial regulation, 15
financial sector, 162
  reforms, 68, 163, 167
financial security, 242
financing infrastructure investment,
  211–12
firms, financial, 163, 164
food insecurity, 240
food production in GMS countries, 10
foreign aid, 108
foreign direct investment (FDI), 2, 4,
  22, 36, 45, 68, 92

  in GMS, 141
  inflows into GMS countries, 142,
    143
  in Lao PDR, 39, 40, 124
  in Thailand, 210
  trends in, 137, 143
foreign investment in Cambodia, 124
Foreign Investment Management
  Committee (FIMC), 124
foreign trade
  in Myanmar, 50, 58–62
  of Yunnan, 105–6
forestry resources in Lao PDR, 41, 42
Formoso, B., 243
fossil fuel resources, 217
"four-I" approach, 87, 99
free trade agreement (FTA), 96, 148,
  155
  external tariffs of, 145
freight transport
  modal share in, 181
  regulations, 184
  in Thailand, 180
FTA. *See* free trade agreement (FTA)
FUNCIPEC Party, 20

G
garment exports in Cambodia, 23, 24
gas exports from Myanmar, 61
GDP. *See* gross domestic product
  (GDP)
GE. *See* government effectiveness (GE)
geographical proximity, 168, 169
GFC. *See* global financial crisis (GFC)
Gini coefficient, 66
global financial crisis (GFC), 2, 22,
  120, 149, 153, 162–63, 165, 168
GMS. *See* Greater Mekong Subregion
  (GMS)
GMS/CLMV integration, 99
GMS–Yunnan economic cooperation.
  See Yunnan–GMS economic
  cooperation

GNI. *See* gross national income (GNI)
GoL. *See* Government of the Lao PDR
(GoL)
Golden Boten City, 236, 251n1
Golden Kapok Flower, 236
goods, free flow of, 201
governance, 172–73
  policy recommendations to
    promote, 205–12
governance indicators, 174–80
government effectiveness (GE), 174,
  176
Government of the Lao PDR (GoL),
  32, 36, 44
Greater Mekong Subregion (GMS),
  1, 18, 32, 46n1, 47, 84, 104,
  172, 216. *See also* Lao People's
  Democratic Republic (Lao PDR)
in 2009, 77
Asian future of, 29–30
"bridging the development gap" in,
  25–26
Business Forum, 44–45, 46n2,
  208–9
capacity building, 210–11
China's trade with, 105
cooperation, 85–88
Corridors Programme, 44
cross-border political conflicts, 12
development stages of, 2
economic cooperation with Yunnan,
  108–9
economic corridors, 197, 203, 206,
  210
economic development, 7, 76
economic growth and restructuring
  in, 122
economic growth in, 2, 14
economic integration in, 13
Economic Partnership, 94
economic variables in, 5
economies, 85, 86, 88–94, 90, 101,
  147

electricity consumption in, 217
eleven sectors for cooperation in,
  104
energy cooperation with China,
  106
energy sector, 222–23
economic development, 2–7
evolution of trade and investment
  policy in, 123–25
expanded cooperation, 222–23
exports, 138
FDI, 141, 142, 143
financial market development of,
  166
financial support, 112
flagship programme, 86–87, 94
GDP growth in, 120, 121
governance indicators, 174–80
governance issues in, 15
gross domestic product of, 1
growth of, 83
growth rebalancing in, 149–54,
  155
inflation rates in, 36, 37
infrastructure development in, 7–8,
  15
infrastructure fund, 208
infrastructure investment plan in,
  78–79
infrastructure projects, 7
institutional arrangement, 207–9
institutional set-up of, 220–22
integration, 96, 99
intraregional trade, 90, 92
labour markets in, 6
LDC, 25–26
logistical performance index of, 128
Ministerial Conference in Vientiane,
  17n1
policy framework, 223–25
policy implications for, 99–101
political developments in, 12
political stability, 12

potential of carbon emission
reductions in, 226–27
power systems, 219–20
PTAs, 130, 131–32
reducing vulnerability to external
shocks, 149–54
resources in, 77
sharing infrastructure cost, 209–10
social and political development,
7–12
social development variables in, 9
socioeconomic and poverty
indicators in, 123
socio-economic development and
cooperation in, 14
socio-political history of, 74
Strategic Framework, 85, 86, 87,
94–99
Summit, 104, 208
Thai exports to, 80
Thai imports from, 81
trade, 91, 104, 133
transport infrastructure, 112–13
transport sector, 208
Yunnan's imports from and exports
to, 105
Yunnan's regional economic
cooperation with, 104
Greater Mekong Subregion Economic
Programme, 156n1
Greater Mekong Subregion integrated
scenario
vs high-growth scenario, 227–28
vs low-carbon scenario, 228–30
Greater Mekong Subregion Ministerial
Meeting, 222
Greater Mekong Subregion Power
Trade Coordination and
Information Centre, 221, 222
Greater Mekong Subregion Program
(GMS), 234, 243
green growth, 95
greenhouse gas emissions (GHG),
225, 230

growth rebalancing
in East Asia, 95
in GMS countries, 149–54, 155
Guangxi Zhuang Autonomous Region,
17n1, 76, 108–9, 117n16

H
Han people, 103
HDI. *See* Human Development Index
(HDI)
health care services, 11
health system in Myanmar, 66, 69
high-growth scenario *vs* GMS
integrated scenario, 227–28
Highway Police Division, 184
Hu Jintao, 109
human capital, 245
Human development index (HDI),
88
for Myanmar, 62, 64
Hun Sen, 76
hydropower, 86
hydropower capacity, 229
hydropower plants in Lao PDR and
China, 78
hydropower resources, 217
hydropower sectors in Lao PDR, 35,
41, 45
hypermarkets distribution
in Bangkok, 192
in Thailand, 191

I
IAI. *See* Initiatives for ASEAN
Integration (IAI)
IGA. *See* Inter-Governmental
Agreement (IGA)
IICBTA. *See* Initial Implementation of
CBTA (IICBTA)
illegal migration, 238, 242
imports
costs and documentary
requirements, 127
from GMS to Thailand, 81

in Lao PDR, 37–38
of Myanmar, 57, 60, 61
from Vietnam to Lao PDR and
    Cambodia, 6
Yunnan's imports from GMS
    countries, 105
Impoverishment Risks and
    Reconstruction Model (IRR),
    239–40
IMR. *See* infant mortality rates (IMR)
Index of Economic Freedom, 50
India, 75
    economies of, 1–2
    financial crisis, 3–4
    regional economic cooperation with,
        111–12
Indonesia, 75
    governance scores of, 178
industrial clusters, 45
industrialization, 86, 230
industrial sector, GDP, 58, 59
infant mortality rates (IMR), 33, 120
    in Myanmar, 62, 63, 67
inflation rate
    in GMS, 36
    in Lao PDR, 37
    in Myanmar, 53, 55, 56, 68
informal sector in Myanmar, 69
information and communication
    technology (ICT), 7, 212
Information Superhighway Network
    (ISN), 78
infrastructure development, 219–20
    in Cambodia, 21
    in GMS, 7–8
infrastructure investment, 95
infrastructure investment plan, 78–79
infrastructure projects in GMS, 7
Initiative for ASEAN Integration
    (IAI), 87, 100
Initial Implementation of CBTA
    (IICBTA), 200
Initiative for East Asian Integration
    (IEAI), 100

Initiatives for ASEAN Integration
    (IAI), 29
inland container depots (ICD), 45
institutional capacity, 224
institutional development, 220–22
institutional integration, 125
Integrated Resource Management
    (IRM), 226
integrated subregional electric power
    market, 216
Inter-Governmental Agreement (IGA),
    220
international integration, 93
international non-governmental
    organizations, 114
international political factors, 115
international public goods, provision
    of, 205–6, 209
international road transport market in
    Thailand, 173, 194–200
international trade, 4
intersectoral diversification, 152
intersectoral specialization, 152
Intra-ASEAN trade growth, 89
intra-GMS FDI flows, 143
intra-GMS inflows, share of, 144
intra-GMS trade, 2
    share of, 136
intraregional trade, 16, 153
intrasectoral diversification, 155
intrasectoral specialization, 152
investment, 1–2, 16
    Lao PDR, 38–39, 41–42
    transformation of savings into, 164
    between Yunnan and GMS, 104
Investment Code, 124
investment deflection, 146
investment policy in GMS countries,
    123–25
investors, ASEAN, 137
IRM. *See* Integrated Resource
    Management (IRM)
IRR. *See* Impoverishment Risks and
    Reconstruction Model (IRR)

ISN. *See* Information Superhighway Network (ISN)

J
Japan
  and ODA, 22
  trade in, 136
Japan External Trade Organization (JETRO), 146
Java-Malay, 75
JETRO. *See* Japan External Trade Organization (JETRO)
Joint Medium-Term Cooperation Work Plan, 225–26

K
key stakeholders
  benefit, 201–3
  and incentives, 207
Khmer Rouge, 19–20
"killing fields," 19
Krugman, Paul, 165
Kunming-Bangkok Highway, 112
Kunming Declaration, 10

L
labour-intensive industries in Lao PDR, 42
labour market reform in Myanmar, 69–71
Labour Ministry policies of Myanmar, 69
labours, skilled and unskilled, 201
land distribution to Khmer Rouge soldiers, 20
land reform in Myanmar, 71
land transport
  regulatory and law enforcement agencies, 184
  in Thailand, 180
Land Transport Act, 184, 195
Langcang-Mekong River Basin, 104
Lao Bao, 198

Lao Expenditures and Consumption Survey (LECS), 32–33
Lao PDR. *See* Lao People's Democratic Republic (Lao PDR)
Lao people, 210
Lao People's Democratic Republic (Lao PDR), 16, 104, 105–6, 119, 216, 236
  Akha communities in, 247
  business environment in, 39–41, 43
  China's aid to, 107
  communication development, 7
  cross-border transport, 201, 202
  economic and social conditions, 32–34
  economic performance of, 35–36
  economic situation in, 13
  economies in, 85
  for electricity, 76
  ethnic minority groups, 243–45
  Exchange of Traffic Rights in, 198
  FDI policy in, 124
  GDP growth rates of, 2–3, 88
  hydropower plants in, 78
  IICBTA, 200
  independence for, 75
  investment, *See* investment
  logistics infrastructure in, 178
  New Economic Mechanism, 32, 124
  population in, 31
  primary commodities in, 139
  regional economic integration, *See* regional economic integration
  road improvements in, 209
  trade in, 90, 130, 136
law enforcement agencies, 184
Law on Foreign Investment, 124
Law on Import and Export Duties, 125
Law on Promotion and Management of Foreign Investment, 124

least-developed countries (LDCs), 21, 31, 32, 47, 57, 112

LECS. *See* Lao Expenditures and Consumption Survey (LECS)

liberalization
market, 205
of rice trade, 53

life expectancy in Myanmar, 62, 63, 64

logistics, 83

logistics development, 178

logistics industry, 173

Logistics Performance Index (LPI), 178

long-term credible investment policies, 176

low-carbon development
in Greater Mekong Subregion, 231
regional energy sector cooperation for, 230–32

low-carbon scenario vs GMS integrated scenario, 228–30

M

Macroeconomic and Finance Surveillance Office (MFSO), 15, 169

macroeconomic trends, 50–57

Mao Zedong, 76

marginalization, 240, 241, 248

marginal productivity of capital, 164, 170n4

market-based integration, programme of, 125

market-driven economy, 11, 16

market economy of Myanmar, 66, 68

market inefficiency, 183–88

market liberalization, 205

material capital, 246

maternal mortality ratio (MMR), 33

MDGs. *See* Millennium Development Goals (MDGs)

Mekong International Bridge, 197, 199

Mekong River, 31, 47, 85, 114–15, 236

Memorandum of Understanding (MoU), 195

MESSAGE. *See* Model of Energy Supply Systems Alternatives and their General Environmental Impacts (MESSAGE)

Metropolitan Police Bureau, 184

MFSO. *See* Macroeconomic and Finance Surveillance Office (MFSO)

military budget of Myanmar, 57

military conflict, 20

military government in Myanmar, 48, 58

Millennium Development Goals (MDGs), 10, 24

mineral resources in Lao PDR, 41, 45

minerals in Myanmar, 49

Ministry of Commerce, 190

Ministry of Interior, 188, 190

Ministry of Transport, 183, 208

mitigation, 249
models, 239–42
process, 242

MMR. *See* maternal mortality ratio (MMR)

Model of Energy Supply Systems Alternatives and their General Environmental Impacts (MESSAGE), 227

modernization, 86, 243

modern trade businesses
impacts on traditional trade retailers, 190
in Thailand, 188

Mon-Khmer, 75

morbidity, 11

mortality rate in Myanmar, 62, 63, 67

most favoured nation (MFN) tariffs, 4, 143, 145, 148

Motor Vehicle Temporary Admission
    Document (MVTAD), 200
Mukdahan checkpoint, 199, 200
Mukdahan-Savannakhet border, 201,
    202
multilateral agreements, 195, 196–200
multilateralism, 16
multiple-rate system, impacts of, 148
multi-tier tariff system, 155
municipal administrators, 194
Myanmar, 16, 47, 104
    border problem with Thailand, 79
    China's aid to, 107
    communication development in, 7
    democratization and political
        reforms in, 12
    economic development trends, 13
    economic profile of, 48
    economic structure of, 57–58
    economies in, 85
    foreign trade in, 50, 58–62
    GDP growth rates of, 2–3, 88
    golden age of, 48
    imports, 6
    independence for, 75
    logistics infrastructure in, 178
    macroeconomic trends, 50–57
    for natural gas, 76
    official trade volume, 48, 60
    political stampedes in, 12
    primary commodities in, 139
    reform needed in, 67–71
    regional economic cooperation with,
        111–12
    standard of living in, 62–67
    trade, 90, 130, 136
    Yunnan's trade with, 105–6

N
NAFTA. *See* North American Free
    Trade Agreement (NAFTA)
Nam Ngum 1 Hydropower Plant, 219
Nam Theun 2 Hydropower Plant, 219

National Bank of Cambodia (NBC),
    23
national development plan, 116
national development strategy in
    China, 110–11, 117n10,
    117n16
National Economic Research Institute
    (NERI), 201
national energy strategy, 223
National Investment Council, 124
national road infrastructure, 173
National Single Window (NSW), 212,
    213n10
National Social and Economic
    Development Plan (NSEDP), 35
National Strategic Development Plan
    (2009–13), 22
    government policies in, 24
National Transport Facilitation
    Committee Joint Committee
    (NTFC), 208
natural gas, 223
    in Myanmar, 49, 76
natural resources, 23, 86, 227
    in GMS countries, 11, 12
    governance of, 27
    of Lao PDR, 41
NBC. *See* National Bank of Cambodia
    (NBC)
"negative externalities", 236, 238, 249
neoliberal engagements, 243–46, 249
NERI. *See* National Economic
    Research Institute (NERI)
New Economic Mechanism, 32, 35
    implementation of, 124
non-discriminatory approach to
    regionalism, 147
non-tariff barriers, 143
non-timber forest products (NTFP),
    33
non-traditional security issues, 94
    in East Asia, 85
noodle bowl effect, 25

North American Free Trade Agreement (NAFTA), 145
northeast Myanmar, minority rebellions in, 233
Northern Economic Corridor, 235, 236
North–South Corridors, 44
North–South Economic Corridor (NSEC), 196
NSW. *See* National Single Window (NSW)
NTFP. *See* non-timber forest products (NTFP)

O
ODA. *See* official development assistance (ODA)
official development assistance (ODA), 21–22, 38–39, 96
opium plantation, 106
Opium Substitute Plantation (OSP), 106, 117n5
own-account trucks, 186

P
Paris Declaration on Aid Effectiveness, 22
Paris Peace Settlement, 20
passenger transport, modal share in, 181
People's Republic of China (PRC), 130, 136, 137, 156n2, 216
per capita income of Myanmar, 49
phased development, 218–19
Philippines, 75
governance scores of, 178
Police Information System, 183
policy framework, 223–25
policy recommendations, 206–7
political conflict, CPP and FUNCIPEC Party, 20
political stability and absence of violence (PV), 174

political stability in GMS countries, 12
political stampedes in Myanmar, 12
poor governance, 176, 183, 187, 189
Portuguese in Malacca, 75
poverty, 11
in Lao PDR, 32, 33
in Myanmar, 62, 63, 64–66, 67
Poverty Headcount Index, 65
poverty rates in GMS, 120
poverty reduction in Cambodia, 21, 23, 24–25, 27
power purchase agreements (PPAs), 218
power sector plans, 225
power systems, 219–20
power trade, 219–21
and interconnection, 218–22
PPP. *See* public-private partnership (PPP)
PRC. *See* People's Republic of China (PRC)
preferential trading arrangements (PTAs), 129
to GMS country, 130, 131–32
membership in, 127–30
price distortion in road transport, 180–83
private sector
development, 26
domestic credit to, 166
in Lao PDR, 39, 41, 43
in Myanmar, 66, 68, 178
participation, 223
risk sharing, 211
privatization of state-owned companies, 20
production deflection, 146
production fragmentation trade, 137
PTAs. *See* preferential trading arrangements (PTAs)
public and private partnership (PPP) programmes, 44

public bus market in Thailand,
185–86
public bus regulations, 184
public goods
provision of international, 205–6,
209
provision of regional, 205–12
public health protection schemes, 11
public-private partnership (PPP), 15,
100, 211–12, 223
public-private partnerships, income
gaps, 88
public sector
in Myanmar, 56
reform, 27
Pyidawtha, eight-year plan in, 48

R
rail transport network, 180, 182
railway transport in Lao PDR, 45
rationalizing tariff, 143–49
raw materials
in Myanmar, 49
sources of, 81
RCM, 232
real economy, 163, 165
rebalancing, growth, 149–54, 155
RE/CF/EE development, 225–26
Reddy, Y.V., 163
Red River, 233
regional cooperation, 86, 96, 100,
222–23, 228, 231
mechanisms, 113
Regional Development Cooperation
Programmes, 98
regional economic cooperation, 116
for China, 111
frameworks, 176
in Yunnan, 104
regional economic integration, 84, 96
in Asia, 3
constraints for, 43–44
development of, 44–46

regional energy sector cooperation,
230–32
regional financial cooperation, 166–69
regional financial integration, 168
regional integration, 25, 29, 205
regionalism, 16, 146
non-discriminatory approach to,
147
Regional Power Trade Coordinating
Committee (RPTCC), 220–21,
232
regional public goods
provision of, 205–12
underinvestment of, 201
region infrastructure network, 206,
210
regulatory agency, 184
regulatory quality (RQ), 174, 176
renewable energy (RE), 224, 225,
229
resource mobilization, 100
resources
in GMS, 77
of Thailand, 76
Retail Trade Law, 194
"reverse remittances", 23
rice trade, 53, 58
risk sharing in government and private
sectors, 211
RL. *See* rule of law
road freight transport service, bilateral
agreements on, 195
road maintenance cost and Lao PDR,
210, 213n9
road map, 222
for Greater Mekong Subregion, 223
for monetary and financial
integration, 168, 170n7
road networks
in GMS countries, 7
in Lao PDR, 34, 44
road pricing framework, 180–83
road's social footprints, 236–38

road transport
in GMS countries, 7
price distortion in, 180–83
Royal Thai Police, 183, 184
RPTCC. *See* Regional Power Trade
Coordinating Committee
(RPTCC)
RQ. *See* regulatory quality (RQ)
rubber, 237, 247
rule of law (RL), 174, 176
rules of origin (RoO), 147
rural areas in Lao PDR, 33–34

S
Savan-Seno Economic Zone, 45
scale of industry, diseconomy of,
183–88
Second GMS Summit, 10
service sector in Lao PDR, 35, 41
Sexually transmitted diseases (STDs),
240
SEZs. *See* Special Economic Zones
(SEZs)
Singapore, governance scores of, 178
Single Stop Inspection (SSI), 212
Single Window Inspection (SWI), 212
small and medium enterprises (SMEs),
41, 44, 45–46
social action plans (SAPs), 241
social capital, 236, 249
social change process, 239, 240, 241,
249
social development
in health care, 27
in Lao PDR, 32–34
policy, 10
social disarticulation, 240, 241
social factors, analysis of, 236
social marginalization, 241, 243
social market economy in Myanmar,
68
social protection, 95
social sector in Myanmar, 69

social transformation, 239
socio-economic corridors, 241
development of, 249
socio-economic development
in Cambodia, 21, 23, 24, 25
in Lao PDR, 31
performance of, 88–94
socio-economic growth, 16
SOEs. *See* state-owned enterprises
(SOEs)
Southeast Asia, 76, 108
communication and cooperation
with, 109
Southern Economic Corridor (SEC),
196
Southern Seaboard development
project, 176
South Korea, governance scores of,
178
spaghetti bowl effect, 25, 147
SPDC. *See* State Peace and
Development Council (SPDC)
Special Economic Zones (SEZs), 45,
210
spillover effects, 169
stakeholders, 99
benefit, 201–3
and incentives, 207
standard of living in Myanmar, 62–67
state economic enterprises (SEEs), 57
State Law and Order Restoration
Council (SLORC), 48
state-owned enterprises (SOEs), 124
State Peace and Development Council
(SPDC), 48, 66
State Railway of Thailand, 211–12
STDs. *See* Sexually transmitted
diseases (STDs)
"Strait of Malacca dilemma", 106
strategic environmental assessment
(SEA), 225
Subregional Development Cooperation
Programmes, 98

subregional integration, 25, 29, 99
Surat Thani, energy development
    project in, 176
sustainability, 94

T
Taiwan, governance scores of, 178
tariff
    in CLMV countries, 143, 145
    rationalizing, 143–49
    and tariff dispersion, 150–51
tax
    collection, 28
    from garment factories, 23
    in Myanmar, 57
    tax rate in Lao PDR, 41
    on trucks, 210
telecommunications projects, 78–79
Thai economy, 4
Thai exports, growing markets for, 80
Thailand, 16, 74, 104
    bus industry in, 185–86
    corruption problem in, 207
    cross-border issues in, 79
    cross-border transport, 201, 202
    domestic transport market in, 173
    economic level in, 75–76
    Exchange of Traffic Rights in, 198
    exports to GMS, 80
    FDI in, 6
    GDP growth rate, 2–3, 7
    GMS relations, 13
    governance indicators of, 174–80
    governance scores of, 178
    growth of, 83
    history, 75
    hypermarkets distribution in, 191
    IICBTA, 200
    impact of 1997/98 Asian financial
        crisis, 119
    imports from GMS, 81
    international road transport market
        in, 194–200

investment reforms in, 123
logistics industry in, 173
manufactured products in, 140
modern trade businesses in, 188
poverty rates in, 120
primary commodities in, 136
PTA, 129
regulation problems of retail trade
    sectors in, 193
road and railway networks in, 180,
    182
trade in, 123, 130, 136, 137
trade with Cambodia, 4
truck industry in, 186–88
Thailand–Lao PDR, cross-border
    transport, 195
Thailand–Malaysia, cross-border
    transport, 195
Theun-Hinboun Hydropower, 219
Tiananmen incident, 76
tourism, 1–2, 24
    in Lao PDR, 41, 42, 45
toxic assets, 163
trade, 1–2, 84, 233
    agreements, 125–30
    chain, 97
    deflection, 146
    in GMS countries, 123–25,
        133–35
    Guangxi with GMS, 104
    in Lao PDR, 36–38, 41–42
    liberalization, 96
    in Myanmar, 50, 58–62
    relations, 86
    trends in, 130, 136–37
    between Yunnan and GMS, 104
    Yunnan with ASEAN and GMS,
        104
trade-investment nexus, 143
trade liberalization, 32
trade logistics in GMS countries, 178
traditional trade businesses, 194
traditional trade retailers, 190

traffic law enforcement agency, 184
Traffic Police Division, 183, 184
Traffic Police officers, 188
Transit and Inland Customs Clearance
      Document (TICCD), 200
transit countries, 201, 207, 209
transit pricing, 209
transportation projects, 79
transport corridors, 44
transport costs
   corruption and, 203
   of cross-border transport, 203–4
   by road, 203, 205
transport sector, GMS, 208
truck industry
   diseconomy of scale of, 189
   weak regulatory and law
         enforcement in, 186–88
Twelfth Five-Year Plan of China,
      111–12

U
underemployment in Myanmar, 69
unemployment
   in Cambodia, 23
   rate in Myanmar, 56
unilateral policy reforms, 155
United Nations Economic and Social
      Commission for Asia and the
      Pacific (ESCAP), 11
United Nations Framework
      Convention for Climate Change
      (UNFCC), 226
United Nations Fund for Population
      Activities (UNFPA), 51
United Nations Transition
      Administration (UNTAC) in
      Cambodia, 20
UN-led peace process, 124
UNTAC. *See* United Nations
      Transition Administration
      (UNTAC)
urban areas in Lao PDR, 33–34

V
VA. *See* voice and accountability (VA)
Vanclay, F., 239
vehicle taxation system, 180, 213n3
Vejjajiva, Abhisit, 152
Vietnam, 2–3, 104, 105–6
   demographic structure, 96
   Exchange of Traffic Rights in, 198
   exports, 92
   FDI inflows, 92
   financial market reform in, 168,
         170n5
   GDP in, 2–3, 7, 88, 120
   governance scores of, 178
   IICBTA, 200
   imports, 6
   independence for, 75
   manufactured products in, 140
   poverty rates in, 120
   primary commodities in, 136
   renovation reforms in, 124
   trade in, 90, 93, 130, 137
   trade reform of, 125
Vietnamese army, 19
vocational training in Myanmar, 70
voice and accountability (VA), 174,
      176, 178

W
wages in Myanmar public sector, 56
water resources of Myanmar, 67
water sources in Lao PDR, 31, 33,
      42
weak governance, 173, 176
weak urban town planning, 188–94
World Bank, 239, 246
   report, 174
World Trade Organization (WTO),
      4, 21
   membership in, 127–30
World War II, 75, 233
Worldwide Governance Indicators
      (WGI), 174

WTO. *See* World Trade Organization
   (WTO)

Y

Yangon
   consumer price index for, 53
   drinking water in, 67
Yunnan
   economic cooperation with GMS
      and ASEAN, 108–9
   economic crop plantation in,
      117n5
   economic indicators in, 104
   economic relations, 104
   ethnic minority groups in, 103
   foreign-aid projects, 108
   foreign trade, 105, 106
   and GMS, investments between,
      105–6
   imports from and exports to GMS
      countries, 104
   multinational water issues, 103
   population of, 103
   in regional economic cooperation,
      104

regional economic cooperation with
   GMS countries, 103
rivers in, 103
strategic location of, 103
trade with ASEAN and GMS, 104
trade with Myanmar, 105–6
transportation infrastructure,
   112–13
Yunnan–GMS economic cooperation
   bridgehead strategy, 109–12
   domestic divergences, 114
   economic development level, 112
   environmental and social problems,
      114–15
   improvement of infrastructure,
      112–13
   international politics, factors of, 115
   regional cooperation mechanisms,
      113
Yunnan Province, 14, 16
exports from, 6
GDP in, 7

Z

zero-trade barrier, 231